Understanding Theatre

Third Edition

W.K. Waters
Emeritus Professor of Theatre
Stephen F. Austin State University
Department of Theatre

THOMSON LEARNING™
CUSTOM PUBLISHING

Understanding Theatre

Editor: Rebecca McGuire
Production Manager: Staci Powers
Production Coordinator: Lisa Donahue
Marketing Coordinator: Sara L. Hinckley

Printed in the United States of America

Thomson Learning Custom Publishing
5191 Natorp Blvd.
Mason, Ohio 45040
USA

For information about our products, contact us:
1-800-355-9983
http://www.custom.thomsonlearning.com

International Headquarters
Thomson Learning
International Division
290 Harbor Drive, 2nd Floor
Stamford, CT 06902-7477
USA

UK/Europe/Middle East/South Africa
Thomson Learning
Berkshire House
168-173 High Holborn
London WCIV 7AA

Asia
Thomson Learning
60 Albert Street, #15-01
Albert Complex
Singapore 189969

Canada
Nelson Thomson Learning
1120 Birchmount Road
Toronto, Ontario MIK 5G4
Canada
United Kingdom

Visit us at www.e-riginality.com and learn more about this book and other titles published by Thomson Learning Custom Publishing

ISBN 0-155-67729-2

The Adaptable Courseware Program consists of products and additions to existing Custom Publishing products that are produced from camera-ready copy. Peer review, class testing, and accuracy are primarily the responsibility of the author(s).

Preface

Understanding Theatre has been designed to fulfill the needs of a basic, one-semester Theatre Appreciation or Introduction to the Theatre course. Though the text has been arranged to provide a background in basic theatre principles (chapters 1-3), followed by a discussion of the script both as a literary work and as a work performed (chapters 4-11), and concluding with discussions of the various aspects of production (chapters 12-23), instructors will find that the various chapters may be used independently and dealt with according to the individual instructor's needs. Several chapters deal specifically with the historical background of certain periods (chapters 10-13). These have been included to provide background for plays assigned from those periods. Additional historical information has been provided at the beginning of each chapter dealing with production. In an effort to increase the students' theatre literacy, important terms have been initially introduced in **boldface** type. These terms are explained in the text and also included in the glossary beginning on page 181.

The text is planned to incorporate the use of a separate play anthology which will provide the student with examples of dramatic works from various periods, forms and styles. It is recommended that plays such as the following be used: *Oedipus Rex, The Second Shepherd's Play, Hamlet, Tartuffe, The Death of a Salesman, Happy Days, Death of a Salesman,* and *Raisin in the Sun.* In addition, the student should be expected to view such live productions as are available to him during the semester. Video recordings of many plays are available, however such should be used only when no live presentations are accessible.

The textbook has also been designed to provide class assignments and exercises which will encourage the student to apply the information covered by specific chapters. These may be removed from the text in order to be submitted to the instructor.

The author expresses his appreciation to the Stephen F. Austin State University Department of Theatre faculty and students for their help and assistance in creating this text. His thanks go to Dr. C. W. Bahs, Dept. Chairman, Allen Oster, Kerro Knox 3, Velta Hargrove, Kevin McClusky, Tomy Matthys, Dr. William Parsons, Dr. Alan Nielsen, and the graduate students who graciously tested the text in their teaching of Theatre Appreciation. Of great help was Mr. Ken Kennemer, Director of the University News Service whose proof reading and editing assistance were most valuable.

One final note: the author is well aware of the current drive for political correctness in all textbooks. He realizes that the generic masculine may be offensive to some individuals; however, the substitution of grammatically incorrect pronouns is even more offensive to many others. Therefore, the generic "he," "his," and "him" will be used throughout referring to positions in the theatre which may well be served by either men or women.

WKW

Five Great American Hamlets

Edwin Forrest
1806-1872

James E. Murdock
1811-1893

Edwin Booth
1833-1893

James Wallack
1818-1873

Lawrence Barrett
1838-1891

Credits: Booth, Courtesy the Library of Congress; all others from Laurence Hutton, *Curiosities of the American Stage* 1891

Table of Contents

Index to Class Assignments

The following pages are designed to be removed from the text and submitted to your instructor according to the directions given:

1
Introduction

"I think I love and reverence all arts equally, only putting my own just above the others; because in it I recognize the union and culmination of my own. To me it seems as if when God conceived the world, that was Poetry; He formed it, and that was Sculpture; He colored it, and that was Painting; He peopled it with living beings, and that was the grand, divine, eternal Drama."

Charlotte Cushman

This is being written as a guidebook toward developing an appreciation of the theatre. Appreciation is not something that can be given to any individual, but it is something that can be gained by each individual through experience and study. The *American Heritage Dictionary* describes the appreciator as one who:

1. Recognizes the quality, significance, or magnitude of something
2. Is fully aware of or sensitive to something
3. Is thankful or shows gratitude for something
4. Admires greatly or values something

Whether it be one or all of the above, the development of appreciation for "something" depends on the individual's knowledge about it and his ability to apply that knowledge under a variety of circumstances. It is this knowledge and this ability in relation to the theatre that we shall attempt to develop throughout this course.

The concentration in this course will be upon the living and live theatre; that vibrant part of our culture which has enthralled and entertained the human race for well over 3,500 years. To aid us in the development of an appreciation for this art form, we will view it in as many of its forms as possible in the time allotted and will investigate the elements of which it is composed. It is through this knowledge that one can gain an appreciation for the art of the theatre.

In order to achieve this, we will start our study with a discussion of some of the elements which differentiate the theatre from other though similar art forms. We will then discuss the various purposes of the theatre as it has existed within our society for these many centuries. Starting with the playwright, we will see how these various purposes are fulfilled through his work and the work of the interpreters of the script; i.e., the actors, directors, designers, and finally, the audience.

As an art form, the theatre is unique in that it makes use of all the arts. The actions of the actors are choreographed just as are the movements of the dancer, and the movements have meanings that reveal the actions and relationships of the characters as do the actions of the dancers in story-telling ballets. Related to the movement is the sculptural arrangement of the actors in three-dimensional space to reveal character relationships and various plot elements. The arts of painting and design are incorporated into the visual presentation of the play through the use of scenery, costumes and the arrangement of actors on the stage. Music is incorporated into the action through the voices of the actors and the choice of words as well as through the literal use of melodic themes to identify characters, moods, locales and time periods. In a well-conceived, well-directed production all these elements are integrated into a whole which is complete in and of itself.

The Relationship of Theatre to Motion Pictures and Television

For most of us, television and the motion pictures are the primary forms of entertainment. They are generally available throughout the western world and are fairly inexpensive. The living theatre, however, is not so easily accessible and often comes at a price that is out of reach for many of us. It is, however, more accessible than many of us may think, for it thrives in our schools and in the community theatres which exist throughout the country. In larger cities and on university campuses, professional troupes of actors may be seen on a fairly regular basis.

Though both television and the motion pictures have been derived from the living theatre, there are major differences between such mechanized or "canned" forms of entertainment and the theatre. Obviously, each has its place within our society and our culture, but each has its own qualities which differentiate it from the others. Some of these qualities are purely physical, but many are aesthetic and of such magnitude as to almost defy comparison.

A Comparison of Live Theatre to Television and Motion Pictures

Within our culture, there are three primary forms of dramatic art: live theatre including opera, television, and the motion pictures. Of these three, live theatre is the oldest while the motion pictures were first projected for a audience in 1896 and television made its bow in public broadcasts in the 1950's. Having many things in common, these media also have differences– distinct qualities and contributions which they make to our culture.

 **Theatre**	 **Motion Pictures & Television**
1. Most of the drama as we know it relies heavily on the written script. It is, therefore, verbally oriented. The live theatre is primarily a servant to the word, i.e., verbal action. Though the visualization of the situation and action is very important, it is not as important as it is in the motion pictures.	1. Television and motion pictures are visually oriented, particularly the motion pictures. For motion pictures, the directors, writers, and actors depend on the visual impact of action far more than does the live theatre. Many film scripts are primarily verbal descriptions of the action to be shown and place minimal emphasis on dialogue. Television often places more emphasis on dialogue than do films because of the size of the picture.
2. Because a play depends more upon the verbal than the visual, many plays use few settings or rely on "space staging" in which several locales are suggested on stage at one time through the use of scenic units and/or lights.	2. Both motion pictures and television can easily, efficiently, and realistically present as many locales as are needed.
3. The effect of a live performance of a play lies in the talents and the control of the actors. Though trained	3. The effect of a performance of a motion picture and of most television presentations (excepting those

Theatre (cont.)

by the director and thoroughly rehearsed, once the play has gone before an audience, it is the actor's immediate response that gives life and spontaneity to the performance.

4. In live theatre there is a sense of communication between the actor and the audience. It is the actor's job to provoke certain responses from the audience and to react to those responses building upon them. The performance, therefore, is a communal activity in which the performer and the audience are of equal importance. No two performances of the same work are identical. The audience in the theatre is active and a part of the performance.

5. In live theatre, audience attention is voluntary or self-controlled. Being voluntary, it becomes the actor's responsibility to hold the attention of the audience and make sure the audience sees what it must see and hears what must be heard.

6. Characters in live drama are as large (both physically and psychologically) as the actors can make them or as the director, through their placement in relation to other characters and elements of the set, wishes them to be.

7. The live theatre is essentially a make-believe environment. Attempts at being totally realistic are often "given the lie" by the very artificiality of the medium.

8. Live theatre is labor intensive; i.e., the actors, technicians, etc. must be present for each performance. The audience for each performance is limited.

9. The art of the live theatre is achieved when the illusion of a spontaneous series of actions occurs in each performance. Live theatre, being a time art, exists only during performance, and each performance is different and therefore new.

Film & Television (cont.)

done live) is controlled by the director and the film and/or tape editor. They choose what the audience will or will not see and put it together in its final form. Much of what the actor does the audience never views.

4. Because both film and television are mechanical reproductions, there is no relationship established between performer and audience. All performances are identical it being impossible to establish a true actor-audience relationship. The audience for these media is passive and absorbs but does not participate in the performance.

5. In film and television the audience attention is also voluntary to a certain extent. In these media, however, the camera acts as the eye of the audience and the audience will see only what the director wants it to see. In a similar way, the microphone acts as the audience's ears allowing the audience to hear only that which it should hear.

6. Characters in film and television are often made larger than life through the use of close-ups, camera angles, and/or special effects. They may also be dwarfed through similar devices.

7. Being basically photographic, film and television can give a greater illusion of actual reality. Attempts at fantasy are often "given the lie" because of the basic reality of these media.

8. Television and the motion pictures are labor efficient. The actors, and most of the technicians required need only be employed for the initial preparations for the performance. Performances may be repeated again and again for any number of audiences at little or no additional cost. The size of the motion picture audience is restricted by the size of the theatre. The size of the television audience is only restricted by the number of television sets available for viewing.

9. Film and television give the illusion of spontaneity on first viewing, but because they are essentially a "canned" or preserved art form, the illusion of spontaneity is lost with successive viewings.

The Theatre and Its Purpose

Ask anyone on the street why he goes to the theatre, the motion pictures, or watches television and he will probably say, "I want to be entertained." And he is correct. But what is entertainment? Then he may add to his response any of a number of other reasons: "I go to escape into another world." "To laugh." "To feel." "To relax." He may even possibly say, "To learn." And in all cases, he is correct, for theatre can accomplish all these purposes and has done so for centuries.

In each case, the respondent is still saying that he goes to the theatre to be **entertained**. And in each case, entertainment can take on a different face for the viewer/participant. The *American Heritage Dictionary* states the verb "entertain" means:

1. To hold the attention of with something amusing or diverting.
2. To consider; contemplate.
3. To hold in mind; harbor.
4. To give admittance to; receive.

Entertain comes from the latin *tenere* which means "to have, to hold," and this is what the theatre has done successfully for many years.

Historically, the theatre has served a variety of functions within society. It has been a means:

through which the ancient gods could be honored and worshipped;
through which man could make direct contact with the gods;
by which the history of a culture, a nation, could be taught;
by which men could honor other men and their achievements;
by which attention could be focused on social and political problems;
for healing the sick;
of exposing and hopefully correcting human foibles;
of relaxation and escape.

The theatre has been used as a source of inspiration or discouragement, of healing or destruction, of approval or criticism, and of agitation or relaxation. It has been praised and revered for its power, while at the same time being condemned and despised for the same reason. Because of its power, it has served as a tool of free men and of despots alike. Its practioners have been deified and condemned, glorified and damned, applauded and hissed. For whatever purpose or use to which the theatre has been put, the responses to it and its practitioners have not been neutral.

The Greek playwright Aristophanes (c.445-c.385 B.C.) summed up his reasons for admiring the playwright, and in turn the theatre, when he had one of his characters state that the playwright should be admired "If his art is true, and his council sound; and if he brings help to the nation, by making men better in some respect." Shortly thereafter, the philosopher Plato (c.427-c.347 B.C.), advocated banning the poet from his utopia because he believed that playwrights, actors, etc., presented lies like truth and therefore deceived and misled the people.

The Christian theologian Tertullian (c.155-c.220) condemned the theatre as a place of sin and blasphemy and warned his listeners that to frequent such a place would contaminate them, "For the show always leads to spiritual agitation...–the whole entirely out of keeping with the religion of Christ. . .The polluted things pollute us. . ." Yet, during the Middle Ages, the Christian church brought back the theatre in its efforts to teach the stories of the Bible through dramatizations and the moral principles of the faith through demonstration.

The Origins of the Theatre

As with the origins of many of man's activities, the origins of the theatre are hidden in the mist of the past. They are, however, present within each individual's life, for the practices of the theatre are native to all of us. They are rooted in the natural desire of all men to imitate. As children we imitate our elders and we unconsciously compose playlets as a part of our play. We often find reality limiting and mundane and seek to enlarge upon it through the use of our imaginations–and we find such enlargements by others to be engrossing and entertaining. We tell stories, both real and fictional, and assume the characters during the telling, imitating their movements, voices, and comments.

In *The Dramatic Imagination*, scenic designer Robert Edmund Jones creates an imaginative view of our first theatre when he conjures up a vision of our ancestors telling stories about their lives and actually dramatizing them for the instruction and enjoyment of their fellows. He writes:

> Let us imagine ourselves back in the Stone Age, in the days of the caveman and the mammoth. . . It is night. We are all sitting together around a fire–Ook and Pow and Pung and Glup and Little Zowie and all the rest of us. We sit close together. We like to be together. It is safer that way if wild beasts attack us. And besides, we are happier when we are together. We are afraid to be alone. Over on that side of the fire the leaders of the tribe are sitting together–the strongest men, the men who can run fastest and fight hardest and endure longest. They have killed a lion today. We are excited about this thrilling event. We are all talking about it. . .
>
> The lion's skin lies close by, near the fire. Suddenly the leader jumps to his feet. 'I killed the lion! I did it! I followed him! He sprang at me! I struck him with my spear! He fell down! He lay still!'
>
> He is telling us. We listen. But all at once an idea comes to his dim brain. 'I know a better way to tell you. See! It was like this! *Let me show you!*'
>
> In that instant theatre is born.
>
> The leader goes on. 'Sit around me in a circle–you, and you, and you–right here, where I can reach out and touch you all.' And so, with one inclusive gesture he makes –a theatre! From this circle of eager listeners to Rheinhardt's great Schauspielhaus in Berlin is only a step in time. In its essence a theatre is only an arrangement of seats so grouped and spaced that the actor–the leader–can reach out and touch and hold each member of his audience. Architects of later days have learned how to add convenience and comfort to this idea. But that is all. The idea itself never changes.
>
> The leader continues: 'You, Ook, over there–you stand up and be the lion. Here is the lion's skin. You put it on and be the lion and I'll kill you and we'll show them how it was.' Ook gets up. He hangs the skin over his shoulders. He drops on his hands and knees and growls. How terrible he is! Of course, he isn't a real lion. We know that. The real lion is dead. We killed him today. Of course, Ook isn't a lion. Of course not. He doesn't even look like a lion. 'You needn't try to scare us, Ook. We know you. We aren't afraid of you!' And yet, in some mysterious way, Ook *is* the lion. He isn't like the rest of us any longer. He is Ook all right, but he is a lion, too.
>
> And now these two men–the world's first actors–begin to show us what the hunt was like. They do not tell us. They *show* us. They *act* it for us. The hunter lies in ambush. The lion growls. The hunter poises his spear. The lion leaps. We all join in with howls of excitement and terror–the first community chorus! The spear is thrown. The lion falls and lies still.
>
> The drama is finished.

While Mr. Jones' story is an imaginative recreation of the past, it does bear the essence of truth about the theatre. It is more exciting and entertaining to be shown through action the activities of man than to simply hear about them. In order to show those actions, characters–in this case the leader and the lion–must be created and enacted. If the performance is to have meaning, there must be an audience present to witness it. Thus we come to four basic requirements for all theatre, requirements which have been present since its inception:

1. An idea–a theme and story of man in action to be demonstrated
2. The actors–those who assume characters to demonstrate the story
3. An audience–those who view and respond to the demonstration
4. A place–any place where people can gather and witness the demonstration

The modern Polish stage director, Jerzy Grotowski, goes so far as to say that only two of the above ingredients are necessary–the actor and the audience.

The actions of Ook and the Leader fulfill several of the purposes of the theatre mentioned earlier. They do entertain; they teach through demonstration; and they relate the experience of others and show their achievements.

Pueblo Indian Dancers costumed to perform a dance interceding with the gods for rain. This form of theatrical presentation makes use of what is called sympathetic magic in which the performance elicits the god's help.

Early theatre, and indeed much present day theatre, served other purposes as well. In ancient civilizations, some would call them primitive, it was believed that man could make contact with the gods through imitators who were in actuality actors. As these imitators assumed the characteristics of their chosen deity, they were believed to come into contact with the gods directly and it was believed that they could then carry messages from man to the spirit world. Such actors were called *shamen* and they held a high position within their society similar to the position sometimes granted to priests, ministers and rabbis today. Indeed, many of our modern religious rituals are directly related to rituals of the distant past and require the reenactment of specific events recorded in religious history.

Such was the *Abydos Passion Play* which was written and performed in Egypt as early as 1,500 B.C. This play, which was performed annually for centuries, not only told the story of the Egyptian gods Isis, Osiris, Horus and Set, but explained allegorically the changing seasons on earth.

Just as the Egyptians found an explanation for their world through such a story enacted as a play, so did other early civilizations. Similar stories can be found in the annals of almost all religious movements, and many of them were dramatized both to inform the people and in honor of the gods they worshiped. This was the case with the ancient Greeks who mounted their plays initially in honor of Dionysus and whose actors were, in a sense, lay priests and, as such, were held in high regard within their cities.

Early theatre, then, may be said to have been used both to teach and as a part of the ritual of worship. The actions portrayed on stage became a metaphor for the experience of man in his relation to nature, to the gods, and to his fellow human beings. In many ways, this is true of the theatre today, for the plays placed upon the modern stage not only imitate life, but become symbolic of the status of man in today's society.

A scene from an Egyptian Drama. A scene from a holy play re-enacting the story of the conflict of the solar deity Horus with Set, the god of evil and murderer of Osiris. The play was probably created more than 5000 years ago and was used by the Egyptians as a part of their ritual of worship.

In the examples of theatre given above, that of the cave-man and of the Egyptians, there are elements present which are necessary to all good theatre. These include make-believe on the part of the actors as well as the audience, imitation of characters and actions on the part of the actor, and conflict, for without conflict there is no drama.

(Below) Mandam Bull or Buffalo Dance. A painting by American artist George Caitlin shows the American Indian taking on the characteristics of the animal he is to hunt. Introduced here is an element of evil, the black dancers who act as disruptive influences in the performance. Finally, they are quelled by means of a magic medicine pipe and chased from the village by squaws.

George Caitlin, *Bull Dance* Mandan O-Kee-Pa Ceremony, 1832. Oil on Canvas, 24 1/2 x 28", L.1965.1.505, *Courtesy of the Museum of American Art, Smithsonian Institution, Gift of Mrs. Joseph Harrison, Jr.*

Methinks I scent the morning air.

Hamlet, Act I, Sc. 5

If you have tears, prepare to shed them now.

Julius Caesar, Act II, Sc. 2

Theatre Appreciation
Student Survey

Name__________________________

Please Answer the following questions as fully and honestly as possible:

1. What is the best live performance of a play that you have seen? If you have not seen any, answer "None."

2. What made it best? Why did you enjoy it?

3. Have you ever acted in a play? (circle one) yes no

4. Have you participated in the technical aspects of a live performance? yes no

5. Briefly describe your reactions to your participation, if any, in a live performance. Were they positive or negative? In what way(s)?

6. What is your favorite painting or graphic art?

7. What is your favorite piece of music?

8. What is your favorite place to be or view?

9. What is a favorite leisure activity that you enjoy frequently?

10. Do you have a favorite play or playwright?

11. Why do you go to the theatre, the movies, or watch TV?

12. What is your favorite movie?

2
The Audience and Its Responsibilities

Earlier, it was pointed out that live presentations require the efforts of both the actors and the audience. The actors are responsible for stimulating audience response, and the audience, in turn, stimulates the actors. The audience, therefore, is an active participant in the theatrical experience. In order to do so, the audience subconsciously enters into a contract with the performers. It agrees to initially view the performance with an open mind, to "suspend its disbelief" or, as one writer put it in the days of cloakrooms, "to check disbelief at the door along with the coat and hat." The performer, in turn, agrees to establish a situation, character and a style and to remain consistent to it. Even in the most symbolic and highly stylized kind of production, the performer must maintain consistency if he is to be believed and understood.

In order for the audience to play its role well, it must accept what are normally called **conventions**. A convention is sometimes defined as "an agreed upon falsehood." We, as audience members, know that what we are seeing on stage is not reality. It is make-believe, and we agree to make-believe for the sake of the event. We agree to accept the actor as the character he is playing for the sake of the believability of the play. We agree to accept the suggestion of trees on stage as real trees. We agree to accept wooden frames covered with canvas (**flats**) as real walls. We agree to accept the **proscenium arch** which frames the stage as an imaginary "fourth wall" behind which is the actual locale required for the action of the play. If the actor tells us that we are in the Forest of Arden, the Castle of Elsinore or Dunsinane, we agree that we are there. In short, we agree to overlook the artificialities of the theatre and accept as reality the premise upon which the artists have chosen to work.

"Don't worry, Jimmy—they're just actors ... and that's not real ketchup."

In turn, the theatre artists agree to remain true to what they have told us is truth. If a young actor playing the role of a decrepit ancient suddenly walks upright with a youthful gait, he has broken his contract with us. If a wall painted to look like heavy blocks of stone wavers every time an actor walks past it, we see the artificiality and stop believing. If an actor moves through that imaginary fourth-wall, the illusion is destroyed. If a light suddenly goes on or off before or long after the actor gets to the switch, we laugh at the incongruity and the magic spell of make-believe is broken.

The experienced audience member in the live theatre knows that, unlike reading a novel or watching television at home, he is a part of a group. He therefore accepts his position within that group, the audience at the theatre. He knows also that the actors are working, for the most part, without mechanical and/or electronic aids. Just as he expects the actors to treat him with respect, neither playing down to him nor ignoring his presence, he will treat the actor with respect so long as the actor remains true to the conventions established at the beginning of the performance.

Good actors are always aware of the audience. Though they must give the illusion of being a specific character in a specified situation, they are sensitive to the audience's response or lack of response and work continuously to mold and manipulate that response. Live theatre is interactive in the best sense of that word and in a way no other art form can duplicate.

The Audience As Critic

If the audience is truly to profit from a play, it will inevitably act as a critic, for it will evaluate what it has seen, not just the quality of the work performed, but the ideas behind it. A play of depth and meaning, whether it be comedy, tragedy, farce or melodrama, has an idea or ideas which it seeks to communicate to the viewers. Sometimes these are readily evident, but more often, they require an effort from the viewer. It is this effort which the critic must put forth. Criticism, then, is an act of evaluating; i.e., making judgments based on analysis and thought. It is both positive and negative, and it relies on a set of criteria established by the critic and/or society as a whole.

During the semester in which this course is being taught, you will be asked to view a number of plays and to write critiques on them. The following approach will serve as an aid to you in writing those critiques. It is based on an approach outlined by Johann Wolfgang von Goethe (1749-1832) as one which he recommended for evaluating any work of art. He recommended that the critic answer three questions:

1. What did the artist(s) set out to achieve?
2. How well did he (they) achieve it?
3. Was it worth the effort?

What did the Artist(s) Set Out to Achieve?

In order to answer this question, the critic needs an understanding of the background of the artist. Out of what social climate did the work of art develop? Was it involved in and does it reflect any historical movements and/or events? What philosophical approach influenced the artist(s) and does the work of art reflect this? Who was the artist and how does this reflect his psychological response to the world about him? What is the artist's attitude toward his fellow men and how is it reflected in this work.

One must always remember in dealing with theatre that a play is produced as a result of a collaborative effort. Whereas the script will reflect the playwright's views of man and how man exists and behaves in his own time and society, the produced play may well reflect the attitude of the director as well as the actor in conjunction with the playwright or in spite of him. For instance, Moliere's *Tartuffe* (1669) may be seen as an attack on religious hypocrisy, greed and gullibility as he felt it existed within the society in which he lived. The same play in the hands of a 20th century interpreter such as the Russian director Vsevelod Meyerhold (1874-1940) became an attack on religion in general and capitalism specifically. Shakespeare's *Julius Caesar* may be seen in terms of Shakespeare's own time when it was a strong statement in support of the monarchy and in opposition to revolution; or it may be seen, as it was in the 1937 production mounted by Orson Welles, as a statement warning about the advance and dangers of Fascism and Nazism in Europe. Similarly, Shakespeare's *The Merchant of Venice* may be staged as a romantic comedy with Elizabethan overtones of racial prejudice; or, as in a recent production, it may be viewed as an indictment of both Christian and Jewish attitudes, prejudices, and religion in general.

The critic, therefore, must investigate the reasons (intent) for the creation of the work of art and seek to find the central theme of the work as currently presented. This is not always easy, for any work of art with depth may affect its viewers and listeners in a variety of ways. Their personal experiences, even those incurred on the way to the theatre, will influence their view of the performance and their understanding of the message. The true critic attempts to set aside personal prejudices and tries to view the work objectively when recording his impressions.

How Well Did the Artist Achieve His Purpose?

In answering this question, the viewer must consider the various aspects of the work of art. In regard to theatre, he will need to consider all aspects of the production.

Was the play well-written? Was it logical? Did it communicate its ideas to the audience with clarity and at the same time entertain the viewers? Was it well structured? Was it complete in and of itself? Were the characters well-drawn? Was the action of the play detailed in such a way as to clarify the theme?

Was the play well staged? Did the arrangement of the actors within the setting complement the theme and progressive discussion of the theme clearly? Were character relationships well established? Did the overall rhythm of the play complement its theme and produce the audience response the script apparently desired? If the director reinterpreted the play in terms of his own view of society, was his reinterpretation justified in terms of the script and did he make his point of view clear to the audience?

Were the actors cast appropriately for the roles they were portraying? Were they effective individually and as a group in interpreting the play and its theme? Were they believable in terms of the play and the director's vision of the play? Were they consistent in their presentations of their characters?

Did the sets provide the necessary locale for the action of the play? Did they establish a mood or feeling that complemented the mood and feeling of the play? Did they establish a particular period or era that was required by the play? Did they provide an opportunity for the artistic arrangement of the actors so that the total picture would be satisfying? Did they support the play rather than dominate it?

Did the costumes complement the characters the actors presented within the context of the play? Did they reflect any requirements placed upon them by the script? Were they consistent with regard to the locale represented, the era being portrayed, and the mood of the play itself?

Did the lighting complement the action of the play and allow you to see necessary actions made by the characters? Did it contribute to the overall mood of the play? Did it fulfill any requirements made of it by the script? Did it contribute to or support the rhythm of the play. Was it obtrusive?

Were the sound effects appropriate for the various scenes and actions portrayed in the play? Did they support the actors and help to clarify the actions required? Was the music suitable in establishing the period, mood and rhythm of the play?

All of the above questions can be answered with a simple "yes" or "no." However, the critic goes beyond that. He justifies the evaluations by citing specific examples and demonstrating with those the basis for his judgment. It is the justification of an evaluation which makes a critique valid. Anyone may accept or reject anything. The true critic knows **why** he likes or dislikes something.

Was It Worth the Effort?

It is in this section of the critique that the critic makes an overall evaluation of the artistic work. Here he evaluates the validity of it by judging whether or not the idea behind the work was worth investigating on the part of both the artist and the viewer. Many playwrights have a lot of ideas or themes they would like to investigate, but the best playwrights often find that some of those ideas or themes are a waste of their time. They may be too shallow or transparent to be given the consideration a full-length play would focus upon them. Playwrights often have notebooks crammed with unfinished plays–unfinished in many cases because the themes or ideas which inspired them lacked the depth or importance necessary for consideration. Unfortunately, some have published these playlets which often prove to be of value only to aspiring writers or students of the playwright's evolving style and of little interest to others. A good play normally deals with an idea which has depth, is challenging, and provides an opportunity for the playwright to reveal it through the actions of interesting characters in a series of scenes which reveal a progressing view of the theme.

A play must also be of value to the viewer. After all, as a viewer you are being asked, normally, to pay admission to view the work. Of more importance, however, is that you are investing a part of your time, your life, in the viewing. Good plays normally are worth viewing, for their characters and themes are such as to provide an entertaining evening with at least a modicum of meaning. A good play poorly presented, however, may be so distorted that its characters and ideas are lost in the mayhem perpetrated upon it. On the other hand, a poor play brilliantly produced, acted, directed and executed may offer to the viewer an exciting and stimulating evening in which the viewer benefits by observing and appreciating the skills of the production team and/or the performers.

In the final analysis, the critic must come to his own decision about the worth of a particular production, but he should know and be able to say **why** he has made the decision.

Conclusion

It is probably impossible for any critic to write a completely just review. We all carry our personal prejudices and tastes within us at all times; they are very much a part of us. Ideally we should set these aside when evaluating something, but in reality, this is probably impossible. However, by using Goethe's approach outlined above, one can approach the task of criticism with objectivity. If we remember that our aim is to enlighten the reader, to view the play for what it is and not for what we would like it to be, and to be open to new ideas and approaches, our criticism and evaluation can be meaningful and of value.

Let's skip the epilogue and beat the crowd."

This was the most unkindest cut of all.

Julius Caesar, Act II, Sc. 2

How is it with you that you do bend your eye on vacancy?

Hamlet, Act III, Sc. 4

Theatre Appreciation

Critique Evaluation Sheet

Play_________________

Name___________________________

Mechanics (30%)

Spelling	____
Punctuation	____
Grammar	____
Clarity	____

Content (70%)

Artist's intent	____
Intent achieved	____
Worthwhile	____
Theme	____
Plot	____
Acting	
diction & volume	____
movement	____
gestures & mannerisms	____
Believability	____
Costumes	____
Lights & Sound	____
Set	____

Suggestions or Comments

Total____

Remove from Text and use as cover page for critique.

Theatre Appreciation

Critique Evaluation Sheet

Play________________

Name__________________________

Mechanics (30%)

Spelling ____

Punctuation ____

Grammar ____

Clarity ____

Content (70%)

Artist's intent ____

Intent achieved ____

Worthwhile ____

Theme ____

Plot ____

Acting

diction & volume ____

movement ____

gestures & mannerisms ____

Believability ____

Costumes ____

Lights & Sound ____

Set ____

Suggestions or Comments Total____

Remove from Text and use as cover page for critique.

Theatre Appreciation

Critique Evaluation Sheet

Play_________________

Name___________________________

Mechanics (30%)

- Spelling ____
- Punctuation ____
- Grammar ____
- Clarity ____

Content (70%)

- Artist's intent ____
- Intent achieved ____
- Worthwhile ____
- Theme ____
- Plot ____
- Acting
  - diction & volume ____
  - movement ____
  - gestures & mannerisms ____
  - Believability ____
- Costumes ____
- Lights & Sound ____
- Set ____

Suggestions or Comments

Total____

Remove from Text and use as cover page for critique.

Theatre Appreciation

Critique Evaluation Sheet

Play_________________

Name___________________________

Mechanics (30%)

- Spelling ____
- Punctuation ____
- Grammar ____
- Clarity ____

Content (70%)

- Artist's intent ____
- Intent achieved ____
- Worthwhile ____
- Theme ____
- Plot ____
- Acting
  - diction & volume ____
  - movement ____
  - gestures & mannerisms ____
  - Believability ____
- Costumes ____
- Lights & Sound ____
- Set ____

Suggestions or Comments

Total____

Remove from Text and use as cover page for critique.

3
Reading a Play

For the uninitiated theatregoer, reading a play script can often be a somewhat daunting assignment. Like a musical score, the play is incomplete until performed. Most of us are used to reading short stories and novels in which the characters are fully and minutely described and the background and action are detailed through word pictures. Few playwrights go to such an extreme. Most leave the description of characters, locale, and action to the directors, designers and actors who will present their plays. When we read a script by Sophocles or Shakespeare, for instance, we are left to the devices of our own imaginations. In many of his plays, Shakespeare indicates location through the dialogue of the characters. Here are a few examples:

Taming of the Shrew, Act I, Scene 2: Petruchio speaks:
"Verona, for awhile I take my leave
To see my friends in Padua, but of all
My best beloved and approved friend,
Hortensio; and I trow this is his house."

The Tempest, Act I, Scene 1: Stage direction:"a tempestuous noise of thunder and lightning heard."
From this point on the characters address each other as "Boatswain" and "Master," etc., thereby makng clear we are on a ship at sea.

Henry V, Act II, Prologue: The Chorus speaks:
"Unto Southampton do we shift our scene."

As readers we must be prepared to use our imaginations. From their actions and personalities, we can create mental pictures of the various characters. From what they say, we can imagine the voice, its pitch and quality, and the expression of the character. From the characters' actions and verbal references, we can picture the locale. In most cases, we will have to relate what we read to our own experiences–our frame of reference. Therefore, the visualization of the play and the action within it will be different for each of us. We become an active part in the creation of its final form, not passive observers allowing the imaginations of others to create for us.

Here are some hints the reader can use in reading a play script:

1. In your mind create the locale of the play with as many details as possible. You can embellish the original locale as you read along and as the characters are required to take certain actions within the setting.

2. Study the list of characters given at the beginning of the play. Try to remember not only their names but their relationships as indicated by the playwright. Create a mental image for each character–height, coloration, hair style, girth, dress, etc.

3. As you read watch for changes of thought within a speech. These can often indicate gesture and movement.

4. Remember that all the characters in a scene are within view of the audience. They not only act, they respond to others' actions. They are human beings with human emotions.

5. Imagine someone you know and apply his reactions, where appropriate, to the characters' reactions. How would you react if you were in similar circumstances?

6. Character names, especially when foreign to us, can give problems. Pronounce them aloud. If you don't know the correct pronunciation, create one.

Here is an example of one approach which can be taken in reading a scene. The play is *Romeo and Juliet* by Shakespeare and the scene is from Act II, Sc. 5. The reader will need to be able to answer six questions in order to view the scene in his mind:

1. ***Who's there?*** The author tells us that Juliet enters, so we at least know who is present at the opening of the scene. Prior to this time we have learned that Juliet is young, about 14, that she is pretty, that she is witty, and that she is either infatuated or deeply in love with Romeo.

2. ***Where are they?*** The author tells us that the play takes place in Capulet's, Juliet's father's, orchard. So, we may picture for ourselves that the scene is possibly wooded or in a garden-like area with trees. In the nurse's first line, she tells her manservant to "wait at the gate," thus giving us another clue about a possible setting. Later in the scene we will find that the nurse is out of breath and exhausted, so we can add a bench so that she can sit.

3. ***What time of day or year is it?*** Juliet's lines indicate it is noon.

4. ***What are they doing?*** Juliet's lines tell us she is wating for the return of the Nurse.

5. ***What's new? What's wrong?*** The Nurse is late in returning.

6. ***What does the audience see and hear?*** The reader is the audience and is witnessing Juliet's impatience and concern. If it identifies with her, it has some of the same feelings she expresses.

Prepared by the events that have previously occurred in the play and by glancing ahead in the script, the reader has an idea of the situation, characters, locale, and the arrangement of the scene within the locale. Now he is ready to visualize the action of the scene.

Juliet's Lines	Imagined Actions
[1]The clock struck nine when I did send the nurse; In half an hour she promised to return.	1 Juliet is impatient, nervous, possibly pacing as she waits.
[2]Perchance she cannot meet him.	2. She stops as a new idea strikes her.
[3]That's not so.	3. She corrects herself and begins to get angry again.
[4]Oh, she is lame!	4. Discouraged, she slumps on the bench.
[5]Love's heralds should be thoughts, Which ten times faster glide than the sun's beams Driving back shadows over lowering hills.	5. She becomes the strict teacher, announcing how things should be.
[6]Therefore do nimble pinioned doves draw Love, And therefore hath the wind-swift Cupid wings.	6. Her imagination takes over, perhaps with her hand she traces the flight of the birds through the air.
[7]Now is the sun upon the highmost hill Of this day's journey,	7. Standing, she looks off into the distance where she can see the placement of the sun.
[8]and from nine till twelve Is three long hours; yet she is not come. Had she affections and warm youthful blood, She would be as swift in motion as a ball;	8. An angry gesture of frustration
[9]My words would bandy her to my sweet love, And his to me.	9. A shift in attitude as she thinks of her "sweet love."
[10]But old folks, many feign as they were dead– Unwieldy, slow, heavy and pale as lead. Enter *Nurse* [and Peter)	10. Again discouraged, she sinks on the bench disheartened
[11]O God, she comes!	11. Jumps up and runs to the nurse excitedly after phrase.
[12]O honey nurse, what news? Hast thou met him?	12. Moves around behind the nurse and happily begins urging her to the bench
[13]Send thy man away.	13. She notices Peter and addresses nurse

The scene above can be visualized in a number of different ways, but always the reader must see the action in terms of the intent of the lines and the personality of the speaker. Given a relatively mature Juliet, the actions and movements would differ considerably compared to a Juliet seen as an active, imaginative and vibrant teenager.

In some modern plays, the playwrights go to great lengths to describe the characters' environment and the characters themselves. For the second act of *The Weavers* by Gerhart Hauptmann (1862-1946), the author describes the set and characters as follows:

> A room in the house of Wilhelm Ansorge in Kaschbach in the Eulengebirge. It is a narrow room, not six feet high, the floor is decayed and the rafters black with soot. In the room are two young girls: Emma and Bertha Baumert, sitting at their looms; Mother Baumert, a stiff-limbed old woman, sitting on a stool by her bed, in front of a spooling reel; her son August, twenty-years-old, an idiot, with a small body and head, and long, spidery limbs, sitting on a footstool, also spooling yarn.
>
> The weak, rose-colored light of evening forces its way through two small windows, holes in the left wall which are partially studded with paper and straw. It falls on the whitish blond loose hair of the girls, on their bare lean shoulders and thin waxen necks, on the folds of their coarse blouses which except for a short skirt of the roughest linen, constitutes their entire clothing. The warm glow falls fully upon the face, neck, and chest of the old woman; a face emaciated to a skeleton, with folds and wrinkles in its bloodless skin, with sunken eyes which are inflamed and watery as a result of the lint, the smoke, and working by lamplight; a long goiter neck with folds and sinews; a sunken chest which is packed in cloths and scarves.
>
> A part of the right wall, along with the stove and the stove bench, the bedsteads and several loudly tinted holy pictures, also stands in the light. On the bar of the stove rags are hung up to dry, while behind the stove all the old worthless rubbish is piled. On the stove bench are several old pots and cooking utensils; potato peelings are laid out on a paper to dry. From the rafters there hang skeins and reels of yarn. Baskets with spools stand beside the looms. In the back wall there is a door without a lock. Leaning against the wall beside the door is a bundle of willow switches. Several damaged quarter-bushel baskets lie about near them. The room is filled with the sounds of the looms, the rhythmic movement of the lathe which shakes both floor and walls, the shuffle and clicking of the rapid shuttle moving back and forth. Mixed into this is the deep constant whirring of the spooling-wheels which resembles the humming of bumble-bees.

Even with such a complete description of the locale and the characters as given by Hauptmann, the reader must employ imagination and hear the lines spoken by the actors in his own mind creating the expression of each line as it is read. For this reason, it sometimes helps to read a play aloud and, with experience, become engrossed in portraying all of the characters.

Juliet coaxes the Nurse to tell her of news from Romeo in this scene from a Stephen F. Austin State University production.

Class Assignment
Reading a Play

Name: ______________________________

Using the assigned play as your source, answer each of the six questions the reader should consider. Apply these to the opening scene of the play:

1. Who's there?

2. Where are they?

3. What time of day or year is it?

4. What are they doing?

5. What's new? What's wrong?

6. What does the audience see and hear?

Remove from text and turn in to instructor.

4
The Play

Every play has certain basic elements. The playwright chooses which of these elements he wishes to emphasize and arranges or structures the play on the basis of his choice. In the Fourth Century BC, Aristotle, tutor to Alexander the Great and one of Athens' leading scholars, chose to apply the scientific method to the analysis of the most successful plays of his time. Scientific research requires that the analyst seek out the recurring elements within various examples of the subject he is studying. For Aristotle, this meant that he would try to find the outstanding similarities existing among the most successful plays of his time. He was not attempting to make a value judgment with regard to the plays, rather he was seeking to analyze them objectively and through that analysis provide information to others about those elements repeatedly appearing in the plays which, over the years, had proved themselves capable of pleasing audiences.

Aristotle discussed his discoveries in his monograph *The Poetics*. What he found in c.335 BC is as true today as it was when originally stated. He discovered there were six elements common to all successful plays. The following is a discussion of these elements with a definition of each. In following chapters we will analyze the elements individually. The elements are listed below in what, according to Aristotle's observations, appear to be their order of importance.

Plot

Aristotle discovered that all of the most successful plays had plots which dominated the play as a whole; that is, all other elements within the play were present to support and carry out the actions of the plot.

The plot is the action of the play which is demonstrated through a series of individual scenes, all interrelated, in dramatic form before an audience. It is this action which holds the play together, revealed the playwright's theme, and provided the action necessary to all drama.

Character

Of next importance in the view of Aristotle are the characters within the play. They are created by the playwright to carry out the actions of the plot. They are the agents who move and speak before us. Since a play, Aristotle had discovered, concerns man in action, these are the means by which the actions of the play are communicated to the audience.

Thought

This element may be described in two different ways:

1. Thought refers to the ability of the characters to think and respond in such a way that they may carry out the actions of the plot believably.

2. Thought may also be defined as the theme or idea demonstrated by the plot. For instance, the parables found in the New Testament and many of the stories from the Old Testament are and have been made into plays. Though each is complete in itself and shows man in action in a certain situation, each also carries a greater meaning symbolizing the relationship of man to man or man to God.

Diction

Characters express themselves and their thoughts through dialogue, i.e., words. The words they choose reveal not only their attitudes, education and social background, etc., but move the action of the play forward thus contributing to the plot. Diction also helps to identify the characters. A dialect, for instance, indicates nationality, regional origin, social level, etc.

Music

For Aristotle, this had a very elemental and literal meaning. In the Greek theatre, we are told, when a playwright was commissioned to write a play, he first sought the services of a lyre or flute player to compose an accompaniment to his new work. Some of the ancient scripts indicate that choral odes were often sung as were some of the speeches.

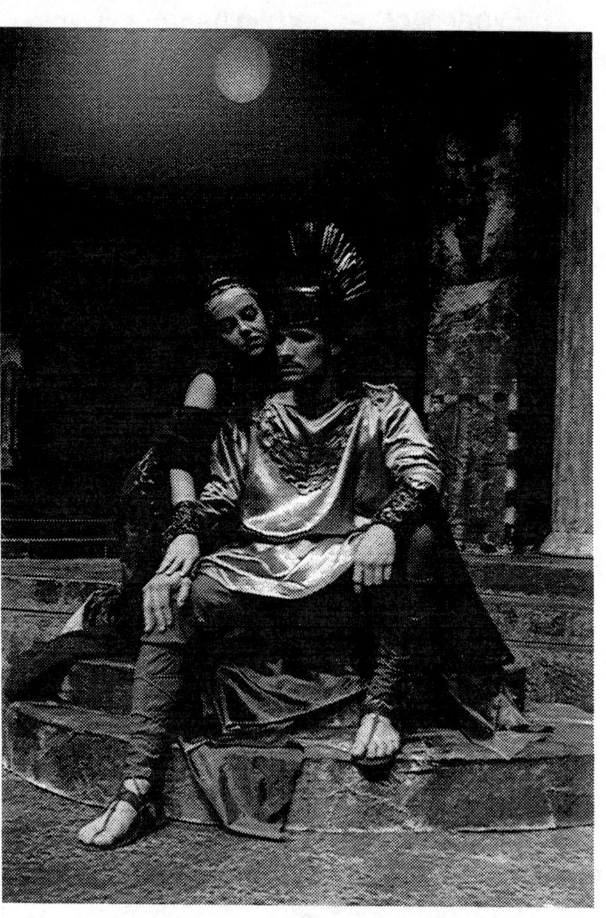

Medea and Jason in the Stephen F. Austin State University production of Robinson Jeffers' version of the ancient Greek story. Here, through word and action, Medea attempts to win back her unfaithful husband.

Today, we still use music in the production of a play. It may provide accompaniment to the action, as it did with the Greeks, may be used as a functional part of the performance, or may provide an interlude between scenes.

The diction used within the play has a musical quality as do the actors' voices.

The function of music in the theatre will be discussed in more detail in a Chapter 21.

Spectacle

Spectacle is everything we see. It includes the actors, their expressions, gestures and movements. It includes the scenery, lighting, costumes and properties used on the stage or in connection with the performance. Though Aristotle states that his observations show this to be the least important element of the six, he does emphasize that since a play is an imitation of an action, both intellectual and physical, spectacle is important.

Aristotle saw in his own time, as we may see today, that various presentations, even of the same play, may emphasize different elements. For instance, a play by Shakespeare may be presented as a character study or as a spectacle verging on pageantry with the script altered to allow for the selected emphasis to dominate.

In some plays, particularly in the modern theatre, playwrights concentrate on character using the plot action primarily as a device for revealing it. Plays written specifically as a vehicle for a particular actor may place more emphasis on character than on plot. *The Magnificent Yankee* (1946) was written as a vehicle for character actor Louis Calhern and used scenes from the life of Oliver Wendell Holmes to achieve this. As a play, the plot structure was very weak, but as a *tour de force* for an actor, the play was very successful. It ran for two full seasons in New York City. In some cases, scripts of established plays will be cut and altered to allow the talents of a star to shine more brightly. Some star performances are totally plotless. For instance, Lilly Tomlin's one-woman performance, *In Search of Signs of Intelligence in the Universe*, has a central theme, but no story or plot line outside of that found in individual scenes.

In the plays of William Shakespeare, there are moments when the action is suspended so that the poetry of the moment may dominate. During the nineteenth century, playwrights often indulged themselves in flights of rhetorical fancy suspending all action in the play as a barrage of words spouted forth to dominate the stage.

George Bernard Shaw's comedies are often seen as thought-provoking debates. Though Shaw was a master craftsman, it is his use of words and the battles of ideas which he brings to the theatre which are most often admired. The third act of *Man and Superman* is a debate between Don Juan, Doña Anna and Lucifer. Shaw calls his play *Misalliance* a "debate in one act."

Music obviously dominates many musicals and operas. In some cases, scripts are contrived to serve only to move the production from one musical number to another. In the best of these works, however, the plot dominates as it does in the greatest of plays.

It is not unusual for spectacle to dominate in today's theatre. The musical *Cats* is a good example of this. With a minimal story line, the production places most of its emphasis on the chorus of dancers, their movements, and the stage effects. The same may be said for *Starlight Express* with its roller-skating principals and chorus. During the nineteenth century, many producers went to extravagant lengths in their staging of major dramas and operas. Charles Kean (1811-1868), for instance, inserted pantomimic and scenic spectacles into the plays of Shakespeare for scenes which were only described in the dialogue and were not intended to be acted out upon the stage. Kean was not alone. He was in competition with a theatre in London in which the opera *Il Trovadore* was being presented with the entire cast on horseback!

What have I done that thou darest wag thy tongue so rude against me?

Hamlet, Act II, Sc. 4

Are you a native of this place?

As You Like It, Act III, Sc. 2

5
The Elements of Plot

The plot of the play is drawn from a story and is usually only a segment of that story. As the Chorus tells us in *Oedipus Rex*, the story of Oedipus begins with his birth, continues through his youth, young manhood, and into his reign as king of Thebes. The plot of the play, however, considers the action occurring on only one day in the life of Oedipus. It is what is normally called a **climactic** or **linear plot**. A climactic plot usually deals with a limited amount of time, possibly twelve to twenty-four hours or less. It is often limited in the place or places represented. Its scenes are arranged in such a way as to have a cause/effect relationship, i.e., one scene leads directly to or causes the next scene of action to occur. The final effect of the climactic plot is achieved as a result of the rising line of action coming to a climax.

A second kind of plot is referred to as a **panoramic plot** or **episodic plot**. This plot uses a variety of scenes and may have more than one story within it, a **sub-plot**. Though all will be brought together meaningfully at the end of the play, one scene does not necessarily lead to the next. This kind of play often covers much more time and makes use of more locales than does the climactic plot. Its final effect results from the cumulative actions of the various scenes or episodes as their actions are brought together by the playwright at the end of the play in one final action. *Hamlet, Romeo and Juliet* and most of the plays by Shakespeare and his contemporaries are episodic or panoramic. Most novels are written with panoramic plots and many films make use of this plot structure as well. Aristotle says that a plot is episodic when there is neither probability nor necessity in the sequence of its episodes.

Climactic or Linear Plot	**Episodic or Panoramic Plot**
cause and effect	theme and variations
one major action	multiple actions
arrow	circle
classical symphony	jazz improvisation
restricted locale	multiple locales
short story	novel
sit-com	feature-length film

Whether plays have climactic or panoramic plot structures, they are composed of a number of elements which enable them to create the desired effects within the audience.

Exposition

Exposition usually occurs early in the play and establishes the situation and such background information as the audience will need to understand what is occurring. In Greek tragedy it is often given by the Chorus and is one of that group's primary functions. In Sophocles' *Antigone*, for instance, the first scene of the play establishes the characters of Antigone and her Sister Ismene and the situation in which they currently find themselves. Antigone:

. . .our friend Creon has decided
To discriminate between our brothers' corpses.
Eteocles he buried with full honors
To light his way to hell in a blaze of glory.
But poor, dear Polynices,–his remains
Are not allowed a decent burial.
He must be left unmourned, without a grave,
A happy hunting ground for birds
To peck for tidbits. This edict applies
To you, –and me, of course. What's more, friend Creon
Is on his way here now to supervise
Its circulation in person. And don't imagine
He isn't serious,–the penalty
For disobedience is to be stoned to death.

This speech is totally exposition, but it doesn't give the audience the entire background of what is happening. That responsibility is left to the chorus, and in the first choral ode the relationship of Eteocles, Polynices, Antigone and Ismene is explained as are the actions of Eteocles and Polynices which have brought Creon's edict into being.

Exposition may be handled by a playwright in many different ways and using many different devices. It may come as a set speech at the beginning of a play as Shakespeare uses it in the opening of *Romeo and Juliet* or it may be brought into the play on a "need-to-know" basis as it is in *Oedipus Rex*. Whichever way is chosen, exposition is necessary if the audience is to be prepared to understand and follow the action which is to come.

Courtesy of the Stratford, Canada, Festival

Oedipus Rex as staged by Sir Tyrone Guthrie and designed by Tanya Moiseiwitsch for the Stratford, Canada, Shakespeare Festival in 1955. Guthrie staged the tragedy using conventions of the Greek theatre, particularly the masks. The lines were delivered in a ritualistic style with the chorus chanting its odes. Douglas Campbell is seen above as Oedipus surrounded by members of the chorus in this scene of discovery as the chorus pleads with Oedipus for help in facing the plague which threatens Thebes.

Discovery

Aristotle says that discovery is a change from ignorance to knowledge. Discovery takes place on two levels within a play. The first and most important level is discovery by the audience which usually begins at the beginning of a play. When the curtain rises, the audience "discovers" the locale, the era, and the mood of the play through the work of the scenic designer. When the first character enters, the audience discovers a great deal about him from his appearance, what he says, and his attitude. For the audience, in fact, discovery never stops in a well-written, well-directed play.

On the second level, but just as important, is discovery by the characters. From the moment the action begins, the characters make discoveries. Antigone's speech, quoted above, is made to her sister Ismene, who has not previously learned of Creon's edict. In turn, Antigone learns, as does the audience, something of Ismene's character when Ismene refuses to assist Antigone in defying the edict.

Point of Attack

This is the event within the story at which the playwright chooses to begin the play. Beginning late in the story, as in *Oedipus,* the likelihood is that the play will have a climactic plot. If Sophocles had chosen to begin *Oedipus* at an earlier point in the protagonist's life, the plot would probably have been panoramic.

Inciting Incident

At the beginning of a play, the playwright presents a wide range of possibilities for his characters. The major character, the protagonist, however, finds himself faced with a situation which requires that he make a decision upon which he will act. That decision provides the inciting incident. It is that point in the play from which there is no turning back. For instance, Hamlet is told by what appears to be the ghost of his father that he, King Hamlet, was murdered by his own brother, Claudius, who is now king. The ghost demands vengeance for the murder and Hamlet, as the son of the murdered king, is responsible for carrying out the demand. He swears on the cross-hilt of his sword that he will do so. From this point on, Hamlet is committed to a specific line of action and though he may question it, his commitment dominates his future actions.

Foreshadowing

The plot of a play has a beginning, a middle, and an end; and the end is inherently in the beginning. All actions and events within the play must be motivated and plausible if the audience is to believe the action of the play and the characters in it. Every event in a well-structured play leads inevitably to the conclusion; therefore, every event foreshadows that which is to come. In some cases, the foreshadowing is fairly specific. During his first meeting with the ghost of his father, Hamlet is told that he must take care not to harm or unduly upset his mother, for she, his father believes, is innocent. When in a later scene Hamlet does level accusations at his mother, the ghost reappears to remind Hamlet of his instructions and to urge him to move ahead in his mission of vengeance.

Complication

Complications occur throughout the play. There is, in fact, normally a complication introduced in each scene of a play. A complication is any event or series of events which will delay or prevent the **protagonist** from achieving his goal. It may be the result of the actions of other characters, the protagonist's own lack of resolution or assurance, or purely a matter of circumstances. Antigone is faced with an edict from Creon which she believes is in defiance of the laws of the gods. She believes her sister Ismene will assist her in defying the edict.

Ismene, however, refuses and Antigone must deal with this complication. For Creon, Antigone presents a complication with her rejection of his edict. Later in the play, Hyman, Creon's son who is in love with Antigone, finds himself in direct opposition to his father, thus presenting both Creon and himself with further complications. Any form of conflict within the play inevitably results in complications.

Crisis

A well-written dramatic work normally involves the emotions not only of the characters but of the audience as well. As in real life, each complication which must be faced produces a crisis; that is, a heightened emotional condition. Thus, in each scene of the play there may be a crisis in the life of the protagonist. As one crisis is added to others, the emotional tension produced is heightened. This is certainly true of tragedy and drama. In comedy, the same may be said to be true except that with each crisis in the life of the protagonist, greater laughter is produced as the protagonist becomes more and more open to ridicule.

Reversal

This is often referred to as "that point in the play in which the hunter becomes the hunted." More literally, it is that point in the play in which the fortunes of the protagonist are reversed. For Willy Loman in *Death of a Salesman*, it is that point in the play at which his oldest son loses faith, respect and trust in his father. In *Hamlet,* it is that point at which Hamlet has his first opportunity to kill Claudius but decides against it. From that point on Hamlet is the "hunted" for Claudius knows that Hamlet knows of Claudius' guilt. In classical tragedies the reversal always comes as the result of a decision made by the protagonist–a decision based on ignorance but one for which he must take responsibility. Some critics refer to the reversal as the technical climax of the play.

Climax

The highest point of emotional response on the part of the protagonist and the audience. The climax comes as a result of the compounding effects of the crises which have occurred within the play. In the most successful plays, there is only one climax. Other climaxes are often referred to as "anti-climactic" because they weaken the overall effect of the major climax and therefore are detrimental to the play as a whole.

Denouement

"Denouement" is a French term which is variously translated as "the loosening of the knot" or "tying up the loose threads." The denouement is the conclusion of the play in which the fate of the protagonist and all the complications previously shown are resolved. In a well-written play, the denouement immediately follows the climax. Here, all the accumulated tensions of the play are relaxed and the viewer is "cleansed" of the emotional trauma he has experienced.

Theatre Appreciation
Class Assignment-Parts of the Plot

Name:____________________

Using *Oedipus Rex* as your source, choose a speech or stage direction which will illustrate the playwright's use of each of the plot elements indicated below:

1. Inciting Incident:

2. Exposition:

3. Discovery:

4. Foreshadowing:

5. Complication:

6. Reversal:

7. Crisis:

8. Climax:

9. Denouement:

Remove from text and hand in to instructor.

6
Character

1. The combination of qualities or features that distinguishes one person, group, or thing from another.
2. A distinguishing feature or attribute, as of an individual, a group, or a category.

As has been discussed earlier, characters are the agents created by the playwright to carry out the actions being dramatized within the play. As such, they are created to fulfill certain functions and must have the characteristics required to make them capable of meeting the play's requirements. Characters are usually defined by those qualities which differentiate one individual from another. When we refer to someone as being aggressive, we are comparing that individual's bent with the bent of others; we are seeing him as being more aggressive than the average person.

We learn about characters within a play from three different sources:

1. What the character says or does
2. What others say about him
3. What the playwright tells us

From the information garnered from these sources, we can analyze a character on several levels. Below is a discussion of the "levels of characterization." It should be understood that a fully developed character is multi-layered; that is, he will probably be composed of all of the elements beginning with the lowest on through to the highest level of characterization.

1. Basic Physiological Traits

This is the lowest level on which any individual may be identified. It is concerned with the character's sex, age, coloration, height, hair, eyes, weight, and general physical conformation. For instance, King Richard the III, the leading character in Shakespeare's history play may be seen as:

a. male
b. probably in his late 20s or early 30s
c. possibly short of stature
d. caucasian of relatively c rk complexion
e. in spite of his position, h s sometimes seen as sloppy in ap arance
f. a twisted body with a hunc l back
g. in spite of deformities, he hletic. Note the duel with Richmon

All characters are identified on this lev those who play what are normally referred to as **wal es**. The amount of detail revealed, however, will vary c pending on the function of the character within the pla

Courtesy, Hoblitzelle Theatre Arts Library, University of Texas at Austin.

John Barrymore in the title role of *Richard III.*

Bert Lahr in *Waiting for Godot* in which he plays a tramp, an individual with little other perceivable social function to serve.

2. Social Function

Every one of us has one or more social functions to fill. We normally have a profession, something we do for a living. We have various relationships with various people. Richard III is found to be not only a king, but a subject, a lover and seducer, a swordsman, a revolutionary, a son, a nephew, etc. We all play roles according to our particular social function at the time. Consider the role Oedipus has been playing in relation to Jocasta and how that changes as he finds his true identity.

All characters are identified on this level but some only nominally. In *Richard III* there are many characters who have only one function to play–a soldier. We learn no more about them than that. We identify them on a basic physical level and only minimally on the level of social function.

3. Habits and/or Mannerisms

All of us have basic habits or mannerisms which identify us in the eyes of others. We have our own way of walking, our own speech pattern, certain peculiarities in our gestures that, though they may be imitated, are specifically our own. A character may fidget with his coat or clothing when under pressure, may have a habit of winking when he feels he has been particularly brilliant, may twirl his glasses when affecting boredom or relaxation, may glance in a particular way at his watch when impatient. These are the things a character does unconsciously but consistently.

Habits and mannerisms are the source of most of the material used by impressionists. Note Jimmy Stewart's speech pattern, the way James Cagney hitched up his pants in some of his films, Richard Nixon's "V" sign, and many of the individual peculiarities of the people around us.

Often playwrights give us little information regarding a character's habits with the result that this part of the characterization is left to our imaginations and to the imagination of the director and actor. The fact that few or no references to particular habits and mannerisms are to be found in many scripts does not negate their importance, particularly in regard to major characters. These are the little, sometimes almost imperceptible, things which can definitively separate one character from another. Usually, the more a character is identified, the more important he is to the action of the play.

Paul Robeson in the title role in Eugene O'Neill's *Emperor Jones*. The manner in which Robson slouched and wore his clothes helped to identify the character he was playing.

4. Attitude or Bent

All major and many minor characters are characterized on this level. It is often on the basis of a character's attitude that he chooses what he will do and how he will do it. Often, he does not make conscious choices, but rather reacts and acts upon situations as a result of his "bent" to do so. His actions will reflect his attitude toward

a. himself
b. life
c. the situation
d. other individuals

The actions will reflect what the character wants and his wants are often a result of his attitude.

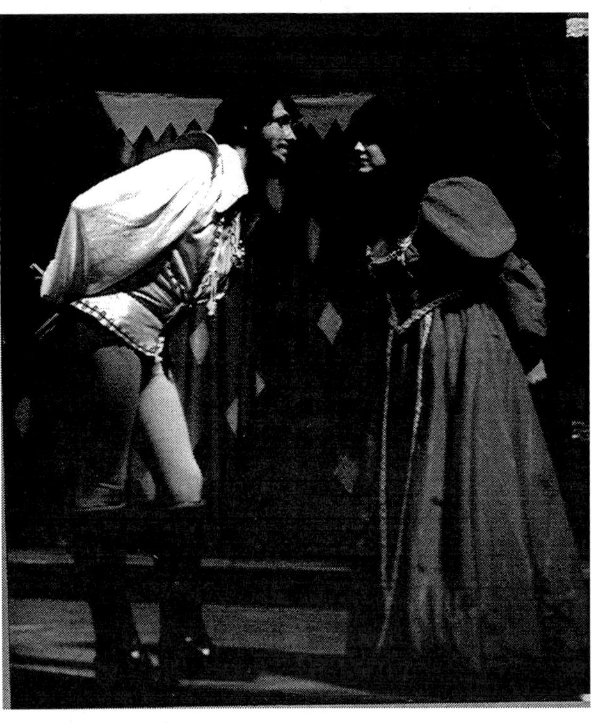

Petruchio and Katarina in the Stephen F. Austin State University production of Shakespeare's *Taming of the Shrew.* Their body positions suggest the attitudes of the characters toward each other.

In *Romeo and Juliet*, Mercutio's actions are a basic reflection of his attitudes. He is whimsical, brash, prideful, self-assured, sees life as a delightful adventure, lives without fear, sometimes unfeeling, often imprudent, and, as his name implies, mercurial.

Hamlet with Ophelia in a scene from the Stephen F. Austin State University production of *Hamlet.* Having found that Ophelia has lied to him, Hamlet's emotions dominate his actions.

5. The Ability to Make a Moral Decision on an Emotional Level

Very few characters are placed in a position by the playwrights to make moral decisions of any kind. Though we may see their decisions as being moral or immoral in our eyes, the character's decisions often are a result of his attitude or bent. In the eyes of the character, therefore, there is no question of right or wrong, but rather a reaction to a situation based on basic attitude. To make a moral decision, the character must choose between two courses of action and that choice must be on the basis of a set of principles higher than those he has created for himself or those stipulated by society. To make a moral choice implies belief in a higher power whose rules are unchangeable, immutable. The choice may be emotional, but the debate between right and wrong must take place and the audience must witness it. On this level the choice is an emotional one and is not necessarily rational either for the character or in the eyes of the audience.

In *Antigone*, Antigone responds to Creon's edicts basically on an emotional level. Her love for the brother to whom Creon will deny a proper burial and her respect for the gods moves her to make her decision to defy Creon in spite of any and all consequences. She never wavers in her choice of action, never reasons, but emotionally chooses the direction in which she will move. Creon, on the other hand, initially responds purely on the basis of attitude. He then reacts and chooses to condemn Antigone to death on the basis of his emotional response to her defiance. Finally, however, he is forced to make a choice on the basis of reason, i.e., intellect. This brings us to the highest level of characterization.

6. The Ability to Make a Moral Choice on an Intellectual Level

This is the very highest point to which a character may be developed. The ability to make a choice on an intellectual level does not rule out the emotions, but indicates a higher level of reaction. In this case, the character makes his choice on the basis of his knowledge which is usually either a misunderstanding of the facts or incomplete. This is the level to which the greatest of the tragic protagonists rise. It is the highest point of development to which any man may rise and one that many of us rarely employ. In tragedy, the tragic protagonist finally makes his choice using reason as does Creon in *Antigone.* By that time, however, the reasoned choice comes too late to save the protagonist from his fate.

Following the trial, Gratiano forces Shylock to kiss the cross in this scene from *the Merchant of Venice.* For Shylock, this requires a moral decision which is rare in what is essentially a comedy. However, Shylock makes what is for him an immoral decision. This prevents Shylock from being the "good" person required of a classical tragic hero. A Stephen F. Austion State University production.

It is rare for any character other than the tragic protagonist to be developed to the highest level. In fact, there are commentators who claim that without exception no characters other than the tragic hero are so developed. It is also rare for any character in a tragedy other than the protagonist to be faced with making a moral choice. In *Hamlet,* Claudius chooses his course of action purely as a matter of self-preservation. Laertes challenges Hamlet to fight as result of his conviction that Hamlet has been responsible for his father's and his sister's deaths, but not out of any moral consideration. Hamlet, alone, considers the morality of what he is doing and how he is doing it. He believes in Claudius' guilt, but will not act until he has indisputable proof of it. He believes what the ghost has told him, but knowing that "the devil hath power to assume a pleasing shape" he seeks proof that the ghost of his murdered father is an "honest" ghost and delays action–a delay which will ultimately cost him his life.

Conclusion

Playwrights choose their characters carefully in order to demonstrate the actions of their stories. They know only too well that too many characters too highly developed will keep the attention of the viewer from being focused on the character or characters who have been designed to demonstrate the theme of the play. As a result, they develop the characters in their plays carefully. Playwrights are also aware that contrasting characters are required if the audience is to easily identify each one and find all interesting.

For the actor, it is important to understand the level to which the character has been developed. He must find all the facets of the character which will enable the character to do what he must do, and he must reveal those facets to the audience as the play progresses. If he gives qualities to the character that are not required by the action of the play, he may destroy the playwright's focus and thereby twist the meaning, intent, mood and progress of the action. An actor who attempts to portray *Hamlet's* Horatio as having the depth of a Hamlet will inevitably take attention away from the main course of action with which Shakespeare was concerned. An actor who attempts to reveal a hidden and honest conscience in Claudius may create a sympathy for the usurper which will, in turn, dilute the sympathy the audience feels for Hamlet. The audience should be able to recognize Claudius, but probably should not identify with him. If *Hamlet* is to achieve its full effect, the audience must not only recognize Hamlet, but must also identify with him.

The playwright is also conscious of the fact that if he is to maintain focus on his principal characters and if they are to be readily identified by the audience, they will have to be created with obvious and recognizable differences. Generally, the director will make sure that the characters differ physically and vocally, but within the script itself there must be sufficient contrasts between characters to set them apart from each other.

The contrasts between characters becomes increasingly important when dealing with the **protagonist** and **antagonist.** Derived from the Greek, these words are often used to identify specific characters within a play. The protagonist is usually viewed as the hero or leading character within the play. This character has a direct line of action he desires to follow. The **antagonist** is the protagonist's nemesis. He opposes the protagonist, bringing conflict into the drama as the two forces are pitted against each other.

Much more may be said about character, but that will be left to future chapters and the discussions of the different forms of drama.

"I have no reason to doubt your abilities as a director, sir, but may I be so bold as to suggest that Hamlet did not have a thing for his mother?"

Mort Gerberg, Diners' Club Magazine, September, 1964

Theatre Appreciation
Class Assignment

Name:________________________________

Analyze a character assigned by your instructor according to the six levels of characterization.

1. Basic Physiological:

2. Social Function(s):

3. Habits & Mannerisms:

4. Attitude(s):

5. Ability to Make a Moral Decision Based on Emotions:

6. Ability to Make a Moral Deicision Based on Intellect:

7
Tragedy & Related Forms

At this point in our discussion of the theatre and the script, we turn our attention to dramatic forms: tragedy with its related forms, drama and melodrama, and comedy with its related forms, farce and satire. A dramatic form or structure is used by a playwright to achieve a specific purpose, a specific effect, and a particular response from the audience. It is a label placed on a play or series of plays for the sake of ease in study and analysis. Few, if any, plays are pure in form. For instance, Aristotle's definition of tragedy applies totally to only one play, *Oedipus Rex.* Though there are other plays which may be called tragedy, none of them totally meet all the recommendations contained in *The Poetics* as does *Oedipus Rex.* There is danger, therefore, in pigeon-holing a play into any specific category since many plays have elements of several forms within them.

Tragedy

There is no happiness where there is no wisdom;
No wisdom but in submission to the gods.
Big words are always punished,
And proud men in old age learn to be wise.

Sophocles' *Antigone*

Playwrights choose their subjects and structure their plays to achieve a specific impact on the audience. In defining tragedy Aristotle tells us:

> "A tragedy is an imitation of an action that is serious and also, as having magnitude, complete in itself; in language with pleasurable accessories . .; in a dramatic, not in a narrative form, with incidents arousing pity and fear, wherewith to accomplish its catharsis of such emotions."

For the Greeks, tragedy was the "queen" of dramatic presentations. It was believed that through tragedy mankind could receive instruction on moral behavior, responsibility, and his fate. It was also believed that as a result of **catharsis**, man could be cleansed of unhealthy and unproductive emotions. In fact, many of the Greek theatres were established in healing centers where patients were taken to view tragedies as a means of aiding them in their recovery. The great theatre at Epidauros was such a place, serving this purpose from the Fourth Century BC until well after the time of Christ with patients coming to it from all over the civilized world.

The Greek Attitude & Tragedy

To understand Greek tragedy, one must have a brief introduction to Greek beliefs regarding man, the gods, and life. According to scholars Whitney Oates and Eugene O'Neill, Jr., there are three basic assumptions found as the basis for Greek tragedy. These three assumptions dominate most serious drama up to the modern age when changes in scientific understanding and man's place in the universe have come increasingly into question. The assumptions are:

1. Man has dignity
2. Man has free will and responsibility for his use of that will
3. The existence in the universe of a superhuman factor

The classical tragic hero and his actions are based on the above assumptions. He is usually seen as a "great" man; that is, one whose position in society is high and whose decisions and actions will influence many others. Aristotle says that he must be a "good" man, meaning that he has and attempts to abide by a moral code. He chooses his actions on the basis of their moral correctness, attempting to act in such a manner as to benefit all mankind. Yet, the tragic hero has his flaws. He is human. A character drawn without flaws would be difficult to identify with and would not deserve any ill fate. Since the tragic character suffers, he must have flaws within him which justify his suffering if the audience is to empathize with him and learn from his experiences. Through the suffering, he learns. As he learns, he grows, becoming a better man than he was at the beginning of the dramatic action.

It should be noted that the "tragic flaw" referred to above is a flaw of degree. That quality within a character which may lead him to make his errors of judgment may be and often is a necessary quality. It is commonly agreed that Oedipus' flaw is that of pride. Pride, however, is a necessary element within the character of a man. It is only when pride is taken to an excess, as in the case of Oedipus, that it becomes a flaw.

Having free will, the tragic hero will make choices, moral choices; choices based on his knowledge and his desire to be morally correct. He must take action on that basis. Unfortunately, being human, he will lack complete knowledge of himself, the situation, and the will of the gods. Because of this, he will make errors in choosing his course of action. Even so, he makes his choices and is responsible for the outcome.

The acceptance on the part of the tragic hero that there is a power greater than himself is directly tied to his actions. Not knowing and not understanding the total will of the gods, i.e., the superhuman factor, he will unwittingly defy them. In the case of Oedipus, it is evident that his entire life, as were the lives of his parents, has been involved in an effort to avoid the prophesies which have come from the gods . The decisions of his parents and those made by Oedipus have been made on the basis of partial knowledge. When Oedipus left Corinth in a futile effort to thwart the prophecies of the gods, he actually placed himself in a position to fulfill those prophecies. The result was that when, on his trip to Thebes, he met King Laius at the crossroads and fought with him, he unwittingly killed his father. When he answered the riddle of the Sphinx and freed Thebes from bondage, he was greeted as a hero by the people, named ruler of the city-state, and given the hand of his mother Jocasta, the queen, in marriage though neither he nor the people knew of the blood relationship. In every case, Oedipus has done the wrong things for the right reasons. His errors are the result of a lack of knowledge, not a willful desire to sin.

Not all Greek tragedies follow the pattern established by Sophocles in *Oedipus Rex*, nor do all Greek tragic heroes rise to the level of Oedipus. Yet, the vast majority of them show us heroes who attempt to follow the will of the gods only to find that they have made errors of judgment for which they will be held accountable. Not only is this true of Greek tragic heroes, but the same pattern of action can be found in later plays which belong in the category of tragedy. In all cases, the tragic hero **suffers** as a result of a decision he has made and **learns** from the suffering. In learning, the hero becomes a greater person; and we, as witnesses, also grow in knowledge and wisdom.

Tragedy, in the hands of the masters, makes a positive statement regarding man and life. It repeatedly demonstrates the levels to which man may rise and often stresses the potentials within humans. Though the tragic hero may suffer, the fact that he usually suffers for a reasonable and just cause raises him above the norm. Added to that is the idea that man can learn from his experiences and, therefore, is capable of growth. In the final analysis, the fact that many tragic heroes die is not the important factor in the meaning of the play. What is important is what a man does, why he does it, what he learns, and what we learn from his life and experiences. These factors become metaphors for our own lives and, if the playwright has chosen his actions and characters well, become universal for all mankind. Tragedy,therefore, makes a positive statement about man and his potential.

Wide World Photo

Eugene O'Neill
1888-1954

Related Forms of Drama

There are other forms of drama which appeal to the emotions of the audience, require identification with the characters, and involve suffering. Two of these are often referred to as **drama** and **melodrama**. Both are serious in tone and deal with the conflicts that occur between humans, but neither reach the philosophical or dramatic heights of tragedy.

Theatre Collection, Museum of City of N.Y.

Tennessee Williams
1911-1983

Of the two, **drama** is generally considered to be the more serious. As a dramatic form, it became an important part of the theatre in the late 19th century though it had been seen on the stage occasionally well over 150 years earlier. It is primarily concerned with ethical rather than moral questions and often deals with current social problems and conditions. Like tragedy, its plot is tightly constructed and well motivated.

Among the best examples of drama are such plays as *Ghosts, A Doll's House, The Enemy of the People, The Wild Duck* and *Hedda Gabler,* all by Henrik Ibsen who is often called the "father of modern drama." More current dramas have come from the pens of such writers as Eugene O'Neill, Arthur Miller, Tennessee Williams, Harold Pinter, Lorraine Hansberry, and Edward Albee.

Wide World Photo

Lorraine Hansberry
1930-1965

Morals vs. Ethics

Morals: Unchangeable and universal rules of behavior prescribed by a source above and beyond man–the gods, God, a Supreme Being. These are considered universal.

Ethics: Rules and laws established by man and society. These may differ as societies differ and may change over time as society changes; therefore, they lack universality.

In many cases, the writer of drama raises problems and questions for which he provides no answers. Ibsen stated at one time that this is the duty of the playwright and the duty of the audience and society is to find the answer to the questions the playwright has demonstrated. Thus, in *A Doll's House,* the audience must answer for itself what the true relationship of a husband and wife should be. In *Ghosts* the audience is left to decide for itself the morality of euthanasia. In *The Wild Duck*, the audience must decide whether a life based on illusion or one based on truth is the ideal. A similar question, though with a different answer implied, is raised by Edward Albee in *Who's Afraid of Virginia Woolf?* Lorraine Hansberry delves into questions not only of family relationships and responsibilities but of social relationships, particularly those related to prejudice.

New York Public Library; Friedman-Abeles Collection

A scene from the original Broadway production of Loraine Hansberry's *Raisin in the Sun* (1954) starring Sidney Poitier and Claudia McNeil. Though the subject of prejudice is raised in the play, Hansberry emphasizes the family and its personal relationships in this drama.

The characters revealed in drama are drawn essentially from real life. They are usually from the middle or lower classes, though this dramatic form has great latitude in regard to the social classes represented. The great majority of these characters are neither ethically good nor evil, but rather are revealed in shades of good and evil. They rarely rise above the level of attitude or bent and are often reflective of social values and pressures. In many cases, they become symbols of those values. Their speech reflects their social position and education and rarely rises to the beauty and poetic levels achieved in tragedy, though in the plays of Williams and Albee, there is often the feeling of prose-poetry.

As in tragedy, the spectacle employed is that which is required by the action of the play and is therefore highly motivated. The great majority of dramas are essentially realistic, though many are often interpreted by directors and designers in a more abstract style.

Melodrama

The term melodrama has fallen into disrepute in the latter part of the 20th Century primarily as a result of the concepts we have of late 19th century "mellerdrama" and the exaggerated acting style often associated with it. Melodrama has been with us since the 5th Century B.C. For a period of time it was referred to as "tragicomedy" because it encompassed in its presentations many of the elements of tragedy with comic scenes interspersed between dramatic scenes. The term melodrama originated in the early 19th century when romantic musical scores were composed to accompany dramatic presentations in an effort to increase the emotional response of the audience. The rise of melodrama in the legitimate theatre was undoubtedly influenced by the growing popularity of romantic operas which stressed elaborate stage effects, violent action and highly dramatic scores.

Melodrama pits good against evil. There are rarely any moral or ethical gray areas , and the audience is always sure of the characters' moral values. The virtuous hero and/or heroine (protagonists) are faced with the threat of both mental and bodily harm at the hands of the villain (antagonist). There is little or no growth in the characters who remain true to their moral bent from beginning to end. The hero is often the victim of a set of circumstances plotted to ensnare him by the villain whose nefarious aim is repugnant to the viewer. Often, in fact, the hero must depend on the actions of others to save him–usually at the last minute. Unlike tragedy and drama, the melodrama ends with the situation being resolved as the hero is rescued and the villain is punished. As a result, this form of drama is related to both tragedy and comedy since the situation is serious and the outcome is happy.

An advertising woodcut for the melodrama *The Poor of New York* as presented in New York City in 1850. In addition to the flames and "smoke" (really steam), the building was rigged to crumble away. Such vivid effects were common in 19th century melodrama and may still be seen on the stage today in such productions as *Phantom of the Opera.*

Many melodramatic plots are contrived in an effort to arouse the emotions of the audience. Melodramatic characters tend to be stereotypes, readily recognized by the audience. Their diction is common and their thought patterns easily comprehended. As the term implies, music is often an important part of the presentation and is designed to appeal to the emotions of the audience. A. H. Quinn comments:

> The essence of melodrama is the freedom from the observance of the strict dramatic law of cause and effect, its intensification and exaggeration of passion. To supply the appeal which true feeling and natural motive make instantly to the audience, melodrama calls in the aid of musical accompaniment to incite emotion and thus weaken, even momentarily, the critical judgement and the appeal of reason.

Spectacle is very important in melodrama, for the threat to the hero is usually physicaand the physical actions within the scenes often carry the play far more than character relationships and dialogue. In some melodramas, spectacle dominates and complex chase scenes, mechanized stage settings, and violent action are often employed. On occasion, rather than placing emphasis on the physical, the melodrama may work on a psychological level creating tension within the audience as the hero or heroine undergoes mental torture perpetrated by the villain. Inevitably, however, the hero will win and the villain will receive his just deserts.

Comparing the Serious Forms of the Play

	Tragedy	Drama	Melodrama
1. **Plot**	Universal theme. Serious, motivated, logically developed.	Serious, semi-universal. Logical & motivated.	Semi-serious, non-universal. Often contrived for emotional response.
2. **Character**	Protagonist fully developed. Grows in knowledge and understanding.	Characters are much as we are. They are often shades of good and bad. Rarely grow.	Characters do not grow and often represent moral types–either good or bad. Stereotypes.
3a. **Character Thought**	Protagonist capable of making moral decisions.	Decisions are made on the basis of attitude or bent.	Morality predetermined. Characters are types.
3b. **Character Theme**	Shows the potential of man.	Often deals with current social problems.	Good vs. Evil on the most elementary level
4. **Diction**	Elevated and often poetic. Makes use of rhetorical devices.	Often used to reveal characters, but reflects native patterns of expression.	Stereotypical, often commonplace. Relatively unimportant since emphasis is on action.
5. **Music**	Often to be found in the language. Otherwise it is totally motivated.	Not too important, but motivated when used.	Exceptionally important. Used to arouse the emotions of the audience.
6. **Spectacle**	Only used as needed to reveal plot and character.	Same as for tragedy, but may be used to emphasize the environment in which the characters live.	Often highly important. May dominate the play and is used to excite the audience; for instance, the chase scene, etc.

8
Comedy

There are three dominant forms of comedy which have developed throughout the history of the theatre and which are still present today–**comedy**, **farce** and **satire**. These forms work on several levels which have been identified as follows and are grouped beginning with the lowest form of comedy and moving to what is considered to be the highest form:

Comedy of Obscenity

This is the comedy which uses shock techniques to produce laughter and often relies heavily on "put-down" humor; that is, the humor of insult. It usually makes use of profane and obscene expressions applied as insults and, at its best, relies heavily on the double entendre particularly with regard to sexual allusions. Lenny Bruce and other comedians of his type often use this form of humor to produce their desired reactions.

Comedy of Physical Mishap

Laughter is produced in this comedy through the physical mishaps which are perpetrated on their deserving victims. Often called slap-stick comedy, it depends heavily on slaps, falls, hits, and other physical mishaps which are suffered by characters as a result of their stupidity, pomposity, general obnoxiousness, etc. This form of comedy may inflict a mild degree of pain on its victims, but never seriously harms them. Much of the comedy of the Three Stooges, Laurel and Hardy, and Jerry Lewis is of this level. In modern plays and films, this form of comedy may be viewed in such works as *Noises Off*, *City Slickers* and most of Mel Brooks' films. Shakespeare uses this kind of humor extensively in *The Comedy of Errors* and *The Taming of the Shrew*. Characters are normally stereotypes.

A Stephen F. Austin State University production.

The "table scene" from Moliere's *Tartuffe* While her husband, Orgon, hides beneath the table, Elmire fends off the advances of the hypocrite Tartuffe. The scene combines physical comedy with that of situation and character.

Comedy of Situation

Laughter here is the result of characters being placed in what are for them improbable situations to which they cannot adapt or in which they would rarely be found. The inability of the character to adapt to the situation, which is not life-threatening or of serious danger, is the source of the humor. Many of our present day situation comedies on television are good examples of this type of humor, particularly *Three's Company, The Nanny, Gilligan's Island,* etc. These characters are often stereotypes. The comedy of situation is well demonstrated in such plays as Shakespeare's *The Taming of the Shrew* and *Twelfth Night,* and in many of the early comedies of Neil Simon such as *The Odd Couple, Barefoot in the Park,* and *The Star Spangled Girl.* The "boulevard farces" of the 19th and early 20th century French theatre, such as those by Feydeau, are excellent examples of situation comedy with a great deal of physical humor and some comments and scenes verging on but rarely becoming obscene.

A Stephen F. Austin State University production.

The Philosophy Professor attempts to teach M. Jourdan, who is the title role in Moliere's *The Would-Be Gentleman* how to form "O" and other vowels. Combining physical humor with that of situation and character, Moliere makes fun of social climbers who place more trust in the surface than the substance.

Comedy of Character

This is a much more serious form of comedy which delves into the foibles to be found within the human being and holds them up to ridicule. It often deals with current problems and/or situations and seeks to reveal the reasons for their existence through comedy and bring about a correction of the causes through ridicule. *M*A*S*H*, Frazier, Murphy Brown,* Cosby, and other such comedies belong in this category. Most of the plays by Moliere are particularly good examples of the comedy of character, particularly *Tartuffe, The Bourgeoise Gentleman,* and *The Misanthrope.* The characters found in this form of comedy are more carefully drawn and more three-dimensional than those to be found in the lower forms listed above. Shakespeare's Falstaff is a good example of comedy of character as are Neil Simon's latest plays, particularly *Biloxi Blues, Brighton Beach Memoirs,* and *Lost in Yonkers.*

Comedy of Language

This kind of comedy is on a fairly high intellectual base. It requires sophistication and knowledge on the part of both the playwright and the audience. Since it often finds its humor in the misuse of language, double meanings, and the pun, it depends on the audience to know and recognize the incongruity within the dialogue. On television, this was well demonstrated in the character and language of Archie Bunker in *All in the Family.* In the theatre, good examples can be found in such plays as Sheridan's *The Rivals,* the play from which we get the word "malaprop." The verbal wit of Oscar Wilde in *The Importance of Being Earnest* is another good example of comedy of language. Shakespeare also makes use of the comedy of language through the witty repartee in such plays as *Much Ado About Nothing,*

A Stephen F. Austin State University production.

In a scene from Wycherley's *The Country Wife,* two of the characters discuss the trickery they plan to play on the citizens of London. Wycherley combines verbal wit with humorous characters and situations in this comedy.

Hamlet, and *Romeo and Juliet.*

Comedy of Ideas

The comedy of ideas is extremely rare and is to be found particularly in the plays of George Bernard Shaw. Such works as *Pygmalion, Major Barbara, Misalliance*, etc. are good examples. In these plays the characters represent specific ideas or attitudes and are placed in competition with each other. Often, the characters in the comedy of ideas become little more than puppets in the hands of the playwright. The comedy of ideas requires a particularly sophisticated and intelligent audience. In many cases, this kind of comedy verges on satire.

Response to Comedy

Whereas tragedy and its related forms demand an emotional response from the audience during the time of performance and often provoke an intellectual response after, comedy demands an intellectual response from the audience at the time of performance. The audience must recognize and understand the jokes if it is to respond to them. Comedy, therefore, demands logic, albeit a kind of twisted logic. It is reasonably unreasonable. If it confuses, there is no laughter because there is no understanding. Even on the lowest level, this appeal to the intellect exists.

In spite of the physical mishaps which occur in this scene from Goldsmith's *She Stoops to Conquer,* no real pain is inflicted on the characters and the emotions of the audiences are not involved.

On occasion, comedy may cause concern or pain within the audience, but if it is to remain comedy, it must provide an escape from pain and that escape will be through laughter. It must avoid causing permanent and/or undeserved pain. The victim of the joke must deserve being the brunt of the humor, but cannot and must not be seriously hurt or harmed.

The pompous man who loses his pride when slipping on a banana peel will bring laughter as he gets up. If he cannot get up, the laughter will cease and the audience will empathize with him. This empathetic emotional response will stop the laughter immediately. Comedy, therefore, must avoid making its characters sympathetic, for sympathy results in empathy.

Some commentators claim that comedy is a pessimistic view of the world. The characters in comedy do not grow or change. Orgon, the dupe of the "religious hypocrite" Tartuffe in the play of that name by Moliere, is a gullible, irrational fool. Tartuffe takes advantage of Orgon's gullibility and, certainly, Orgon learns how his trust in Tartuffe has been used against him. Unfortunately, Orgon is as irrational in his rejection of Tartuffe and religion in general as he had been in his acceptance of his nemesis earlier. Orgon does not grow, is incapable of learning and therefore incapable of growing. If we accept Orgon and other comic characters as representative of man, then the prognosis for all of us is bleak.

On the other hand, over the centuries comic writers have claimed that their job is to hold up the foibles of mankind to ridicule and by doing so to make us see ourselves and change our behavior patterns. Moliere, one of the greatest writers of comedy states:

> To expose vices to everyone's laughter is to deal them a mighty blow. People easily endure reproofs, but they cannot at all endure being made fun of. People have no objections to being considered wicked, but they are not willing to be considered ridiculous.

This, then, views comedy from an optimistic viewpoint; for if it is a corrective form of the drama, then its targets are capable of being corrected.

Comic Devices

Writers and performers of comedy make use of several devices to elicit laughter. One of the most obvious of these is **ridicule** in which the writer or performer makes fun of a character and his behavior. This may be done on any one of the first four levels of characterization. Though not accepted now, in past centuries this was used to make fun of physical characteristics over which the comic character had no control. Today, we make fun of how a character walks, how he talks, how he dresses, etc., so long as what the character does is done by choice and not by necessity. We laugh at the idiosyncrasies of certain professions: the absent-minded professor, the rascally lawyer, the pretentious judge, the dumb jock, etc., Of more fodder for humor are mannerisms that often identify us and separate us from others: the effete man, the nervous nelly, strange speech patterns, etc. Attitudes provide us with targets for humor as we laugh at inane prejudices, the boasting coward, pretentiousness of any kind.

Anyone, in fact, who deviates in any way from what we think of as the norm may become the butt of a joke and often is. For this reason, the playwright often includes a character in the play who represents the norm, or depends on the audience having a norm which is similar to his, the playwright's, own.

Teasing is another comic device often employed by the humorist. Teasing depends on the inability of the victim to realize he is being teased because he is too proud, too preoccupied, or too ignorant to be aware of what is going on around him.

Many playwrights rely heavily on using **incongruity** as a comic device. They usually accomplished this by placing the comic character in a situation with which he cannot cope. His discomfort in that situation is the basis for the laughter which is to come. In some cases, this calls for role reversal: the butler who is smarter than his employer, the woman who is stronger and wittier than the man, or the animal who responds more wittily than its master.

Sources of Laughter

While devices such as those indicated above will provide the means by which laughter is evoked, they usually depend on several sources of laughter which are exploited by comic writers and performers.

Automatism is the chief of these sources. The ability to adapt to various situations is considered to be innate to the human condition. In comedy, the character is pictured as being somewhat less than human, almost machine like, or as having animal characteristics. As with a machine, the comic character is unable to adapt. Ideally, man is supposed to be in charge of his environment and have control over the lesser species. When he does not, he becomes less than human and is therefore subject to ridicule and laughter. A reversal of this situation is also a ripe field for humor, for when animals and machines take on human attitudes and characteristics, they can provide laughter.

A Stephen F. Austin State University production.

Mr. Pinchwife discovers his wife, Margery, disguised as a man on a public street. The inability of Pinchwife to adapt to the situation and the incongruity of Margery's disguise serve as sources of laughter in Wycherley's *The Country Wife*

Repetition is a form of automatism. Machines repeat, humans normally do not. When a comic character continually makes the same errors of judgement, he can become the subject for laughter. This is particularly evident in the use of the "running joke;" that is, a trick which is repeated and successfully pulled on its victim throughout the play. The inability of the victim to learn and therefore to adapt to the situation, a form of automatism, brings on the laughter.

Incongruity is not only a comic device, but is a source of laughter as well. The discomfort of the victim and his inability to adapt as a human should is incongruous.

In all cases, the audience must see itself as superior to the victim. It must know more than the victim and be able to see how to avoid the situation or at least control it. It cannot be stressed too much that at no time does true comedy become overtly cruel, at no time is the victim placed in any serious danger, and at all times, the victim must deserve his fate.

The Comic Character

To create a comic character, it is necessary that the playwright develop a character whose deviation from the norm is deeply enough ingrained to provide a constant source of humor as the character is placed in a wide variety of situations. The character, of course, must be completely unaware of his ridiculousness. Usually, he is vain enough to consider himself the norm and others the deviants. He is self-assured and self-aggrandizing and often feels that all in society, nature, and the world is centered on him. He must be identifiable as a human being and, while insufferable to humanity, not a serious threat to humanity.

Three Forms of Comedy

Comedy

Comedy, as such, is normally considered the comic equivalent to tragedy or drama. True comedy deals with very serious actions and attempts to bring about change through the ridicule of the characters involved in those actions. It finds its character roots in the attitudes of those portrayed.

> Comedy is an imitation of a man worse than the average, not as regards any and every sort of fault, but only as regards one particular kind, the ridiculous, a species of the ugly. The ridiculous may be defined as a mistake or deformity not productive of pain or harm to others.
>
> Aristotle, *The Poetics*

> Comedy is an imitation of an action that is ludicrous and imperfect, of sufficient length, . . . directly presented by persons acting, and not in the form of a narrative, through pleasure and laughter effecting the purgation of like emotions.
>
> *The Tractatus Coislanus*, 1st century B.C., (Lane Cooper, trans.)

Farce

The term **farce** was introduced during the time of the English Restoration (1660-1700). Prior to that time, any play which ended happily and produced laughter was generally called **comedy** though it might contain both farcical and satirical elements. Farce is a comic form which places relatively little emphasis on satire and/or criticism and therefore lacks comedy's significance as a commentator on man and the human condition. The elements of the ridiculous and burlesque are highly important in farce. This form of comedy is the comic equivalent to melodrama, since it relies heavily on contrivances both in character and plot development. It exists purely and simply for the sake of laughter.

Stephen F. Austin State University production.

Farce depends a great deal on exaggerated characters and contrived situations for its laughter. Physical humor is also an important element in this form of comedy as it is in the scene above from *She Stoops to Conquer.*

Farce depends heavily on the exaggeration

of character and incidents to achieve its purpose. Characters are simplified and are often stereotypes, sometimes becoming almost inhuman though having sufficient human qualities to be identifiable and provoke laughter. Action is also simplified, having little if any depth of meaning, but providing ample opportunity for the exaggerated actions of the character to be displayed. Farce of this sort may be easily identified. More difficult to recognize is farce which relies on verbal wit such as Oscar Wilde's *The Importance of Being Earnest* and several of the Restoration comedies. In such plays mental action replaces physical action. Even so, the play is based more on the situation than on the characters which are dominated by the plot.

The Commedia dell'Arte - Renaissance Farce

(See Chapter 16 for illustrations)

During the early part of the Renaissance, which is often dated from about 1350 AD to the early 17th century, and into the 18th century, the **Commedia dell'Arte al Improviso**, the Art of Improvised Comedy, was developed. Totally unrelated to the church and the religious plays of the time, the companies which performed this type of presentation were professional; that is, they made their living as actors. Working from **scenarios**, outlines of dramatic action, the actors improvised their dialogue during the performances. The companies were composed of up to 12-14 actors, each of which specialized in impersonating a specific **stock character**. These stock characters, all of them stereotypes, carried names which were widely known and recognized and included:

The Zanni (Servant clowns)

Harlequin - Witty, crafty, whimsical, a trickster, athletic
Brighella - Dull-witted, cantankerous, scheming
Columbine - the female counterpart of Harlequin
Ruffiana - a courtesan or woman of questionable character

Middle Class Characters

Pantalone - Foolish old man, miserly, gullible, lascivious
Il Docttore - Educated fool. Pretentious. Often spouts fractured Latin. May be a doctor, lawyer, professor, etc.
Braggart Warrior - Brags of his heroism, conquests of women, etc., but when faced with a threat or a woman, he proves to be a coward or impotent.
The Shrew - often married to Pantalone
One or Two pairs of Young Lover - all sweetness and light. Fashion plates. Devoid of ability to think or reason.

The plots of the scenarios often center around getting the young lovers together despite the obstacles placed before them by the older characters. The Zanni usually mastermind the trickery needed to outwit the lovers' elders. All but the lovers wore identifying and traditional masks and costumes.

Satire

Satire is a form of comedy which attempts to bring about social or political change through the use of humor. Its form dates back to the time of the Greeks when Aristophanes wrote his satires on political figures, his society, philosophies of the time, and the works of writers of tragedies. His attack were so viciously funny that on at least two occasions he was sent into exile by the governing powers in Athens. Some historians credit his play *The Clouds*, which attacks sophists and particularly Socrates, with having brought that great thinker to trial and having influenced the Athenian public so deeply as to cause them to condemn Socrates to exile or death. His play *Lysistrata* pillories politicians and others who found war an answer to their problems.

During the 17th century, the French playwright Moliere raised satire to a highly artistic level with his criticism of religious hypocrisy in *Tartuffe*, social climbing in *The Would-Be Gentleman*, medicine and the doctors practicing it in *The Imaginary Invalid*, social pretentiousness in *The Ridiculous Young Ladies*, miserliness in *The Miser*, and duplicity in *The Misanthrope.* Since satire is such a powerful weapon of ridicule, it can also be dangerous. Satirical plays have, it is true, brought about social and political change, but they have also brought repercussions down upon their authors and performers. It is not unusual for the satirical playwright to suffer as did Aristophanes. Moliere was excommunicated from the Roman Catholic Church for *Tartuffe.* The plays of George Bernard Shaw initially could be produced only in private theatres. Shaw's *Arms and the Man*, a satire on war and its practitioners, could not be performed in the public theatres in England for many years.

There is a major problem with satire. Often, it is concerned with immediate situations and, therefore, fails to speak to all time. It is normally not universal. Moliere, however, selected his targets for the ridicule of satire from basic human foibles which were timeless and seem to exist today just as much as they did in his own time.

"Author, Author!"

Comparing the Comedic Forms of Drama

	Comedy	Farce	Satire
1. **Plot**	Serious theme Semi-universal Logical	Not serious Non-universal Contrived	Serious theme Non-universal Often dated
2. **Character**	Characters are much as we are. Have a flaw for ridicule.	Stereotypes No development Readily recognized	Characters represent social or political types chosen for ridicule.
3a. **Thought Character**	Decisions are made on the basis of attitude.	Few decisions are made. Those that are are on the level of habit or bent and possibly attitude.	Decisions are made to reveal political or social stupidity or hypocrisy.
3b. **Thought Theme**	Man is seen as ridiculous but capable of reform as a result of ridicule.	Little or no thought. Ridicule is used for the sake of laughter.	A social or political theme aimed at bringing about action as a result of ridicule.
4. **Diction**	Carefully chosen to reveal human flaws and provoke laughter.	Stereotypical and normally unimportant. Though some wit may be used.	Used to reveal social and/or political flaws for ridicule.
5. **Music**	Motivated. Same as for drama, but used to emphasize humor.	Used to point a joke. Usually not too important.	Used to point a joke and contribute to social/political statement.
6. **Spectacle**	Only used as needed to reveal plot and character.	Important–much of the humor is visual; i.e., physical, slapstick	Used to visually establish political and/or social comments

9
The Musical Theatre

One of the most popular forms of theatre has been the musical theatre. As was noted earlier, music has always been a part of the drama. Choruses were apparently sung and/or chanted to a musical accompaniment in the Greek Theatre. The Romans used music extensively in their mimes and pantomimes. In the presentations of Biblical stories and episodes in the Church during the Middle Ages, choral passages were often sung.

It was, however, during the Renaissance that music began to take on a more important role in the theatre. In 1594, in Florence, Italy, at the Academy, an attempt was made to stage Greek tragedies as the scholars believed they had originally been mounted. Accepting the recorded references to music being used in the Greek stagings and taking the term "chorus" literally, an effort was made to mount the tragedies with full musical accompaniment, choruses, and **recitatives**. According to his tombstone in the Church of San Croce in Florence, the founder of Italian **opera** was Giorgio Paoli. His innovations soon became popular and composers, who were to become more noted, Monteverde and Gluck, came to the forefront in the development of this art form.

This is not to imply that music did not play an important role in presentations outside of opera at this time and in succeeding years. Many of the actors in the Commedia dell'Arte incorporated musical numbers into the improvised plays they performed. In Elizabethan England musical numbers were often included in the plays, both tragedy and comedy, with most of the numbers being drawn from well-known folk tunes. In 17th Century France, Moliere and others included musical interludes, songs and ballets in their presentations. In these cases, however, the music was either used as an interlude or was carefully incorporated into the plot. It did not dominate the presentation as it did in opera.

As there are different forms of drama and comedy, there are also different forms of musical theatre. Also, as with the dramatic forms, few of these are absolutely pure and each musical theatre presentation may make use of characteristics from several of the forms.

Opera

Opera, especially early opera, is often dominated by music. In many cases it was composed to show off the beauty and versatility of the performers' voices with arias and choruses provided specifically for that purpose. Opera requires highly developed and classically trained voices capable of being heard over a full orchestra and filling an auditorium while maintaining a beauty and purity of tone without the aid of artificial amplification. Because of the dominance of music, many operas have no spoken dialogue but require that all words be sung whether in highly melodic arias and choruses or in the form of a **recitative**; that is, sung speech.

Most operas are highly dramatic, making use of the music to arouse the emotions of the audience, and many are based on essentially melodramatic scripts. Most of the major operas, called "grand operas," also require large casts and extensive staging. The operas or music-dramas of Richard Wagner, for instance, often require an orchestra of 100-120 musicians, the same number of vocalists or more, and multiple full-stage settings as well as special effects. On the other hand, Mozart's *Don Giovanni* requires a minimal number of singers, sets, and a relatively small chamber orchestra. Verdi's very popular Italian operas run the gamut in their requirements. *Rigoletto*, for instance, requires only a cast of 30 or fewer while some productions of this composer's *Aida* have gone to the extreme of including a large cast of vocalists, camels, horses, elephants, and the Egyptian pyramids.

Contrasting with grand opera is another operatic form sometimes referred to as light opera or **opera buffa**. These works are usually comedies set to music, but they retain many of the requirements of grand opera. Words are delivered in arias, choruses, and recitative. Some scenic spectacle is often required. Usually the orchestras are smaller than those required for grand opera, but the vocal requirements are often as demanding and the training required of the singers is just as arduous. Light opera is best exemplified by such works as Mozart's *The Marriage of Figaro* and *The Magic Flute*, Donizetti's *Don Pasquale,* and Prokofief's *The Love of Three Oranges.*

Operetta

The word "operetta" means "little opera." As with opera, the operetta is also demanding on the singers. Operetta, however, incorporates dialogue with or without musical accompaniment. It is rarely serious, usually comic, and often does not place an undue amount of emphasis on spectacle. The music, however, is of the highest importance and often dominates the plot, characters and other aspects of the production. The songs are highly melodious and often quite singable even by those without classical voice training. Among the best known operettas in English are those of W. S. Gilbert (1836-1911) and Arthur Sullivan (1842-1900) whose *H.M.S. Pinafore, The Mikado,* and *The Pirates of Penzance* are the most popular.

Also highly popular have been what are often referred to as **Viennese Operettas** because of their origin in Vienna, Austria. Developed toward the end of the 19th century, these operettas require highly trained voices, but incorporate music which is very melodious and songs which can be sung by skilled amateurs. The plots tend to be fairly predictable and romantic and primarily serve as a means of moving from one musical number to another. The Folksoper in Vienna specializes in this kind of musical theatre presenting the lighter works of Mozart, Smetana, Johann Strauss and others throughout the year as well as some musicals from the American theatre. The Viennese operetta was particularly popular in America at the end of the last century which encouraged a number of American composers and writers to work in this medium, particularly Victor Herbert (1859-1924), Rudolf Friml (1879-1972), and Sigmund Romberg (1887-1951).

Ballad Opera

The **ballad opera** is a minor genre of musical theatre which draws on folk songs and melodies. The earliest of these was *The Beggars Opera* by John Gay, first presented in 1728. Immensely popular in its own time both because of the music and because of its political implications, *The Beggars Opera* gave rise to a number of imitations. One of the most successful 20th century ballad operas is *Down in the Valley* by Kurt Weill (1900-1950) which makes extensive use of American folk songs.

New York Public Library Collection, Astor, Lenox, and Tilden Foundation

Florenz Ziegfeld's *(1867-1932) Ziegfeld Follies* were among the most popular of musical revues to be mounted between 1907 and the late 1920s. Large casts, sumptuous staging and costumes as well as noted vaudeville headliners were featured in each annual production.

Musical Revue

The **musical revue** has always been popular in the American theatre and in England. Often built around a central theme, the revue is primarily a collection of songs, musical numbers, and dances. There is rarely any plot or story line involved in this form of musical theatre. It became an important form of musical theatre for young composers trying out their talents during the 1920s and may still be seen in cabarets, night clubs, and on television. It was with the musical revue that such composers as Irving Berlin (1888-1992), Richard Rodgers (1902-1979), George (1898-1937) and Ira (1896-1983) Gershwin, Jerome Kern (1885-1945), and Cole Porter (1891-1964) got their start in show business.

African-American musical revues were also popular starting in 1921 with *Shuffle Along* which featured the songs of Eubie Blake (1883-1983). This marked the first Broadway Afro-American production, but it had been preceded by several revues mounted in Harlem. After 1921, annual new productions were mounted the next several years. One, *Blackbirds*, introduced dancer Bill "Bojangles" Robinson (1878-1949) to the Broadway audiences in 1928.

Related to, but different from, the musical revue was the **burlesque** show which featured musical numbers and comedy burlesques of serious dramatic presentations. Originally mounted and accepted as family entertainment, the burlesque degenerated into more scatological performances. What had originally been a form of innocent titillation became less innocent and far more overt in its appeal to the prurient.

Minstrel Shows

During the 19th century and up to World War II, the **minstrel show** was a popular form of musical entertainment. Based on Afro-American music, the minstrel show introduced to multi-racial American and European audiences the ethnic rhythms and harmonies often associated with the Black social condition in the United States. The earliest minstrel shows were performed by Afro-American companies of singers and comedians. Later, however, these productions were mounted by white actors wearing stereotyped make-up. Because of the stereotyped images projected from the stage, minstrel shows fell into disfavor after World War II and are no longer being staged.

The Book Musical

The musical comedy or musical play has been called the one dramatic form contributed to world theatre by America. Its origins are somewhat obscure, but the first of these presentations is often attributed to an 1866 production called *The Black Crook.*

A scene from *The Black Crook* as shown in an advertising woodcut for the original production. This combination of a melodrama with ballet is often credited with introducing the American musical to the theatre.

From Stanley Appelebaum, *Advertising Woodcuts From the Nineteenth Century Stage* Dover Publications

The Black Crook started out as a melodrama; that is, a play accompanied by music. The producers, finding that the play did not have the quality they expected, were desperate to find a means by which to save their investment. Just at that time, a French ballet company arrived in New York to start an American tour only to find the theatre it was booked to perform in had burned down. In an effort to save *The Black Crook*, its producers approached the now-stranded ballet company with the idea of incorporating the dancers into the failing melodrama The spectacle of the melodrama combined with the spectacle of the dance attracted audiences which, in spite of the response of some critics, were delighted with the presentation. Perhaps as much an attraction as anything was the fact that for the first time on the American stage a bevy of beautiful maidens, 100 in all, revealed the shapeliness of their legs (called "limbs" by the more genteel). The clergy, in particular, was agast at the offering and sermonized against it, a fact which probably did more to popularize the presentation than the quality of the performance itself. At one time there were ten touring companies crossing the United States performing this new blend of drama, music and dance.

Though there were many imitations of *The Black Crook,* the popularity of the Viennese operettas still outshone this new form of theatre. It was the contribution of George M. Cohan (1878-1942) that truly made the musical theatre an American idiom. Cohan, who with his father, mother, and sister had been popular on the American vaudeville stage as a singer and dancer, began writing musical plays based on American themes. Combining American themes with American popular music, Cohan's approach caught the fancy of his audiences and established the American musical as a viable form of theatre. Even so, the musical was still primarily a collection of songs and dances tied together with a relatively weak plot and just enough dialogue to get from one musical number to the next, a dramatic form referred to as a **musical comedy.**

In 1927, Oscar Hammerstein II and Jerome Kern joined forces as librettist and composer to mount a serious musical production of Edna Ferber's novel *Show Boat.* Though dance was held to a minimum, compared to earlier efforts in writing and mounting musicals, *Show Boat* had a relatively strong plot line, fairly well developed characters, and highly motivated songs designed to carry the plot forward and reveal the characters, their thoughts and aspirations. In addition, it dealt with a serious theme–miscegenation–and for the first time on the Broadway

Jerome Kern and Oscar Hammerstein II's original production of *Show Boat* based on the novel by Edna Ferber provided a serious plot combined with developed characters and motivated songs for the American stage in 1927. It was one of the first American musicals to consider serious social subjects and to present Afro-Americans on the legitimate stage as real, not stereotypical, characters.

stage presented African-American characters sympathetically and with a depth that had not been seen in the stereotypes previously offered. It was one of our earliest **musical plays**.

In 1931, George S. Kaufman (1889-1961)and Morrie Ryskind (1895–) authored the first American satirical musical, *Of Thee I Sing*, with music and lyrics by George and Ira Gershwin. Taking American presidential campaigns as their theme, the authors pinioned the various politicians and political parties that they believed were appealing to the American public purely on an emotional rather than a reasoned basis. *Of Thee I Sing* was the first musical to be awarded the Pulitzer Prize. It is still revived every four years in conjunction with presidential campaigns. During the 1984 campaign, *Of Thee I Sing* was presented in a truncated version on national television. In 1992, it was revived by at least five regional theatres. The show has had countless other revivals in regional, community, and university theatres. As with most satires, *Of Thee I Sing* speaks to an issue and is generally appropriate only when presidential campaigns are in full swing.

During the 1930s, experimentation with the musical form continued at the hands of some of the finest librettists and composers America has produced. Richard Rodgers and Lorenz Hart (1895-1943), in addition to other musicals, adapted Shakespeare's *The Comedy of Errors* into the tuneful *The Boys From Syracuse* (1938). In 1940 with *Pal Joey,* they introduced the first anti-hero to the musical theatre. Maxwell Anderson (1888-1959) and Kurt Weill adopted a theme from American history for their *Knickerbocker Holiday* and then mounted a musical version of Alan Payton's novel about race relations in South Africa, *Cry the Beloved Country.*

It was in 1943, however, that the American musical truly came of age. It was then that Richard Rodgers and Oscar Hammerstein II joined forces under the auspices of the Theatre Guild to write a new American musical which would totally incorporate plot, music, song, and dance (tap, modern dance, and ballet) as one complete whole. Based on a 1920s play by Lynn Riggs, *Green Grow the Lilacs*, the new musical version was staged by director Rouben Mammoulian (1897-?) with choreography by Agnes DeMille (1905-c.1992). *Oklahoma!*, as it was retitled, had a strong plot line, and its songs and dances carried the story forward. The production set a standard for the American musical for years to come.

In the best of these musical plays the plot dominates. Songs are written to carry the story forward either directly or by revealing the inner-most thoughts and wishes of the characters.

The Billy Rose Theatre Collection, New York Public Library for the Performing Arts, Astor, Lenox and Tilden Foundations

"Everything's up to date in Kansas City," sing the cowhands in the original production of *Oklahoma!* (1943). For the first time in the musical theatre dialogue, song, and dance (ballet, modern, and tap) were brought together and used with motivation to further the plot line. *Oklahoma!* by Rogers and Hammerstein, set the pattern for many of the successful musicals of the 1940s, '50s, and '60s.

The dances are carefully integrated into the plot and are often used to reveal symbolically the action of the play or the thoughts of a character. These elements are usually so tightly woven together that the songs and dances lose much of their original meaning if they are removed from the plot line and forced to exist on their own. The spectacle is directly related to and in support of the plot. Unfortunately, the pattern or organization of the musical in the hands of some has become little more than a formula thus weakening the genre as a whole.

In an effort to move away from such formula musicals, some producers, directors, composers and libretticists have developed what are sometimes called **concept musicals.** These are musicals which investigate an idea through the use of a variety of songs, dances, scenes, etc. Panoramic plots usually dominate these musicals which depend on the cumulative effect of the various scenes for their total impact. Among these, *Chorus Line* (1975) has been one of the most successful.

Martha Swope, Photographer

The final scene from *Chorus Line*, a musical which relies on a series of monologues and dances to discuss the plight of musical comedy dancers. Held together by a very thin plot, *Chorus Line* relies on the cumulative effect of the individual and group numbers for its final impact.

In more recent years, there has been more experimentation with the musical theatre just as in the dramatic theatre. In the hands of some, the musical has evolved into an almost operatic form with little or no dialogue other than that set to music. This is particularly true of the musicals of England's Andrew Lloyd-Webber and America's Stephen Sondheim. Lloyd-Webber's *Starlight Express* and *Cats* rely heavily on a combination of music and spectacle with very little attention being paid to character and plot. Sondheim, conversely, normally uses a strong story line in such musicals as *Sweeney Todd* and *Into the Woods*.

10
The Greek Theatre

One of the most famous plays in the history of drama is Sophocles' *Oedipus Rex*, the work which Aristotle considered to contain all of the elements of the play in their most ideal relationships. Like other plays of the classical Greek era, *Oedipus Rex* was based on an ancient story well known to the Greek audiences. It was the interpretation of the story and its presentation inn dramatic form which made it so popular and has contributed to the fact that the play is still performed in the theatre and on film. The play was so highly thought of during the Fourth Century BC that the government in Athens reportedly subsidized any revivals of it that were mounted. It is upon this play that Aristotle based his full definition of tragedy.

In order to understand (appreciate) *Oedipus Rex* and other Greek plays, it is necessary to know something of the Greek theatre and the **conventions** to which the Athenian audiences were accustomed. These conventions include:

1. The chorus
2. No more than three actors could appear on stage at one time
3. All roles played by male actors
4. The use of masks
5. No violence on stage
6. Deus ex Machina

The Chorus

For modern audiences, the most difficult of these conventions to accept is the chorus. The use of a chorus in the Greek theatre was a part of the tradition of the theatre and dates back to its earliest days when performances were composed of **Dithyrambic Odes**; that is, songs sung and danced in honor of the gods and/or Greek heroes of the past. It is believed that Greek theatre evolved from sung presentations when dramatizations of the subject matter treated in the songs were added to the performances.

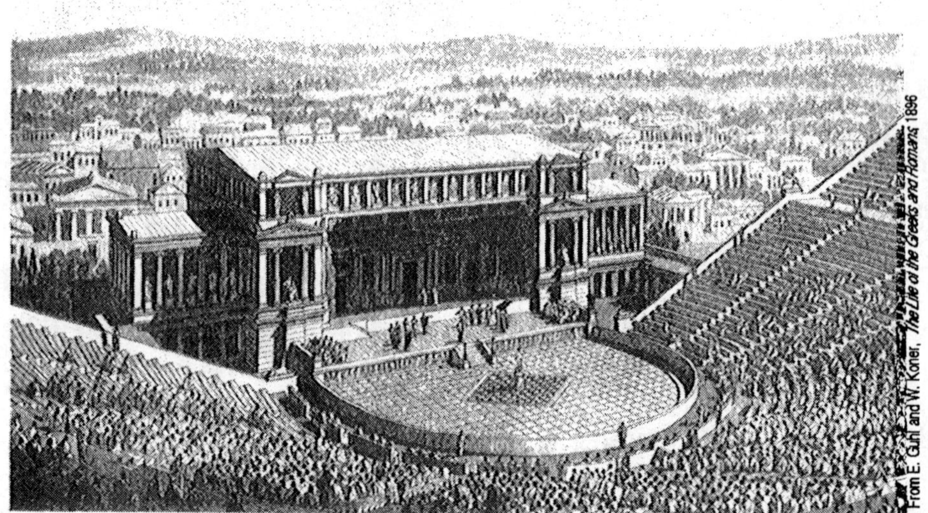

From E. Guhl and W. Koner, *The Life of the Greeks and Romans*, 1896

A conjectural reconstruction of the Theatre of Dionysus located at the foot of the Acropolis in Athens. This view of the theatre shows it as it may have appeared in the 4th century BC.

The Greek chorus serves several purposes within the play. Initially, it is responsible for informing the audience of the background of the play, the **exposi-**

tion. In many cases it takes on the role of the audience itself commenting on the action taking place within the play. The chorus also acts as a character in the play itself, speaking to and sometimes debating a course of action with a character. In some cases it also serves as a representative of the playwright by speaking for him. The Chorus also provided for an indication of a time lapse during its odes. This allowed acts to take place off stage during the choral interlude. It also provided time for an actor to change his costume and mask in order to reenter to portray a different character. Finally, the Chorus often reverts to its original purpose and delivers odes to and in honor of the gods.

In *Oedipus Rex* the Chorus serves all these purposes, but its major purpose is to serve as a guide to us, the audience. In order to achieve this, the Chorus was given a special place within the Greek theatre to perform, the **orchestra,** which was placed between the audience area (the **theatron**) and the stage (**logeon**). In this space, the chorus could chant its odes and move in dance-like formations. In the early days of the Greek drama, the chorus was composed of about fifty performers. As the drama developed, more emphasis was placed on the characters, dialogue became more important, and the number of the chorus members dwindled to about twelve to fifteen.

The Actors

We are told that the first actor in the history of the theatre was Thespis, who was a choral leader in the Sixth Century BC, but who stepped out from the chorus and assumed a role. Thespis (it is from his name that we have derived the modern term "Thespian" referring to those who act) began a trend which was soon followed by others. In many cases, the playwright assumed the role of the actor, as did Aeschylus (523-456 BC) whose plays are the earliest to have been preserved. Aeschylus, however, added a second actor. This provided a greater opportunity for **conflict** to be shown within the play and for **dialogue** to be developed. Sophocles (c.496-406 BC) is credited with adding a third actor to Greek tragedy thus providing opportunities to dramatize more complex situations within the play. *Oedipus Rex* can be

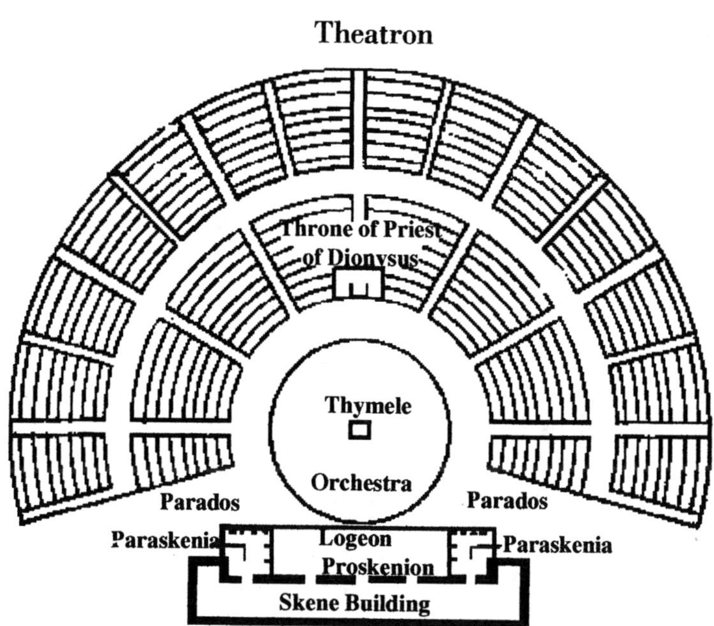

A ground plan of the classical Greek theatre from the 5th century BC. Note the full circle **orchestra** where the chorus performed; the altar sometimes called the **thymele** in the center of the orchestra; the **logeon** or stage behind which is the **skene** or scene building; the facade of the scene building is called the **proskenion** from which we get our modern term **proscenium**; the **parados** were entry ways for the audience and chorus; the **paraskenia** were projections on either end of the scene building. The seating area was called the **theatron**.

performed by three actors playing a variety of roles, the choral leader (Priest) and the chorus quite effectively. By law, the number of actors a playwright could use was limited to three in 468 BC. These have come to be known by the following titles:

Protagonist - the first speaking actor: In modern day theatre, we consider the leading character within the play to be the protagonist. He is the character who normally sets out on a specific course of action.

Deuteragonist - the second speaking actor: In the modern theatre, this actor portrays a character who is in oppposition to the protagonist and seeks to change or alter the protagonist's selected course of action.

Tritagonist - the third speaking actor: In the modern theatre as in the past, this actor portrays a character around whom much of the action may center, but who is often the subject of the actions of the pro and antagonists.

Note: the word **agon** appears in each of the titles listed above. In Greek "agon" meant debate or argument. Thus, with the addition of a second and third actor, the argument and conflict within the play could develop more efficiently.

The Greek tradition of using only three speaking actors on stage at one time is, perhaps, hard for a modern reader and audience member to understand. However, we have something similar in the modern theatre. It is not unusual for a large cast to have one actor play several roles. This is called **double casting**. Of course, an actor cannot play the roles of two characters that appear on stage at the same time. For instance, since Oedipus is in every scene of *Oedipus Rex*, the actor asigned that role cannot play any other role. The actor playing Creon, however, can play at least one and perhaps two other roles.

Since tragedies were presented in honor of the Greek gods, particularly Dionysus, and were performed in theatres dedicated to those gods, only male actors could be used. The actor was a kind of lay-priest serving the gods through his art. In the Greek culture, women were not admitted to the priesthood though they often had religious duties to perform. They were not considered to be citizens, for the Athenian culture was male oriented and dominated. For the drama, therefore, this meant that **all roles** had to be played by men, even the female roles portrayed on stage.

The Masks

All roles in the Greek tragedies were performed by actors wearing masks which were made of linen, cork, or a lightweight wood. These were used to indicate the role being played and assisted in permitting one actor to portray several roles within a play. Since no masks have survived, having been made of perishable materials, historians base their knowledge on vase and wall-paintings and sculptures

which have survived from the period. These would indicate that many of the masks were larger than life-size and were painted with a fair degree of realism. There is some speculation that built into the mouth of the mask was a megaphone which would assist the actor in projecting his voice. After all, the actors were performing out doors, to audiences of between 12,000 and 20,000, and in a space much larger than a modern football field. Though the acoustics in many of the Greek theatres were excellent and the actors were trained from childhood, the task of communicating with such a large audience must have been highly challenging.

On-stage Violence Prohibited

Since the plays were being performed within the theatres which were the sacred precincts of the gods, violence was prohibited. Such acts, it was believed, would profane the religious nature not only of the performances but the very areas in which they took place. This is not to imply that the Greek plays lacked violence. Rather than being committed on the stage, the conventions of the theatre required that a messenger tell of the violence. Some of the most dramatic and graphic speeches in all of Greek tragedy are those delivered by messengers.

It is a true today, as it was in the time of the Greeks, that violent acts presented live on stage before the audience are often totally unbelievable. If the director, actors, and playwright want the audience to truly believe that a character has been killed, it is often wise to have the killing take place off stage. Though "stage blood" may be used, it is often viewed as a device or trick by the audience which knows very well that though the character may be dead, the actor portraying the character is very much alive. Another factor which must be taken into account is removing the body from the stage if no curtain is used between scenes. Shakespeare normally provided a way for this to be accomplished. For instance, the bodies of Hamlet, Laertes, Claudius and Gertrude are taken from the stage by soldiers acting under Fortinbras' orders.

There is some evidence that though acts of violence could not be performed on stage, they could be shown through the use of the **ekkyklema**, a wagon that could be rolled out through the central doorway of the **skene** (scene building) at the rear of the stage. On this wagon was placed a tableaux of the action being described by the messenger.

Deus ex Machina

The **deus ex machina** was a crane stationed on top of the scene building from which a god could be lowered to or suspended above the stage. The term may be translated as "god of the machine" or "god from the machine." Today the term is used to refer to a contrived ending for a play in which a new and poorly identified character is introduced solely for the purpose of resolving the complications of the play. In the Greek theatre this mechanical device was often used by later playwrights, most notably Euripides (c. 480-406 BC) who brought in a god or goddess at the end of some of his plays to resolve the situation and provide the **denouement.** Aristotle states that the use of this device is only seen in the less successful tragedies and is the weakest form of denouement.

The Playwrights

Like the actors, the Greek playwrights held an honored position in Greek society. Their plays were written in celebration of the gods the Greeks worshiped and their subject matter was drawn from the stories of those gods and the history of the Greek people. Though there were many playwrights working during the fourth and fifth centuries B.C., only a few of the works of five Greek playwrights exist today. Many of the manuscripts of the Greek tragedies and comedies were lost during the battle between Caesar and Anthony over Alexandria when the great library of that city was destroyed by fire.

Each spring dramatic festivals were mounted in Athens under the auspices of the city. Playwrights were commissioned by patrons to write for these festivals which were really competitions. For the festivals featuring tragedies, the playwrights were required to write a trilogy of plays; i.e. three plays possibly based on one story or one central theme. In addition, the playwrights were required to write an additional play, a **satyr play**. The satyr plays were lewd, lascivious works often parodying the tragedies which were perform earlier in the day.

The first playwright to become established in the Greek theatre was Aeschylus (523-456 B.C.) , who wrote in the early part of the fifth century B.C. It was Aeschylus who introduced the second actor to the Greek theatre. His plays are closely related to the earlier Dithyrambic odes and are very heavily tied to the rituals related to the worship of the Greek gods. From Aeschylus we have the only extant Greek trilogy, *The Oresteia.* Aeschylus was primarily concerned with revealing the conflicts between the gods and man.

The second major playwright was Sophocles (496-406 B.C.) whose *Oedipus Rex* is considered by many the greatest tragedy ever written. Though he was also concerned with the conflicts between the gods and man, he introduced conflicts between man and the state in *Antigone* and other plays. Sophocles' plays are often more dramatic and less ritualistic than those of Aeschylus. The beauty of his poetry is unsurpassed.

Present day tastes find the plays of the third Greek playwright, Euripides (c.480-406 B.C.), more interesting, for he stressed human relationships and conflicts. Though he was not so highly regarded during his own time, his reputation has improved over the centuries. He is particularly noted for the strong and believable female characters he presented in such plays as *Medea, Hyppolytus,* and *The Trojan Women.*

Aristophanes(448-380 B.C.) is the only early Greek writer of comedy to have survived the centuries. An acid-tongued commentator on contemporary society, politics, literature, philosophy and war, Aristophanes is credited with having written some of the most pointed and funny satires of all time. He is particularly noted for *Lysistrata* in which he pointed out the follies of war, *The Clouds* in which he attacked Socrates and the Sophists, and *The Frogs* in which he made fun of his fellow playwright, Euripides.

The last of the Greek playwrights to have been preserved is Menander (342-291 B.C.) whose works in the realm of situation comedy influenced the Roman writers Plautus and Terrence as well as Shakespeare, Moliere and many present day writers of comedy. Only one of his plays survives, *The Grouch,* discovered in 1957 in a Yugoslavian monastery.

Theatre Appreciation
Class Assignment-Greek Theatre

Name:______________________________

While reading a Greek tragedy, assign the various roles to the three actors who would have portrayed them. Remember, no more than three actors may be used, therefore some of these actors will have to play more than one role during a performance of the play. (Members of the chorus and the chorus leader are not considered actors in this case.)

Protagonist:

____

____

____

____

Deuteragonist:

____

____

____

____

Tritagonist:

____

____

____

____

Remove from text and turn in to instructor.

11
Medieval & Elizabethan Theatre

The Medieval Theatre

The theatre has been called "the perennial invalid" because dire predictions have been made almost continuously about its imminent demise. If one had been living in Rome in 476 AD, he would undoubtedly have come to the conclusion that the theatre was undergoing its last gasp. Not only did Rome fall, which resulted in the sacking of the city by the barbarians from the North and the complete disintegration of its economic and social structure, but the arts, including theatre, almost disappeared. The barbarians saw little use or value in the arts and destroyed many of the artistic works which had been accumulated by the Romans over the centuries. In addition, the city of Rome had come under the power of the growing Christian movement which rejected the theatre for several reasons:

1. The theatre had been used to satirize the Christians unmercifully
2. The theatre was rooted in the rituals and worship of pagan gods
3. The theatre "told lies like truth," thus breaking the commandment against bearing false witness.

With such pressures from both the inside and the outside, it is little wonder that theatre was banned and most of the theatres in and around Rome were destroyed. This is not to say that all theatre disappeared. There is evidence that vestiges of it remained in the form of itinerant players and street performers who traveled throughout Europe during the Dark Ages. These included troubadours and minstrels, jugglers, wild animal trainers, and others who eked out a living as best they could traveling from one small court to another performing often for little more than a roof over their heads for the night and a meal or two.

Some vestiges of the old theatre were kept alive, however. Many of the manuscripts of the past were kept in monastery libraries and were known to the few educated men in Europe. During the Renaissance, these were rediscovered and became important as textbooks for the study of Latin and Greek in the Universities which had been founded by various orders of priests. We know that by the 11th century AD, the plays of the Roman playwright Terrence were well known; so well known, in fact, that a German nun by the name of Sr. Hrosvitha wrote several plays imitative of Terrence's work though greatly sanitized.

Ironically, one of the very institutions that condemned the theatre brought it back. The church, seeking ways to instruct its parishioners, who were essentially illiterate and could not speak Latin much less read it, sought a method to teach the scriptures of both the Old and New Testaments. By the tenth century, theatrical elements had evolved in many of the church's rituals and portions of the various celebrations, most notably Easter, were being briefly dramatized by priests in four-line dialogues called "tropes." Though the tropes were delivered in Latin, the visualization of their content revealed through pantomime helped to communicate the scriptural passage to the communicants.

Initially these short plays were mounted within the church as a part of the services. However, as they became more popular and their scope was enlarged, they were moved outside the church and laymen replaced the priests as actors in the presentations. By 1200 AD religious plays were being acted both inside and outside the church. These grew in popularity and scope during the following centuries, reaching their height by around 1500 by which time the actors were all laymen.

Three types of religious plays were developed during this period:

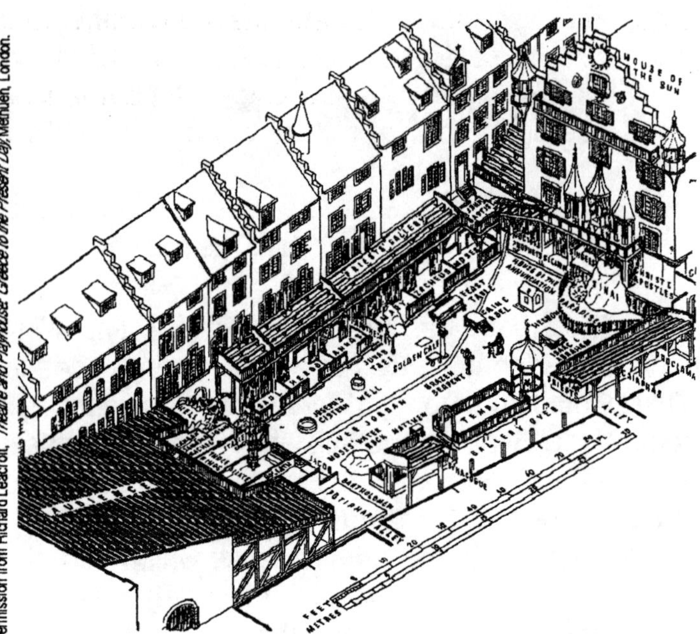

Reprinted by permission from Richard Leacroft, *Theatre and Playhouse: Greece to the Present Day*, Methuen, London.

A diagram of the layout for the Lucerne Passion Play in the early 15th century. In the center of the town square before the cathedral, the various mansions were placed for the scenes which occurred during the last week of Christ's life. The audience was seated around the square and could also view the play from the surrounding buildings. This is an example of a **simultaneous setting.**

1. Mystery Plays - these were plays based on Biblical stories from both the Old and the New Testaments. In some cases, they traced the development of the Christian religious experience from the Creation to the Crucifixion, Resurrection and Ascension, and the Last Judgment. In England and Spain, the plays were often presented in cycles. A cycle play is a short scene or act based on an episode in the Bible. A complete presentation of a cycle of plays could take as many of forty days. Highly popular were the Passion Plays which reenacted the last week in the life of Christ.

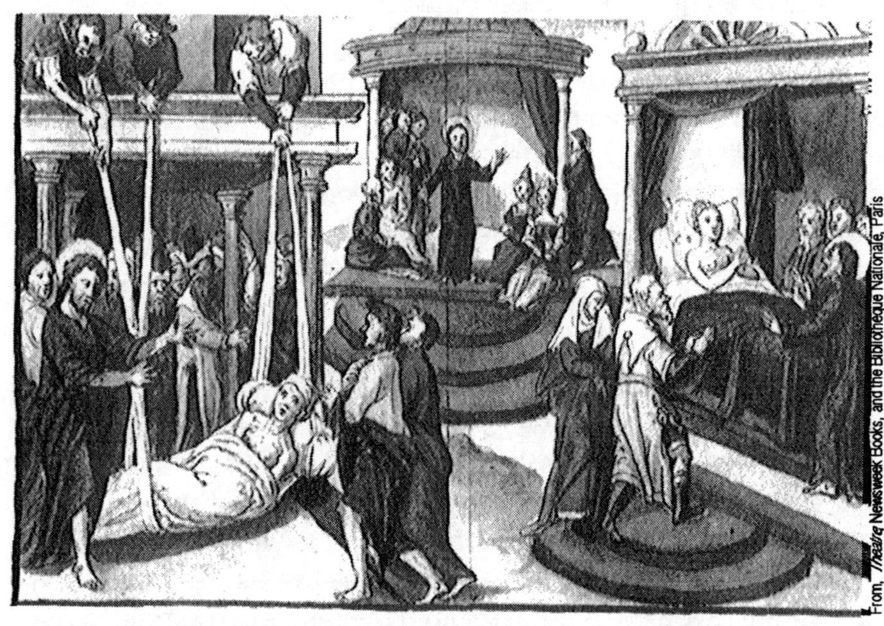

From, *Theatre* Newsweek Books, and the Bibliotheque Nationale, Paris

A composite scene from the Valenciennes Passion Play (1547) showing three episodes simultaneously. See Chapter 17 for a sketch of the full stage for this production.

2. Miracle Plays - these plays were based on the lives of the saints, often martyrs in whose names miracles had occurred.

3. Morality Plays - these plays demonstrated the Church's understanding of good and evil with the characters personifying good and/or evil characteristics. In the best known of these plays, *Everyman*, the leading character is Everyman, who is informed by Death that his time has come and

he must prepare himself for the Last Judgment. Everyman must then face each of the seven deadly sins and all of the good attributes he has developed throughout his life as he searches for someone to witness for him when the judgment occurs. He finally discovers that only Good Deeds is willing and can accompany him to the throne of God at the time of judgment.

With the great number of scenes required for these plays, Medieval man developed several methods of staging the works:

1. Multiple stages - These were initially developed within the church itself with acting areas, **platea**, placed around the nave of the church with the action moving from one platea to another. At each platea there was what was called a **mansion,** which was a set piece representing the locale of the action. The audience, in the nave of the church, moved or turned to follow the action of the scenes.

2. Simultaneous staging - For simultaneous staging,all the mansions were placed on one platform. It was a convention that when a performer entered from a particular mansion, the audience would accept the entire stage as that locale.

3. Wagon stages - In England and Spain wagon stages were often used. Here a wagon carried the actors, costumes, properties and set pieces from one place to another. Upon reaching its destination in a town square, the actors would perform the scene for which the wagon had been prepared. Following that, the wagon would then move to another location while another wagon would take its place for the next scene. This was the manner in which the English cycle plays were usually presented. It was not unusual for comic scenes to be introduced as interludes between the various Biblical episodes.

From Sharp, *A Dissertation on the Pageants or Dramatic Mysteries. . . at Coventry* (1825)

An English pageant wagon, early 16th century, on which was presented a short play drawn from the life of Christ.

The Elizabethan Theatre

The Elizabethan theatre and its literature were derived out of the influence of both the cycle plays and the classical Roman tragedies. The panoramic structure of the cycle plays influenced the panoramic structure of the Elizabethan tragedies and comedies. Both used many characters, were highly episodic, often had more than one story, intermingled comedy and tragedy, were highly poetic, used or implied many locales, began early in the story rather than late as did the classical climactic plays. Many of the plays were related to the morality plays with the characters representing different facets of good and evil.

Roman influences, particularly found in the plays of Seneca, were evident in the subject matter chosen for tragedy. The five-act structure was accepted and practiced, bombastic language was used, violence was often performed on stage, there was often a preoccupation with the supernatural and witchcraft, and insanity appears in many of the plays.

The staging of the plays was also related to the medieval period. Here, instead of having the medieval mansions on stage, the architecture of the theatre buildings provided for a number of acting areas, all constantly in view. The Elizabethan stage was actually an architectural simultaneous stage. **Seven acting areas** were provided according to historian John Cranford Adams and are illustrated in the accompanying sketch of the Globe, the theatrical home for Shakespeare and his colleagues. Following the conventions of the period, the locale in which the play's action took place was identified by the location from which the actor entered the stage and by the lines. If the locale was important, the audience would know it from what the actor said and/or did.

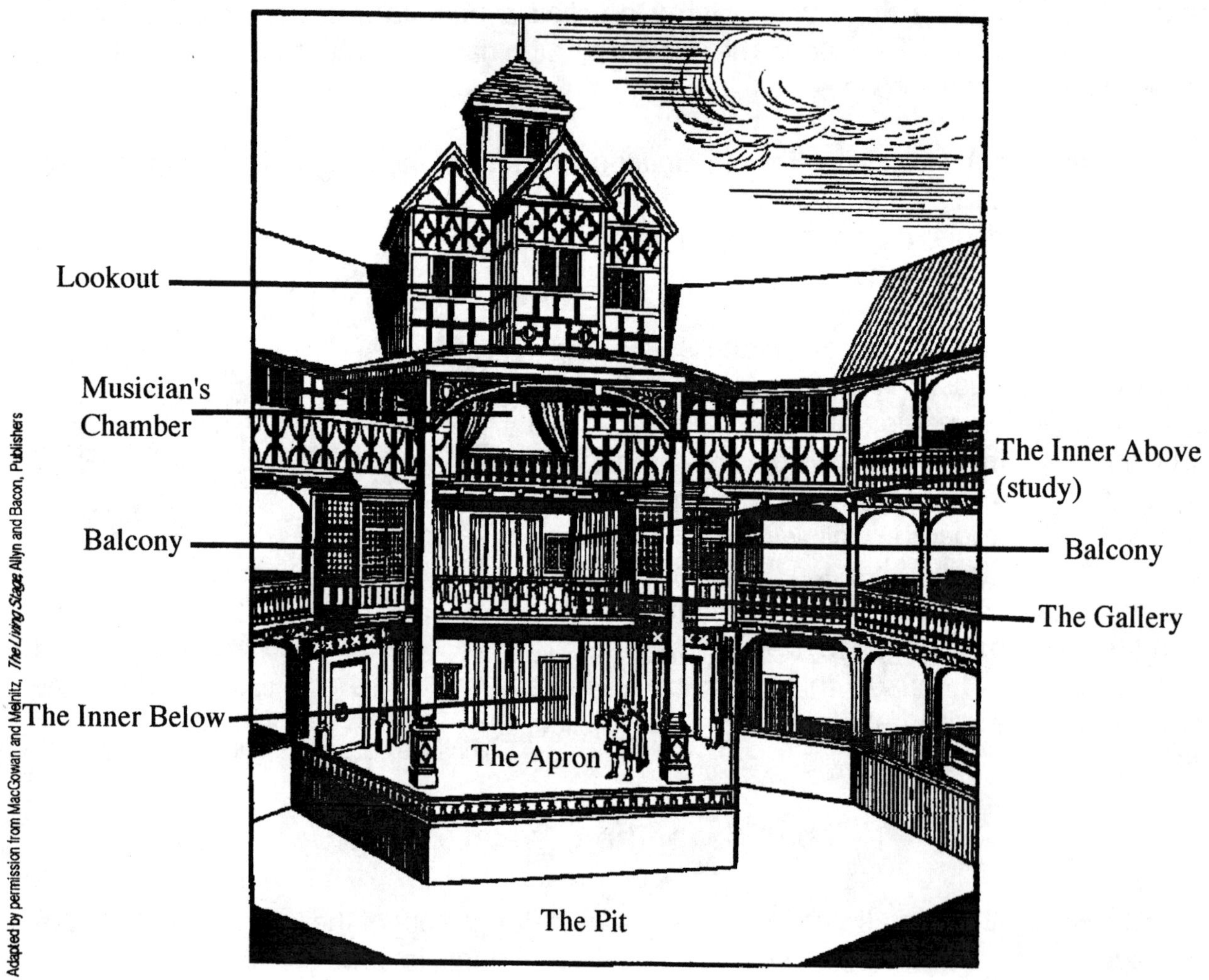

Adapted by permission from MacGowan and Melnitz, *The Living Stage* Allyn and Bacon, Publishers

John Cranford Adams' Reconstruction of the Globe Theatre

Another convention of the Elizabethan theatre was that all roles were played by males. Often the female roles were handled by boy actors apprenticed to older members of the company. Boy actors were favorites with the Elizabethan audiences, so much so that there were full companies of boy actors performing in London until the middle of the first decade of the 17th century. Women would not appear on the English stage until about 1660[83]

The late 16th century was a particularly happy time for England. As a nation, it was secure and stable under the guidance and leadership of Queen Elizabeth. The strongest naval force in the world and England's chief rival for power, Spain, had been soundly beaten as a result of the destruction of the Spanish Armada. France was busy trying to establish order within its borders following the massacre of the Protestant Huguenots and was therefore not a threat to England. Holland and Portugal were more interested in trading than war, and the English Church was under the control of the English monarch and not a foreign pope.

In Elizabethan eyes, the world centered on and in England. Being very much in the vanguard of Humanism, the English saw themselves as God's chosen people, people with a manifest destiny which could not be stopped. The Elizabethans believed that the world was created for man and that man was created to dominate the world, and they believed they could do just that. They readily accepted that there was a supreme being and that He was their benefactor. They agreed that God had given man free will and they accepted responsibilities for exercising that free will and the results. It is this attitude which is demonstrated in the Elizabethan plays.

Though there were many successful Elizabethan playwrights, three stand above the others for their contributions to the English and world theatre. Christopher Marlowe (1564-1593) is the first of these. Well educated, Marlowe brought a talent to the English theatre that had not been present prior to his time. Not only did Marlowe develop his protagonists with more care and depth than his contemporaries, but he did more than any of them to establish blank verse as the medium for drama. He is particularly noted for *Tamburlaine*, Parts I & II (1587-1588), *Dr. Faustus* (c. 1588), and *Edward II* (c. 1592). With *Edward II* Marlowe produced a play which was to become a model for the chronicle plays which followed, particularly those by Shakespeare.

Standing well above all his predecessors, contemporaries and successors was William Shakespeare (1564-1616), who built on Marlowe's models, perfected the iambic pentameter or blank verse line, and composed the greatest library of dramatic masterpieces produced by one playwright since the time of the Greeks. Like many of his predecessors through-

Courtesy of Stratford, Canada, Festival. Douglas Spillane, photographer.

Christopher Plummer as Hamlet in a production at the Stratford Shakespeare Festival in Stratford, Canada, 1957. The stage is a thrust stage surrounded on three sides by the audience, a situation very similar to that experienced by Elizabethan actors. The production was directed by Michael Langhan and designed by Desmond Heeley.

Christopher Marlowe 1564-93

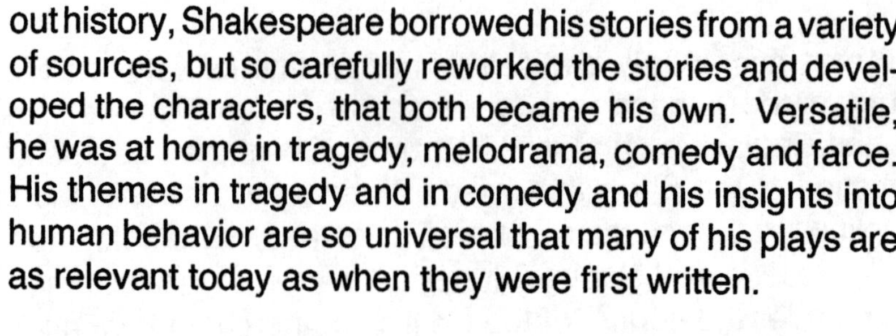

out history, Shakespeare borrowed his stories from a variety of sources, but so carefully reworked the stories and developed the characters, that both became his own. Versatile, he was at home in tragedy, melodrama, comedy and farce. His themes in tragedy and in comedy and his insights into human behavior are so universal that many of his plays are as relevant today as when they were first written.

William Shakespeare 1564-1616

The third of these Elizabethan playwrights was Ben Jonson (1572-1637), who is remembered more for his comedies than for the highly poetic tragedies he penned. Jonson saw comedy as a corrective device, one that should be employed to reveal the foibles of human behavior and, by holding them up to ridicule, could force people to change. As a writer of poetry and court masques, Jonson gained the favor of the King who made him England's first poet-laureate.

Ben Jonson 1573-1637

Mort Gerberg in *Diners' Club Magazine* September, 1964

Theatre Appreciation
Class Assignment

Name____________________________________

Using the Elizabethan play assigned, designate the specific playing area(s) used for each scene in each act. Use the John Cranford Adams reconstruction of the Globe theatre for your source for location names.

Remove from text and hand in to instructor

12
The Modern Theatre

In 1859, Charles Darwin (1809-1882) wrote his book *The Origin of the Species* in which he recorded his observations about life and its origins. A scientist, Darwin based his theories on his observations and claimed that life on earth was an evolutionary process and that man was essentially the product of his environment and heredity with continued existence being based on the survival of the fittest. His writings caused a furor within the scientific, social, and religious communities. His theory was labeled **scientific determinism** and brought about a major change in attitudes toward man, his behavior, and his place in the universe.

If the theory was accepted, as it was by many scientists and writers of the era, it meant that man had little control over himself, his physical well-being, his intellectual ability and his emotions. While man might be able to alter his environment to some extent, his heredity was another thing. That could not be altered. Several writers, theorizing, carried the principles of scientific determinism even further by stating that man was pre-determined or predestined to certain behavior patterns as a result of his genes and the environment in which he existed. In other words, man had no control over himself and very little over the world in which he lived. Man was, to all intents and purposes, either the beneficiary or the victim of outside forces. As such, man was fated to a basic set of inborn behavior patterns. What decisions man made, he was fated to make.

If the reasoning developed out of Darwin's observations was acceptable, what, then, was the responsibility of man for his choices and his actions? Did man act or was he acted upon? Those who accepted the theory of scientific determinism believed that man was acted upon and, therefore, had little or no responsibility for what he did. They felt that man's choices and actions were the product not of his conscious moral choices but of his physical and social background which had given him a predisposition to follow his chosen path. This philosophy is very much with us today. All we have to do is view the world around us and see modern man's responses to it and to himself. Current court cases provide good examples of the application of scientific determinism to human behavior.

The fall-out from *The Origin of the Species* brought other responses. In some cases, the existence of God was brought into question. If man was formed by heredity and environment, he could no longer be considered as being "created in the image of God." If this were the case, some asked, is there a God? In 1929, Joseph Wood Krutch wrote an essay titled "The Tragic Fallacy" in which he claimed that classical tragedy was no longer possible in the modern world. He based his conclusions on his observation that there seemed to be an absence of a Supreme Being in modern philosophy. Without the existence of a Supreme Being and a moral code (not an ethical one), he said, classical tragedy could not be understood, could no longer be experienced, and certainly could not be written.

One of the primary results of the development of the philosophy of scientific determinism was a movement within the arts to reflect man in his environment as fully and honestly as possible. Advocating this approach was the French writer Emile Zola (1840-1902) who castigated novelists and playwrights of his time for their romantic view of the world. He believed that man must face the realities about him if he is to deal with them. Zola, therefore, advocated a style of writing which would be labeled **naturalism**. In a naturalistic work, the author places before the audience all the details of a man's environment as is indicated in the descriptive passage from Hauptmann's *The Weavers* quoted at the end of Chapter 3. If a man is a product of his heredity and environment, the reader/audience must be exposed to it as fully and completely as possible. In addition, writers must deal with the real problems in the world whether public discussions of those problems are taboo or not. The results of this movement can be seen in the plays of authors like Hauptmann and particularly in the works of Norway's Henrik Ibsen (1828-1906). This approach is the basis of much of modern drama.

Henrik Ibsen

Perhaps no writer has had more influence on the modern theatre than Ibsen. Writing in the last quarter of the 19th century, Ibsen introduced realistic drama to the world of the theatre. By discussing major social and personal issues of the day, he opened the theatre to a broader range of topics. His discussions of divorce, euthanasia, venereal disease, inherited tendencies, suicide, women's rights, etc., normally considered taboo subjects by "polite" society, shocked many viewers and brought cries for censorship from the authorities. In many countries, his plays could not be performed in the public theatre, but were restricted to private theatre societies. Once Ibsen opened the door to these subjects, other writers followed his lead and the theatre became a forum for the discussion and demonstration of current social and personal problems.

Tragedy in the Modern Theatre

Arthur Miller

While Joseph Wood Krutch's comments were readily accepted by many writers, others attempted to justify the existence of tragedy in today's theatre. Chief among these was playwright Arthur Miller. Miller's approach moved away from the contest between the will of man and that of God, and dealt with a more inward struggle as man sought to deal with himself and society. "Tragedy is the consequence of man's total compulsion to evaluate himself justly," said Miller. "In the tragic view, the need for man to wholly realize himself is the only fixed star. ."

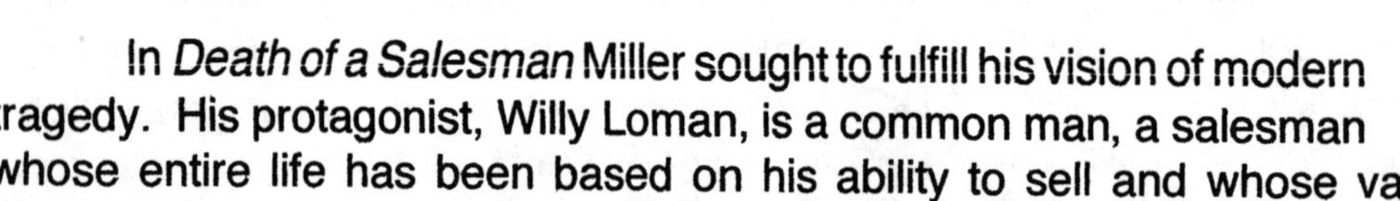

In *Death of a Salesman* Miller sought to fulfill his vision of modern tragedy. His protagonist, Willy Loman, is a common man, a salesman whose entire life has been based on his ability to sell and whose values are essentially materialistic. The play is concerned with Willy's attempts to understand himself and justify the actions of his life in light of his values. For Miller, Willy is a product of a society in which material values have grown to the point of dominating man's activities. Willy, trained by society, seeks love and respect but knows of no resources to achieve those goals other than the materialistic.

Other Modern Dramatic Forms

Epic Theatre

During the 20th century, the theatre has been the scene of a variety of efforts to find new ways of moving audiences and achieving many purposes. This has brought about the emergence of varied approaches to theatre both in Europe and the United States.

Bertolt Brecht

The use of the theatre to instruct has always been one of its main justifications for existence. The Greek playwrights used the theatre to instruct the audiences in their Greek heritage, religious and political. During the Middle Ages, the Church used the theatre to instruct the people in the ideas and concepts contained within the Bible and church dogma. During the Renaissance, the theatre was justified as a means by which the public could be instructed in man's relation to a Supreme Being, to the State, to other men, and the past. Writers of comedy singled out the theatre as a means by which audiences could be instructed concerning proper attitudes and behavior. In the 19th century, a variety of directors saw the theatre as the means by which history could be taught both verbally and visually. In the late 19th century, playwrights such as Ibsen and Shaw saw the theatre as a means to investigate and teach about current problems and attitudes. During all of these periods, however, the writers sought to so engage the viewers in the action on the stage that the teaching would be subliminal and would occur subconsciously while the audience was engrossed in the action of the play.

A Stephen F. Austin State University production.

In Brecht's *The Good Woman of Setzuan,* three gods come to earth to find the reason for their existence which can only be justified if there is at least one good person.

In the 1920s, in Germany and Russia particularly, a new movement related to theatre as an instructive device began to develop. This was what is commonly referred to as the **didactic theatre,** that is, the theatre designed specifically to teach. In Russia, the movement was sponsored particularly by the Soviet government which saw theatre as a means by which its social and political philosophy could be communicated to the masses. In Germany, the goal was much the same, though the didactic theatre was not an arm of the government but was often a means of protesting against prevailing social attitudes and political actions. One of the leaders of this German movement was Erwin Piscator who, with the rise of Hitler, escaped to the United States where he became head of the theatre program at New York City's New School for Social Research. Though Piscator was important, particularly as a teacher, it was his student, Bertolt Brecht, who became famous and whose plays are considered to be among the most important works written during the early 20th century.

Brecht worked in a style which may be called **theatricalism**. He dispensed with and rejected the conventions required to make a suspension of disbelief possible. He wanted his audiences to remain objective while viewing his plays and wrote the plays in such a way as to jar the audiences out of subjective, emotional responses. His characters were designed as symbols of various elements of society or political concepts. His staging was done in such a manner as to continually remind the audience that it was in the theatre not in another imaginary world. He interrupted the flow of action within the scripts by introducing songs, direct comments to the audience, and used other non-illusionary devices such as masks on the actors. In order to maintain the objectivity he sought, he instructed his actors to rehearse their roles using methods which would prevent them from identifying with the characters they were playing. His stage settings were practical but non-representational; and he insisted that the lighting instruments be within view of the audience, thus reminding the audience that it was in the theatre. Like Piscator, he used what has come to be referred to as a **multi-media** approach incorporating motion pictures, slides, and music with the actions of his live actors. Because of the scope of his stories and his methods of staging, critics have often referred to the Brechtian theatre as **epic theatre**.

A Stephen F. Austin State University production.

In *The Good Woman of Setzuan* (1940) Brecht criticizes modern society's tendency to reduce man to the status of a machine in the worship of money and material gain. This is demonstrated in this scene in which the characters become little more than cogs in a machine.

Though many of Brecht's ideas and political comments alienated him from the American theatre scene during the 1940s and 50s, his influence on Western, including American, theatre has been great. Thornton Wilder (1897-1975) employed Brechtian techniques in his masterpiece *The Skin of Our Teeth* (1941). British playwright Robert Bolt (1924–) made use of the Brecht device of a narrator, in this case the Common Man, in his historical tragedy *A Man for All Seasons* (1960). Archibald MacLeish (1892-1982) used the characters of God and Satan as Brechtian-type commentators in *J.B.* (1958). *Big River,* based on *Mark Twain's Huckleberry Finn,* is designed to be presented theatrically so that Twain's comments on prejudice and society can be viewed more objectively and consciously. *Pippin* (1972), the musical, is also a reflection of Brecht's style using a narrator, direct asides to the audience, and many very obvious theatrical devices.

French Information Service

Samuel Beckett

Theatre of the Absurd

Theatre of the Absurd is a phrase coined by critic Martin Eslin in writing about a series of playwrights in France and England following World War II. The theatre of the absurd is a logical descendent of the realistic and naturalistic movements which reflected Darwin's theories and the theory of scientific determinism. It is also a result of the reactions which developed throughout Europe and to some extent America as a

Courtesy of the Utah Shakespearean Festival, Susan Bennett, photographer.

Samuel Beckett's *Waiting for Godot* as staged by the Utah Shakespearean Festival in 1990. Here the designers have used Utah's caprock formation as the basis for the setting, a most suitable way of indicating Beckett's desolate and hopeless world. *Waiting for Godot* was first presented in Paris in 1953 and was soon seen in the major theatrical centers of the western world.

result of the Holocaust and the war itself. World War I had been billed in both Europe and the Western hemisphere as the "war to end all wars." When World War II with its accompanying horrors occurred, the natural result was disillusionment.

The influence of scientific determinism on theatre of the absurd is evident. If we are determined by our heredity and environment, as some believe, and if much of this occurs haphazardly, almost by accident, then there is no master plan for the world or humanity. If there is no master plan, then there is no goal. If there is no goal, then there is no point to our existence. Life, therefore, is absurd. Without God, man is without direction and a moral code. Each of us, therefore, must find his own way, develop his own value system, and act accordingly.

The most influential play to come from the theatre of the absurd is Samuel Beckett's (1906–) *Waiting for Godot* (1953) in which two tramps meet at a crossroad by a single tree to wait for the arrival of Godot. Who or what Godot is is never explained–and Godot never arrives.

Absurdist plays rarely have developed plots. A plot is structured and therefore is not relevant to the absurdist. The playwrights, therefore, present the audience with an experience, one in which the action is often circular; i.e., the characters end the play just in time to begin the same action over again and again and again. There is no discussion of meaning or lack of meaning by these writers, rather they present life on stage as they see it–filled with meaningless actions, verbal non sequiturs, and often inarticulate and incomprehensible exchanges and actions.

New York Shakespeare Festival. Photo by George Joseph.

Irene Worth in the New York Public Theatre production of Samuel Beckett's *Happy Days*. The play calls for the actress to be buried up to her waist during the first act of the play and up to her neck during the second.

The Birth of Dionysus ritual in The Performance Group's production of *Dionysus in '69* (1969) directed by Richard Schechner. The production featured close contact between actors and audience in an informal theatre space. The play is based on Euripides' *The Bacchae*

Experimental Theatre

Beginning in the latter part of the 19th century and continuing today, there has been a great deal of experimentation in the field of theatre. The aim has generally been to find new purposes for the theatre, new forms of drama, and new ways to express oneself dramatically. In the United States this has been seen in the work of a number of **Off-Broadway** and **Off-Off-Broadway** companies and in smaller **fringe theatres** in major cities throughout the world. Some have investigated the techniques of the highly ritualized Oriental theatre; some have attempted to resurrect ancient Greek techniques of writing and staging plays; some have deliberately broken theatrical and social taboos in order to shock their audiences and, hopefully, inspire them to think. Almost all of these group have had serious purposes and many have been involved in political and social protest movements. In many cases the performances mounted by these groups make use of Brechtian techniques but often go well beyond Brecht's approach and involve direct audience confrontation.

Guerilla Theatre

During the late 60s and early 70s, the didactic theatre took another form which has come to be known as guerilla theatre. This was a form of street theatre that was created by playwrights and actors to espouse specific causes. During this period, there were two primary sources of discontent in the United States that guerilla theatre often addressed: the Vietnam War and racism. The presentations were publicly mounted in democratic countries and often performed "underground" (sometimes literally) in more repressive political atmospheres. The practitioners of guerilla theatre accepted no limitations on what they said or did in a performance. They often employed shock techniques, both verbal and visual, in order to make a point. They refused to be bound by literal truth and presented their version of the truth. They called on the audience to take action against a litany of political and social abuses. Their appeal was primarily to the emotions of the audience and their message was invariably highly prejudiced and politicized. Guerilla theatre was usually mounted on street corners, in parks, or in any public place where an audience could be attracted. Because of the controversial nature of its subject matter, this was not viewed as "commercial" theatre and often was produced, directed, and acted by amateurs. It was presented in a variety of styles, some consciously outrageous. Its purpose was propaganda through entertainment.

13
The Theatre of Asia

The theatre of Asia is almost unknown to the general public in the United States though it has influenced twentieth century theatre in the Western world greatly. Playwrights, artists and scholars alike have found within it elements that they have incorporated into modern works as they experimented with "new" ways to reach audiences. Time and space do not allow an in-depth discussion of the great theatrical traditions of the East here, but an attempt will be made to introduce the student to some of the most noted kinds of theatrical performances India, China and Japan have developed over the centuries. Unfortunately, many of these theatrical forms have almost been lost during this century. First, Muslim influence in India discouraged play acting and dramatic story telling, then the British rule of India brought western theatre to that country during the nineteenth century; and current film and television now exert a great influence on the traditional arts. Similar influences affected China at the end of the nineteenth century and well into the twentieth. Japan, perhaps, has been most successful in preserving its traditional theatrical forms, though Western theatre, film and television have also become quite popular there.

Popular throughout the Arab world and much of the East is the puppet play. Samples of such plays may be found in many Arab and Eastern countries and even in Sicily, which was under Arab rule for a period of time. In Java the Shadow puppet play is popular today with material drawn from the folk-tales and literary works of South-East Asia. For these performances elaborately formed puppets are cut from leather and other substances, placed behind a linen sheet with a light and operated from below by skilled puppeteers while one or more narrators tell the stories to the accompaniment of instrumental music and songs.

Dance is also a popular form of theatrical entertainment in Southeast Asia with the dancers, primarily young girls, carefully trained in a series of highly symbolic gestures and movements which have become standardized over the years. The grace and precision with which these movements are executed appeal to Western audiences which, while not being acquainted with the symbolism of the movements, can readily appreciate the aesthetic beauty of the dancers.

India

Dance and drama in India were the dynamic accessories of a culture entirely dependent on a grand scheme of hierarchical ritual affecting every phase of living and given total realization in the community through the institution of caste. As the supreme celebration of ritual it can be said without exaggeration that dance has there attained qualities of dramatic intensity unsurpassed in any civilization.

A.C. Scott, *The Theatre In Asia*

Scholars attribute the development of drama in Asia primarily to India, which influenced the drama of China, Japan and Southeast Asia. Ancient Indian drama is rooted in the Hindu religion and reflects Hindu philosophy. There are three basic types of native Indian dramatic works: **Sanskrit** drama, folk drama, and dance-drama.

Sanskrit drama, which flourished until about 1000 AD., was a form of court drama written in Sanskrit, a language brought to India by Aryan invaders during the second millennium BC.

According to Henry Wells, Sanskrit dramas could be divided into "two major types of plays: the *nataka*, plays of mythological or historical content, and the p*rakarama*, plays with invented stories and less exalted characters." The dialogue was distinguished by having characters of education and position speak in Sanskrit while characters coming from more common backgrounds spoke in the vernacular, the *Prakrits* dialect.

The Sanskrit plays are highly ritualistic and are designed to lead the audience through pleasure to serenity and ultimately to peace. There is no tragedy in these plays, for the Hindu beliefs do not admit to tragedy. In both types of plays, the acting style required is highly regimented with choreographed moments using symbolic gestures and finger movements which are carefully integrated into the action. As in the court productions of the Renaissance in Europe, the Sanskrit plays rely greatly on spectacle as well as poetry with elaborate staging devices often being required. For instance, in the seven-act *Shakuntala*, a Sanskrit play from the fifth century, the King Charioteer flies over the stage in pursuit of an imaginary antelope in Act I and descends from the sky in Act VII after leading India's armies in a successful battle with a rebellious race of giants.

Though the Sanskrit tradition has been preserved in some 700 plays, it was lost to performance with the Muslim invasion of northern India in the eighth century BC. By 1000 BC., Sanskrit drama had disappeared from the stage, suppressed by the Muslims, whose Islamic faith would not tolerate the representation of the human form in art.

Much of the **folk drama** developed and still performed in India came from the work of traveling players; usually families of actors, who performed for the general public rather than the courts. Few of these plays exist in printed form since they relied heavily on tradition and improvisation. They also drew from the Sanskrit plays, simplifying the language and adding references and characters which would be recognizable to the common audiences for which they were intended.

Today, due to the influence of film and television, much of the live theatre in India has been lost except for the dance-drama. The dance-dramas are derived from Indian myths and legends well known to the audiences viewing them. In some cases they are accompanied not only by music but by a narrator or reciter who tells the story as it is enacted on stage by the dancers. The style of dancing is highly regulated with established gestures and movements with which the audience is well-acquainted, a kind of sign language. In all cases, the story being told dominates the dance. (In the West, the dance usually dominates the story, which is often of little consequence.)

China

[The] Chinese theatre is perhaps the purest and most nearly idealistic of all theatres, for it presumes the supreme potency of the actors to carry all burdens. Their words describe the most vivid scenery, their gestures mime the most incredible actions without the benefit of stage properties; they create whole worlds in disembodied air.

Henry W. Wells

More akin to western theatre is the classical theatre of China. Its influence has been felt in both Europe and the United States where twentieth century playwrights have drawn from its themes and its style of presentation. Sweden's August Strindberg was highly influenced by

Chinese drama in the writing of *The Dream Play* and *To Damascus*. *The Dream Play*, in particular, owes much of its stylistic quality to Chinese drama in its extensive use of symbolic scenery and acting. Germany's Bertolt Brecht drew from Chinese drama the style of presentation and the stories for *The Caucasian Chalk Circle* and *The Good Woman of Setsuan*. America's Thornton Wilder, who spent a portion of his youth in China, made use of the Chinese open stage for his *Our Town*.

According to Oriental theatre authority Henry Wells, "The classical Chinese theatre is in every sense a creation without walls." It was designed to be performed wherever and whenever possible indoors or outdoors, on a permanent stage or within a temporary structure. Costumes are elaborate as may be the sets, though on occasion these may be suggested only symbolically. The acting style is highly stylized and the productions often incorporate song, music and dance.

Actor training is demanding and rigorous with many of the actors trained from earliest childhood. Wells says that, "most were brought up with the theatre as their foster mother, having no other education and memorizing all their parts through the ear. These boys barely learned to walk before they were instructed in the artificial manner of walking peculiar to the Chinese stage." Though women appeared on stage during the early years of the Chinese theatre, many soon found it impossible to meet the rigorous physical demands of their profession; the practice of binding a girl's feet at an early age made it impossible to move with the agility required of an actor on stage. By the 18th and through the 19th century only men performed for the public. Today, women again are seen on the stage.

Best known to Western audiences is the **Beijing Opera** (formerly called the Peking Opera and sometimes referred to as the Chinese Opera). This form of classical Chinese theatre is still being performed in Beijing and in Chinese communities on the US. West Coast. Highly stylized, it was derived from the various regional forms of Chinese drama in the late 18th century in Beijing. According to Oscar Brockett, the plays are classified under two headings: "civil plays (dealing with social and domestic themes) and military plays (involving the adventures of warriors or brigands)." The performances are made up of acts or portions of acts from other works and include acrobatic displays between the scenes. Highly symbolic, the Beijing Opera depends heavily on an audience familiar with its various conventions. Actors are handed properties by "invisible" property men throughout the performances. Tables, chairs, and props may become symbolically walls, bridges, trees, etc. The audience's imagination, therefore, becomes extremely important. Actions, the use of voice, and costumes are also highly stylized and, to some degree, regimented by custom. Finally, it is the performance that is of the greatest importance. Actors are permitted a great deal of freedom with the text which becomes little more than an outline for the performance the audience has come to see.

Though the classical style of acting and production has been retained to some degree in China, much of it has been lost due to the western influences of the twentieth century. Under the Communist regime, the theatre has been seen as a propaganda organ primarily of value to promote the interests of the state. With this approach, the government has financially supported the arts, particularly drama, opera and ballet.

Japan

As in India and China, Western forms of theatre, particularly film and television, have become highly popular in Japan since World War II. In spite of these influences, Japan has preserved three forms of its classical theatre: the ***Noh*** plays, the ***Kabuki*** theatre, and the ***Bunraku*** or the Japanese puppet theatre. Performances of these theatrical forms are regularly presented in Tokyo, Osaka, and Kyoto; and Noh and Kabuki presentations are often sent on tour to Europe and occasionally to the United States.

The Noh Theatre

The Noh plays, which originated in 15th century Japan, were originally developed for court presentation and are highly formal and ritualistic. They rely on extreme understatement. Often restricted to one masked actor, physical action is at a minimum. Much emphasis is placed on minuteness of gesture and the use of the voice. The actor, always a male, is assisted on stage by a chorus, seated stage left and a small orchestra seated to the rear of the stage. The chorus comments on the play and discourses with the actor much in the manner of the ancient Greek chorus. Noh plays are usually no longer than a short western one-act play. Three of these are presented in an evening's offering with the second, a *kyogen,* providing a comic interlude between the two serious offerings.

Edward Seidensticker states, "A Noh play is like an Italian opera in that it is an amalgam of drama, music and dance, but in spirit the two are quite different. When the Noh play trails off into silence and players turn and move slowly from the bare stage, it is a silence as if all passion had been over for a long time."

The Kabuki Theatre

Contrasting sharply to the Noh theatre is the Kabuki theatre which is called "the popular theatre of Japan." It was the Kabuki theatre which inspired the staging of Sondheim's American musical *Pacific Overtures.* Though drawn from the Noh plays of the late 15th century, the Kabuki is far more spectacular than its predecessor with ornate costumes, makeup, scenery, and highly physical action. In fact, these elements of the Kabuki are recognized as being the most lavish in the world. Over 300 years ago, well before its introduction to Europe, the revolving stage (the ***mawari-butai***) was invented for the Kabuki theatre thus allowing rapid scene changes to occur during the action. An additional feature of the Kabuki stage and theatre is the ***hanamichi***, also called the flower-walk ramp, which connects the left side of the stage to the back of the auditorium allowing actors to make entrances and exits through the audience.

The plays, drawn from domestic or historical sources, are highly demanding on the actors who are usually trained from childhood on to perform in the Kabuki theatre. In fact, many of the actors come from the families of current and former Kabuki actors and have been trained in movement, voice, makeup, and the traditions of the Kabuki by their fathers and/or grandfathers. (One current actor is a 17th generation Kabuki actor.)

As in the Noh theatre, all roles in the Kabuki theatre are played by men. (Note: A newly formed all-female Kabuki company has been established in Tokyo.) At one time it was customary for an actor to play only the role for which he had been trained. Today, however, actors, other than those playing female roles, the onnagata, are given more freedom in the roles they play. The ***onnagata***, a female impersonator, in the Kabuki theatre is one of the most admired actors, for he must present his character so believably and beautifully that the audience is never aware of his masculine gender. The secret to this lies in the fact that the feminine beauty which has been created on stage has not been created naturally but artificially through the eyes of men objectively looking at the behavior and psychology of the opposite sex.

The conventions of the Kabuki theatre are similar to those of the Noh plays although the orchestra usually is secreted behind a screen. The musicians often accompany the play throughout and the actors speak in a form of idealized elocution using a rhythmic pattern somewhere between speech and song for monologues. In such cases, the action moves almost to the formality of dance. As in the Beijing Opera, the Kabuki makes use of "invisible property men" (***kurogo*** or "men in black," for they are garbed in black costumes and hoods) who assist the actors throughout the play both with the properties and as prompters.

The Puppet Theatre

While puppetry in Japan is over 1000 years old, ***Bunraku*** entered the Japanese culture as a popular form of theatre in the mid-17th century. It is the name used to describe the Japanese form of *ningyo-joruri,* literally puppets and storytelling. Drawing heavily from the Kabuki plays, the Bunraku uses scripts derived from its sister theatrical form. Its uniqueness lies in the fact that the puppets are large, being about 1.3 to 1.5 meters in height, and are operated by three puppe-

From *Schribner's Magazine* 7, 1890.

A Kabuki stage of the late 19th century. Note the markings for the revolving stage. To the left of center is the *hanamichi*, the "flower-walk," which extends through the audience to the back of the auditorium. There is also a small elevator trap to the right.

teers who remain in view of the audience throughout the performance. The first or master puppeteer, the *omozukai*, manipulates the head, eyes, mouth, and right arm; the second, the *hidanzukai*, manipulates the left arm; and the apprentice puppeteer, the *ashizukai*, handles the feet. To become an apprentice, one must go through ten years of training. Another ten years is required to become the second puppeteer. The position and mastery of the art of the omozukai is a life-long task.

Ironically, the Bunraku proved to be so popular during its early years that the Kabuki actors began imitating the actions and gestures of the puppets, thus assuming an almost puppet-like quality themselves. This style of movement became and still is the standard for Kabuki. The puppeteers, however, attempted to develop movements and gestures for their puppets that were as realistic as possible.

Bunraku has enjoyed a resurgence of popularity since World War II. In 1985, the Japanese opened the National Bunraku Theatre in Osaka. The Bunraku troupe there presents about 170 performances a year and tours extensively.

14
Producing the Play

The Commercial Theatre

The production of a play, that is moving the play from script to stage, has become increasingly complex as the theatre has developed over the ages. In the ancient Greek theatre, the play was produced under the guidance of the playwright who sought financing, selected the Choregos to train the chorus, and directed the actors, sometimes acting in the play himself. Today plays presented in the commercial theatre face an entirely different set of problems. Rarely is the playwright, particularly the young playwright, in charge of the production. Rather, that function is normally in the hands of an individual known as the **producer**.

A young playwright attempting to have his work staged submits the script to a producer who decides whether or not the new play is worthy of production and the financial investment which would be necessary. If the producer's response is positive, he **options** the play; that is, he signs a contract with the playwright securing the right to produce the play within a specified time limit. Though this does not guarantee a production, it does give the playwright an initial financial reward for his work. If the producer fails to mount the play within the specified amount of time, he may seek to extend his option, paying an additional sum to the playwright, or he may relinquish all rights to the play. If the producer relinquishes his rights, the playwright is free to submit the work to other producers.

Once a work has been optioned, the producer proceeds to raise funds to finance the new production by finding backers or investors who are usually referred to as "Angels" for obvious reasons. With financing secured, the producer arranges for the services of an artistic staff, director, actors,

Theatre Unions

The following are unions contracted by the producer:

Dramatists' Guild - a Guild representing playwrights, composers, etc., in their relations with producers and directors.

Actors' Equity Association- A union representing actors and stage-managers in their relations with producers.

Society of Stage Directors and Choreographers - an organization made up of stage directors and choreographers that recommends minimum contract terms for its members.

United Scenic Artists of America - a union which represents scenic and lighting designers.

Wardrobe Supervisors and Dressers - a union which represents its members in terms of contracts and grievances

The following are local unions organized in various cities throughout the country and contracted by the theatres in which they work:

International Alliance of Theatrical Stage Employees - the stage hands union. The number of employees on any given show depends on the size of the production.

Treasurers and Ticket Sellers - the number of employees depends on the seating capacity of the theatre.

Other unions represent maintenance personnel, cleaning personnel, ushers, and doormen.

The following are national unions contracted by both the producer and the theatre:

Association of Theatrical Press Agents and Managers

American Federation of Musicians

designers, etc., to mount the new work. In addition, he sets up a business staff to handle all the financial and promotional aspects of the enterprise, including legal considerations, contracts, budgets, payrolls, advertising, theatre rental, and box-office management. He and his staff work closely with the artistic staff and with the various theatre unions which will be involved.

In some cases a well-known playwright with a history of successful productions will become his own producer. Such is the case with Neil Simon. For many years Rodgers and Hammerstein produced not only their own works but the works of others as well. This is more the exception than the rule, however. Also exceptional is the director who serves as his own producer. Hal Prince is a prime example. His long string of box office successes and established reputation, which are reassuring to backers, have given him the power to assemble adequate financing and his own production team.

In the ideal situation, the producer concerns himself with the nitty-gritty day-to-day handling of the enterprise, turning over artistic considerations to the artistic staff headed by the director and possibly the playwright. Working closely with the playwright, the director selects the cast and unifies the approaches taken by the design staff. He then conducts the rehearsals and works with the playwright to refine the script as rehearsals proceed. Often this means that scenes are written and rewritten up to opening night with the necessary adjustments being made in the various technical areas which support the visual aspects of the play. The production, then, becomes a team effort with the playwright and director as co-captains and with the producer in a supporting role.

In the commercial theatre, however, the situation is rarely ideal. The cost of production– one million dollars for a play and up to six or more millions for a musical– is so great that producers and their backers are often leery of taking risks. As a result, the control over the production often rests in the hands of those whose names will bring in the greatest box office. Some producers are so well known for the quality of their presentations that the public will support almost any effort mounted by them. The name of a well-known and successful playwright is often sufficient incentive to attract audiences. In some cases, the very fact that a specific stage director has mounted the production will bring in the box office receipts. More often, it is the name of the actor or actors that attract. Some actors are so well known and admired that their very names on the marquee will assure the success of the play, guaranteeing box office receipts over a prolonged period. It is not unusual for a play to be reworked or rewritten with major changes of emphasis to satisfy a particularly successful director or, more likely, the star upon whom the success of the financial undertaking apparently rests.

The Regional Theatre

More and more in today's theatre the young or unknown playwright first approaches regional theatres for an opportunity to be heard and seen. Since most regional theatres are supported not only by box office but by philanthropic grants and are registered as non-profit organizations, they are in a position to take risks the commercial theatre would avoid. All major regional theatres have one or more play readers whose duty it is to read new scripts submitted for consideration. Once they have made their recommendations, the scripts are turned over to the theatre's Artistic Director, who makes the final selection, often balancing his season of productions between new works and proven plays. Though often supported by outside funds, the regional theatres work under relatively meagre budgets and must depend on continued public support to exist. If the new play proves to be a success on the regional level, it may be optioned for a commercial production. In fact, the vast majority of new plays and musicals presented on Broadway in recent years have originated in regional theatres.

The University Theatre

The University theatre is not bound by the same financial restraints as those which exist in the other producing organizations listed here. Its professional staff is on salary and is paid primarily for teaching. Often productions are subsidized by student activities moneys and funds made available from instructional sources. For the most part, the actors and technicians are students and are unpaid for their efforts. Still, the costs of mounting productions are considerable and what subsidies are available must be supplemented by box office receipts. The choice of plays is, therefore, influenced by the play's ability to draw audiences. Of more importance in the university situation, however, is how a play may be used to train young actors and technicians and how it may serve to provide a rich cultural experience for the university community as a whole.

On occasion, a playwright may enter into an agreement with a college or university and join that institution's faculty as a "playwright-in-residence" with the guarantee not only of a salary but of a trial production of a new script. In this situation, the playwright retains the greatest control over his script as it moves into production. Working closely with the production staff, he has the time to refine his script and the opportunity to test the results of his work in a situation which is not as financially critical as it is in the commercial theatre and may be in the regional theatre. A drawback exists in this arrangement, however, for the playwright may not always have directors with the greatest expertise and experienced, seasoned actors with which to work.

The Community Theatre

The personnel of many community theatres is often composed totally of volunteers with no paid participants whatsoever. These groups present two to four productions during a season, choosing their plays from among those which are well known and will readily attract audiences. Many times actors are chosen as much for their ability to attract certain segments of the community as for their ability to portray certain roles. In such cases, if a new play is mounted by a community theatre, it is often a play written by a member of the community and thus has a built-in audience.

When a community theatre has the financial ability to expand its programs beyond the minimal, it often engages the services of an Artistic Director who advises the theatre's Board regarding its choice of a season and serves as producer overseeing the various aspects of mounting the plays. Depending on the relationship of the Artistic Director to the theatre's Board of Directors, the Artistic Director can play a major part in expanding the program of the theatre and the kinds of productions mounted.

Under the best of circumstances, a community theatre has the backing of grants and tax moneys and has a relatively secure and experienced staff. When this is the case, the theatre is in a position to take more risks and may well offer a wide variety of plays, sometimes even a second season of plays which are new and/or experimental.

Community theatres at this level like to bring in new playwrights who will provide a fresh approach for their audiences. For the playwright, this provides a valuable testing ground for a new work and allows him to hone his skills with very little of the risk involved in a far more public and expensive professional production. Here, the playwright is given the venue in which to work and re-write without much of the pressure that is found in a regional or commercial theatre.

Table of Organization of a Typical Broadway Musical

(Note: Delete references to musicians and choreographers and the chart remains about the same for a legitimate play.)

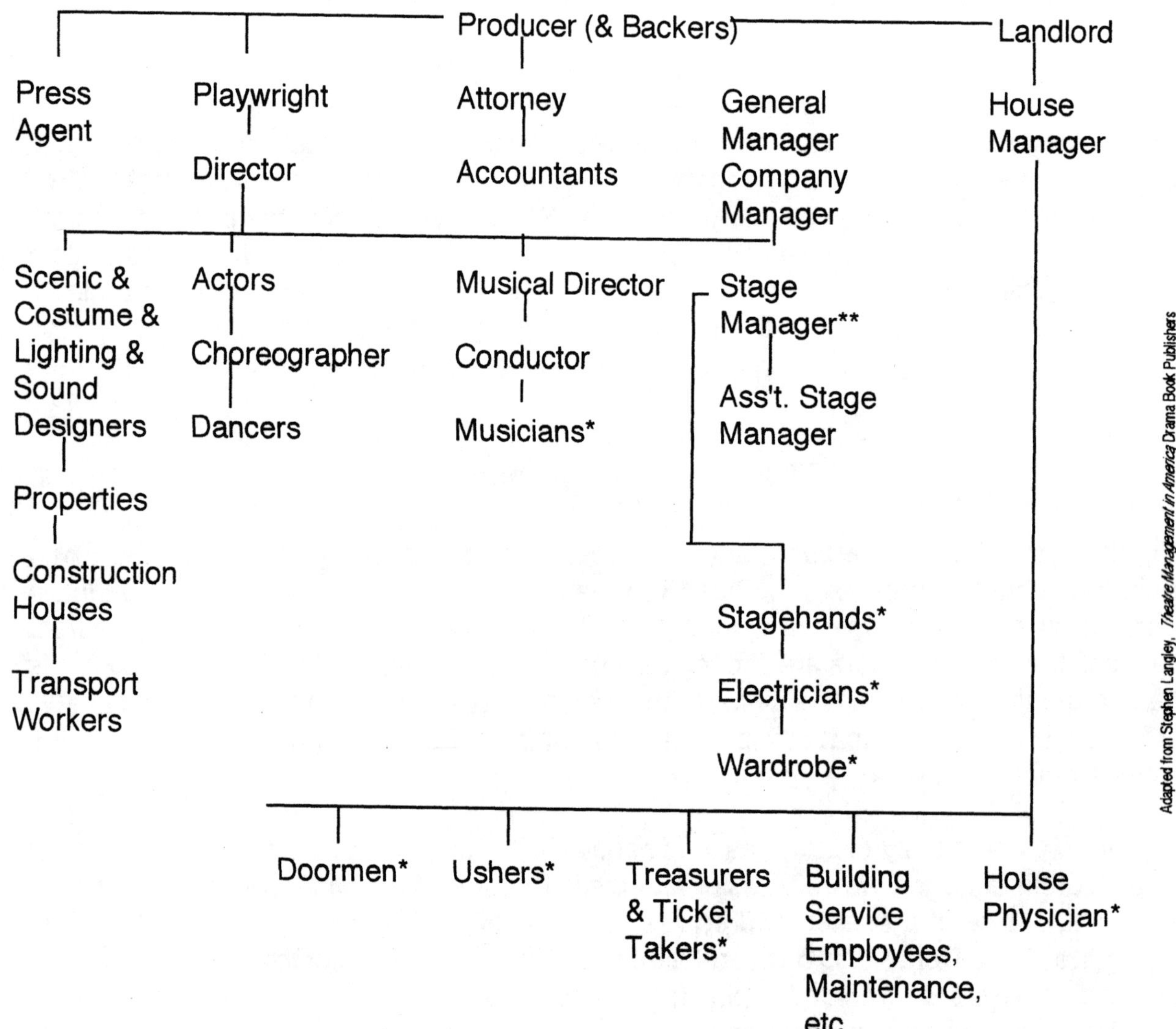

Adapted from Stephen Langley, *Theatre Management in America* Drama Book Publishers

*Often contracted by the Landlord (Theatre owner).

**Once the production has opened, the stage-manager is in charge. Though the director, by contract, will visit the performances occasionally, the stage-manager rules. In addition to running the show, the stage-manager also trains replacement actors as necessary.

15
The Director

The true director comprises within his own person a director-teacher, a director-writer, a director- administrator.
Constantine Stanislavski

In the modern theatre the director is normally responsible for establishing a unifying concept for the production. He chooses the cast, directs the actors in their interpretations of the roles, **blocks** or choreographs the movements of the actors on stage, and establishes the tone and rhythm of the performance. In fulfilling this function, he works closely with the designers–scenery, properties, costumes, lights, sound, make-up–in order to assure a unity of concept, style, and interpretation in all areas. The manner in which he fulfills his responsibilities depends greatly on his own personality and on the power granted to him by the producer.

Historical Background

The position of the director in the theatre is a relatively young one when the history of the theatre is considered from its beginnings to the present. As indicated in the previous chapter, the playwright served the function of both producer and director in the Greek era though part of those responsibilities were often assumed by the **choregos** who trained and often led the chorus. There is some indication that priests served as stage directors during the Middle Ages when the medieval presentations served the purpose of teaching the Bible and church dogma.

With the advent of commercial presentations, the function of the director was often undertaken by the head or owner of the company. In many cases, this individual served as an actor-manager since he not only acted in the company, but managed its affairs as well. With some exceptions, up to the middle of the 19th century the interpretation of plays was traditional with the actors following traditional movements and their arrangement on stage being based almost entirely on the importance of the role being performed. Often, few if any rehearsals were held since movements and actions were based on tradition rather than upon any unified interpretation of the play itself. The actors provided their own costumes and such settings as may have been used were often **stock sets**; that is, basic settings that would be used in play after play.

One of the earliest depictions of a director at work can be found in Moliere's *Impromptu at Versailles* in which the author conducts rehearsals of one of his comedies in preparation for a performance before France's Louis XIV. In this rehearsal, Moliere instructs his actors in the manner and style of their portrayals giving careful attention to the individual details of each performer's role.

During the mid-1700s, England's David Garrick began to establish early vestiges of the position of the director in the theatre. As manager of Drury Lane, Garrick was responsible for the selection of repertoire, the staging of the plays, and the financial well-being of the theatre and the company which performed in it. Garrick shocked his fellow actors when he required them to attend rehearsals, but the quality of his productions soon impressed them with the value of such preparation.

The approaches used by Moliere and Garrick may indicate the early beginnings of the director, but neither man actually served as director. Rather, each was in the position of being what is commonly called an **actor-manager**; that is, an actor who heads and manages his own company. Both performed in their productions and neither seems to have been particularly concerned about dealing with the details of the supporting elements, including the scenery and costume design and style.

From 1850 to 1859, Charles Kean, also an actor-manager, produced a series of contemporary and Shakespeare plays at London's Princess Theatre. For a number of these plays, he added to his work as an actor and manager the responsibilities of a director. He carefully researched each play and its historical period, particularly the Shakespeare productions, supervised the many stage settings he felt the plays required, and also demanded that authentic period costumes be worn. His rehearsals were carefully planned to not only train his actors, but to allow him time to create interesting and meaningful stage pictures that would visually illustrate Shakespeare's text. The care which he expended in planning and mounting his productions had been unequaled prior to this time and became a pattern that a number of others would follow in the future. Still, he was an actor in the productions and his stage pictures were arranged to show him off to the best advantage. (It should also be noted that though he may have controlled all other elements within the productions, he did not control his actress wife who refused to give up her hooped-skirts for the more authentic garb of the period being portrayed.)

New York Public Library, Lincoln Center

George II, Duke of Saxe Meiningen (1826-1914)

Duke George II, the Duke of Saxe Meiningen, is often credited with being the theatre's first true stage director. Having a deep interest in the theatre, the Duke, married to a niece of Queen Victoria's, had seen Kean's productions in London. With his background in art, a scholar's intensity for period research, and a desire to mount major plays fully and with absolute historical accuracy, the Duke used his position as ruler of the Duchy of Saxe Meiningen (a part of the future Germany) to satisfy his desires. He formed his own theatre company to perform in the ducal palace theatre, chose the repertoire, researched the plays, designed historically accurate sets, costumes, and props, and oversaw the rehearsals. He provided his stage-

From Grube, Max: *Geschichte der Meininger* Berlin, 1926

A scene from Shakespeare's *Julius Caesar* as presented under the direction of the Duke of Saxe Meiningen. The Duke was particularly noted for his attention to historical detail, ensemble acting, and his handling of crowd scenes.

manager with detailed drawings showing the arrangement of the actors on the stage for each scene, indicated movements and gestures to be used and, through the services of a vocal coach, controlled the line readings and interpretations. He demanded that all sets and costumes be completed in time for rehearsals and be used in all rehearsals. No time limit was placed on the rehearsal period, the Duke refusing to open a production until it was completed to his satisfaction. He also organized his company as an **ensemble**. Actors were assigned to roles according to their abilities and might play a leading role in one production and carry a spear in another. In the Duke's productions, therefore, there were no stars.

Had Duke George's productions been seen only in his small Duchy, they would have made little impact on world theatre. However, visitors from Berlin, upon seeing the first of his offerings, convinced the Duke that he should tour to the capitol of Prussia. He did so and was so successful there that he soon was invited to other major cities, among which were Moscow, London, and Brussels. He was scheduled to bring his company to the United States in the 1890s, but illness and financial constraints made the U.S. visit impossible. The fame of his company had spread throughout the western world by that time, however, and others were beginning to implement his ideas.

Andre Antoine (1863-1943), who had founded an experimental theatre in Paris, the Theatre Libre, saw the Meininger perform in Brussels and returned to Paris convinced that the Duke's approach should be applied to the plays he was producing. Antoine, therefore, became the first true director in the French theatre. Constantine Stanislavski saw the Meininger in Moscow and adapted the Duke's methods to the theatre that he and Nemirovitch-Danchenko founded, the Moscow Art Theatre. Though the English theatre was dedicated to the **star** approach, such writers, actors and directors as George Bernard Shaw and Harley Granville-Barker advocated an ensemble approach similar to the Duke's. In the United States, Augustin Daly approached his productions using many of the Duke's methods, though he still adhered to the star system. During the first decade of the 20th Century, American director David Belasco firmly established the position of the stage director when he supervised all aspects of his productions including training the actors in the details of their personifications.

Building on the Duke's approach was the Austrian-German director Max Reinhart (1873-1943). Not only did Reinhart oversee the sets, costumes, lights and properties of his shows, he also detailed all line readings, movements, and gestures for his actors. In addition, he approached each show as an entity in and of itself. He felt that no two plays were alike and that each must be directed in a **style** suitable to it. Whereas in the productions of earlier directors all plays had generally been approached in the same style, Reinhart's productions varied considerably.

Much of the reason for the development of the position of the director in the modern theatre lies in the fact that our theatre today is highly eclectic; that is, theatre artists are expected to work in a wide variety of dramatic forms and styles. No longer can tradition alone guide the activities of the actors and the other artists involved in the production of a play for public consumption. There are too many elements and too many individuals involved, all of which need unifying guidance. Playwrights are experimenting with a variety of styles and dramatic forms, resulting in the need for consideration of each play as an entity in and of itself with its own particular qualities and needs.

Approaches to Directing

Each director in the theatre has his own way of approaching a play, working with his artistic staff, and addressing the needs of the actors. As in any art, some directors are more creative than others, some more inspirational than others, some are excellent craftsmen, and some may combine all these elements in their work. In his autobiography, *Minority Report*, playwright Elmer Rice tried to identify the types of directors who work in the theatre. Though he pointed out that all share similar qualities and approaches, he felt that there were basically three kinds of directors:

1. **The Actors' Director**: Rice says that this person is probably one who has come into directing from the acting profession and sees the play he is interpreting in terms of the challenges it provides for each actor. He is therefore at home in plays which have strong leading characters or in plays in which the talents of a star are being emphasized.

2. **The Playwright's Director**: This director, according to Rice, sees his function to be that of interpreting the playwright's intent to the artistic staff, the actors, and finally to the audience. He gears his entire approach to serving the playwright in such a way that the playwright's message is made clear and dominates the presentation of the work.

3. **The Director's Director**: This is the director who views the play as an avenue for his own concepts and ideas and the playwright's efforts as his personal vehicle for expressing his vision of the world and life. It is not unusual for such a director to choose plays from the past so that he is free to alter the dialogue, the action, and possibly even the meaning to reflect his personal concept. Though this aproach to directing has been present in the theatre since the advent of the director, it has become more important in recent years, particularly in Europe where such directors as Robert Wilson and Peter Brooks have made an impact on the theatre with their work. Wilson, a consummate visual artist, has adapted a variety of plays to allow him to incorporate his visual talents. He places great emphasis on the stage picture and often presents his offerings as a series of visual vignettes reflecting his abilities as a sculptor through the three-dimensional pictures created. His actors are required to master stylized, dance-like movements and read their lines almost as though they are elements within a religious ritual.

Being a playwright, Rice readily states that the playwright's director is the ideal. In actuality, there is a place for all of these in the theatre, for each has an important offering to make to his audiences.

Responsibilities of the Director

Whatever the approach, the modern director has several major responsibilities. His first is to interpret the play using any of the means cited above. In interpreting the play, he chooses the approach to be taken finally by all the artists involved in the production–actors, designers, etc. It is normally his responsibility to select and train the actors. He must strive to see that all the elements of the production are in harmony one with the other, including actors, sets, costumes, lighting, make-up, sound, dance, etc. He is responsible for **blocking** or choreographing the movement of the actors.

While the above are the "hands-on" responsibilities of the director, there remains another and very critical one. Throughout the rehearsal period, the director acts as a surrogate for the audience. He must maintain an objectivity toward the production so that he can see whether or not all the combined elements will affect the audience as he intends. If he fails in this, the production may well fail to entertain the audience and will therefore fail to live up to one of the major purposes of the theatre. (Remember the definition of "entertain" from Chapter 1?)

A Stephen F. Austin State University production.

The Madwoman of Chaillot, Act III, as presented at Stephen F. Austin State University under the direction of C.W. Bahs with set by Tomy Matthys, lighting by Kevin Seime, and costumes by Julie Renner. In this staging of the play by Giraudeaux, the director and the designers have worked to create not only an interesting stage picture, but one which contributes directly to relating the story to the audience. Note the composition made possible by the set and the lighting. Attention is focused on the character in the left foreground and her relationship to the other characters.

Some Fundamentals of Play Directing

The director is not only an artist-interpreter, but he is also a craftsman. He must develop and implement a series of techniques which will assist him, his staff, and the actors to communicate with the audiences. Alexander Dean, one of America's early teachers of the art of stage direction, divided the fundamentals of play directing into five parts.

Composition

The first and most elemental of these parts is **composition**. Composition results from the arrangement of the total stage picture–the actors within the set–into an aesthetically pleasing picture. This picture is not necessarily meaningful, but it must be interesting to view and pleasing to the eye. Composition makes use of all the elements that are normally found and studied in the field of art and includes balance (symmetrical and/or asymmetrical), line, color, etc. It is through composition that the director forces the audience to focus on the character and/or action the audience must see to understand the play. In film, the camera serves this purpose, but in the live theatre, it is the arrangement of the actors within the set that accomplishes this task.

Picturization

Having arranged the stage picture into a pleasing composition, the next step is to maintain the picture's aesthetic qualities while giving it meaning. **Picturization**, therefore, refers to the composition which has meaning and helps to tell the story of the play. It will provide visual images of attitudes, individual and group, of character relationships, and activities in much the same way as the artist attempts to create a picture on canvas which will carry a specific meaning to his viewers within the context of an aesthetically pleasing composition. Picturization also requires that the director design his stage pictures in such a way as to place emphasis on the specific elements he wants the audience to see.

By arranging the actors within the setting, the director places emphasis on the one or two he wishes the audience to focus on. Note the dominant characters in each of the three illustrations above and how the arrangements provide that dominance. From Albright, et. al., *Principles of Theatre Art* (Cambridge, 1955.

Movement

A stage picture is not static. It is composed of three-dimensional, living characters in a variety of situations. The picture, therefore, is constantly changing as the story unfolds. **Movement,** in this context, refers to the choreography of action which is devised by the director to reveal the shifting relationships of the characters, satisfy the need for basic practical actions, and reveal individual attitudes. It is through this choreography that the director provides a constantly changing and shifting picturization thereby revealing the progressive stages of the story he and the playwright are telling.

Rhythm

Rhythm is the "beat of life" within the play. Just as a composition in painting has a certain rhythm, so do the stage pictures created by the director, designers and the actors. Each character has his own rhythm, which helps to separate him from the other characters and gives him his own individuality. Each scene within a play has its own particular rhythm, which helps to communicate the mood and idea of the scene to the audience. And finally, the play as a whole has an overall rhythmic pattern, which helps to give it unity of mood and purpose. The challenge to the director is to find these differing rhythms and blend them, preserving each but uniting all in such a way as to give the play its own unified rhythmic pattern. This is often achieved through careful planning of the kind and timing of movements, large and small, and the rhythmic pattern of the lines as they are delivered.

Rhythm is composed of two elements, each of which may have an infinite number of variations: (1) **meter**, the pattern of the recurring points of emphasis within the movements and the lines, and (2) **tempo,** the speed or rate at which the pattern is repeated. Rhythm, therefore, is one of the most complex elements with which the director will deal in the preparation of a play for performance. Because the performance of the play depends not only on the actor but also upon audience response, the rhythm of a play may vary considerably from performance to performance. Part of the director's job as a surrogate for the audience is to sense potential audience responses and devise ways for the actors to handle them and maintain the overall rhythm of the play as it is repeated for a variety of audiences.

Pantomimic Dramatization

Pantomimic dramatization is that element of the performance which helps it create a visual reality. A play exists both verbally and visually. In the ideal situation, the actor not only speaks the lines but moves in such a way as to make the meaning of the lines visually clear to the audience. Pantomimic dramatization is to be found in all the actions present during the performance. The handling of a property can reveal as much about a character and his attitude as the words he speaks. A slight change of body position can reveal a major change of attitude or relationship of one character to another. It is through pantomimic dramatization, normally called **stage business**, that the play is given a depth of meaning beyond the words spoken.

Training of the Director

In serving his functions as both a craftsman and an artist, the director must acquire a wide range of knowledge. As a craftsman he must be well organized in order to meld all the elements of the play into one final, polished performance complete in every detail. He must know how to manage time in the scheduling and planning of rehearsals, finances with regard to the overall production, the practical problems of multiple costume and set changes which may affect the overall rhythm of the production.

As an artist, the director must be sensitive to the play, its structure, the philosophy or history behind it. He must develop a clear concept of what he believes the play is saying or what he and the artistic staff want it to say. He must have an understanding of the psychology of the actors, the characters in the play, and, certainly, of the audience. In order to communicate with the other members of the production team, he should have a background in and understanding of sets, costumes, lighting, and sound design.

Every work intended for performance on the stage involves directing. Since there are various types of drama, there is a directing style and method corresponding to each of these types and–within a given type–to the specific nature of each individual work. Directing is the sum-total of artistic and technical operations which enable the play as conceived by the author to pass from the abstract, latent stage, that of the written script, to the concrete and actual life on the stage.

Jacques Copeau (1878-1949)

Producing a play clearly requires the coordinated efforts of many people, and the [director] is no more than the coordinator. His work may, and I think should, have creative functions, but not always. The important thing is gathering together the different pieces and welding the many disparate elements into one complete unity, which is never, of course, fully achieved in artistic matters.

Tyrone Guthrie (1900-1971)

From the souvenire program.

David Belasco's production of *The Auctioneer* (1901) for which he purchased the entire contents of a New York City auction shop, had it mapped, cataloged, and then reconstructed on stage. Belasco (1859-1931) was one of the first American directors to insist on controlling every element within one of his productions: acting, stage movement, setting, properties, lighting, costumes, and sound. He firmly established the role of the director in the American theatre.

Class Assignment
Theatre Appreciation

Name:

Your instructor will assign a particular scene from a play for you to use in this exercise.

1. What characters appear in the assigned scene?

2. On what character in the scene should the audience focus?

3. On the ground plan below indicate the placement of each character.

4. What is the body position for each character?

Remove from text to turn in to instructor.

16
The Actor

Jerzy Grotowski, the Polish director, has said that the theatre needs only two elements–the actor and the audience. If either one is missing, the theatre cannot exist. Without the actor, the playwright's ideas, words and actions cannot be communicated to the audience–the story cannot be told. The actor, therefore, is the keystone of the theatre.

We all act. Acting is, simply, imitation and revelation. We learn by imitating just as a child learns. Often we communicate through imitation and if it is accurate and fully realized, we reveal something about the object of our imitation. This is the job of the actor, to imitate a character in such depth and with such believability that the character, his thoughts, emotions, and actions are revealed to the audience with precise clarity.

In Chapter 6 we discussed the fact that we play different roles in different circumstances. The individual who is a son, father, employee, boss, etc., behaves differently as he assumes one of his particular roles after another. Our role-playing, however, is unconscious; that is, we don't stop to think about it, we simply assume the role appropriate to the moment. The actor is also a role-player. His role-playing, however, is by conscious choice; but if well done, we, the audience, are not aware of that, but see his actions to be spontaneous, natural and believable. Over the centuries it has been the actor's goal to create this illusion.

Historical Background

Ever since Thespis stepped out from the Greek chorus and assumed a role, the actor has been the medium by which the playwright's actions, thoughts and words have been conveyed to the audience. It is his responsibility to help the audience suspend its cloak of disbelief and enter into the world of the play by so portraying his role that the audience sees and experiences what the character sees and experiences without being aware of the actor who is truly the servant of the character and the play.

The profession of acting has been a long and sometimes difficult road. During the Golden Age of Greek drama and comedy, the actor was a highly trained and greatly honored member of society. Dedicated to the profession as a youth, the actor was trained in philosophy, literature, mathematics, music, voice, and athletics. He was dedicated to the service of the gods, particularly Dionysus, and as a kind of lay priest was a highly respected and honored member of Greek society. Even in time of war, he was given safe passage between warring city states and often carried mes-

sages from and to the various political leaders involved.

Unfortunately, with the rise of the Roman Empire, the actor's training and social position were greatly altered. His education was often skimped and in many cases he was a slave valued by his owner for his talent alone. Rome itself produced few actors, but relied heavily on importing them from areas Rome had conquered. One of the most famous, Roscius, was Jewish, and many of the other practicing actors were from Israel and other areas of the Near East including Greece. Because of their social status, because of the fact that many of the productions in which they appeared were mounted in honor of the pagan gods, and because they were viewed by some as liars presenting themselves as other individuals on the stage, actors and the acting profession was frowned upon by the rising Christian populace. In fact for several hundred years, the Church refused the Sacraments to actors until they had renounced their profession.

During the dark and early middle ages, as we saw earlier, actors most often were entertainers performing as jongleurs, minstrels, or troubadours. Those who did appear in the medieval mystery, miracle, or morality plays were usually amateurs, though there are reports indicating that a few became well known for their portrayals of Biblical characters and may have traveled from town to town performing with locally organized amateur troupes.

As the drama of the Renaissance grew out of the religious plays of the middle ages and the rediscovered Greek and Roman plays of the distant past, more and more professional actors began to appear, some of whom may well have begun their profession in the seminaries and universities in which the ancient plays were used to teach Greek and Latin.

With the rebirth of learning in the Renaissance, the writing of plays imitative of those of the Romans and Greeks, and the emergence of the Commedia dell'Arte, the opportunities for professional actors increased immeasurably. The **Commedia dell'Arte al Improviso**, which literally means "The Art of Improvised Comedy," was one of the earliest professional groups of actors to perform in the early Renaissance. The troups were unique in that they worked from **scenarios** rather than scripts. These scenarios were brief outlines of the action of the play and were posted backstage for the actors to read prior to playing a scene. The plays were improvised by the actors, each of whom played a character he had developed and repeatedly performed. These were **stock characters**, that is, characters which remained the same from play to play reappearing often.

By the end of the 16th century, traveling troupes of players were

Basic Characters of the Commedia dell'Arte

Harlequin

Pantalone

Il Dottore

Inamorata (Lover)

Inamorato (Lover)

formed which presented a **repertory** of plays throughout England and Western Europe. Though viewed with distaste by the socially conscious and by the law, which in England lumped "common players" with vagabonds and rogues subject to immediate arrest and punishment, the popularity of plays and related entertainments helped the actors gain a more secure foothold on the social ladder. For their own protection and in an effort to establish their respectability, troupes of actors often sought aristocratic patrons and announced themselves as such. For instance, the company with which Shakespeare worked was known as the "Lord Chamberlain's Men" and later as the "King's Men." A competing company performing at the Rose theatre was the "Lord Admiral's Men." The company headed by the great French tragedian Montfleury and performing at the Hotel Bourgoyne in Paris in 1641 was called the "King's Players." Later, in 1658, Moliere's company was sponsored by Louis XIV's brother and was called the "Troupe de Monsieur."

During the 18th century, acting companies were normally subsidized and/or licensed by governments in England and Europe, but the position of the actor was still suspect in the eyes of some. In America, particularly in the New England colonies, the theatre was seen as socially suspect and in some cases totally banned with actors subject to arrest if they mounted performances. In the southern colonies, the situation was more relaxed since those sent to colonize that section of the New World often came from a more aristocratic background. Still, performers were viewed with a degree of skepticism and were required to secure permission from governors, mayors, or others in power.

David Garrick, England's great 18th century actor, as Hamlet.

Though in most countries there was no formal training for the actor, small companies provided a kind of apprenticeship situation in which the would-be performer could learn his trade, whetting his skills on the standard repertoire of the time. Many of England's finest actors received their early training in Dublin, Edinburgh, Glascow, or other provincial cities and towns prior to coming to London. Finally, Charles Macklin (1699-1797) began a school for actors in the 1740s in London. Though the school was short-lived, it was one of the first attempts to establish a formal training situation for prospective actors. In France in 1786, the Royal Dramatic School was founded and worked in conjunction with the Comedie Francaise to train actors. Known as the Conservatoire, it is still active today.

In the 19th century France's Francaise Delsarte (1811-1871) established a school of acting based on an analytical approach to the emotions and their relation to body positions. He believed that the laws of stage expression were discoverable and could be analyzed as precisely as mathematical principles. According to Oscar Brockett, "[Delsarte] divided human experience and behavior into the physical, mental, and emotional-spiritual, and he related these to each action, thought, and emotion. He also divided and subdivided the body into parts and related each to the physical, mental, and emotional-spiritual." Delsarte developed over three hundred categories of responses and body positions which the actor was encouraged to learn and carefully rehearse. After mastering this technique, the actor marked next to his lines in his script the exact condition of his character and applied the proper body position to it thus choreographing his movements, posture, and action accordingly. Though the end result was often mechanical, the approach became standard for many actors in France and elsewhere during the late 19th century.

The Delsarte approach was introduced to America by actor, playwright and producer Steele MacKaye (1842-1894) in 1872 in Boston and later in New York City. His early efforts at establishing a school for actors grew into what is now known as the American Academy of Dramatic Art. His students followed his lead and established other conservatories for the training of actors and orators. European, English and American actors used the Delsarte approach well into the 1920s, by which time the more realistic approaches advocated by Constantine Stanislavski became popular.

In 1898, Constantine Stanislavski (1863-1938) and Vladimir Nemirovitch-Danchenko (1858-1943) founded the Moscow Art Theatre and created a training program for actors. Though Stanislavski revolted against the mechanical and oratorical style of 19th century acting as well as the star system, he repeatedly emphasized the necessity for the young actor to learn the basic techniques of body and voice required of the actor. Between 1924 and 1961, Stanislavski published four books explaining his approach in detail. His influence on acting and the modern theatre cannot be underestimated.

The social position of the actor steadily improved throughout the 19th century. In 1895, Henry Irving, then England's reigning tragedian, was granted a knighthood, the first actor to be honored in this manner. Even in the United States, which held on to Puritan attitudes long after they had gradually disappeared in Europe, the actor became more socially acceptable.

Actor training in the 20th century has become more structured. In the early part of the century many actors began their careers working with provincial companies learning by doing. With the advent of the motion pictures, many smaller stock and repertory companies were forced to close thus creating a vacuum in the training of theatre actors and technicians. Now universities and conservatories throughout the world offer training for actors, directors and theatre technicians. In Europe the concept of conservatory training in all of the arts is common. It is less so in the United States where college and university programs offer not only specialized training, but a broader educational background.

The Actor's Tools

Though the actor depends heavily on the script, his primary tools are his mind, voice, and body. Unless these have been thoroughly trained, he will find it difficult to interpret roles adequately and

Delsarte Basic Body Positions

Accusation

Appeal

Grief

Imprecation

Resignation

From Florence A. Fowles, *Gesture and Pantomimic Action* 1897 fulfill the demands they make upon him. If he cannot do this, the character he portrays on stage will be incapable of believably performing the actions required by the script.

The Mind

The demands of the modern theatre are such that the present day actor needs to be well educated. He needs a broad background in literature and literary movements with an understanding of the history of those movements if he is to interpret the range of roles he may be called upon to portray in the modern theatre, particularly in the regional theatres which mount a wide variety of plays both in style and period. Along with a knowledge of literature and literary movements, the actor needs at least a cursory understanding of the philosophic concepts reflected in the plays of various eras. He should also have at least an elementary knowledge of psychology in order to understand the motivations which drive his characters.

The actor must have an active, though disciplined, imagination, for he will often have to create responses and actions which he has never personally experienced. This requires him to have a creative felxibility. He must be moldable and have the ability to transform himself according to the demands of his character.

In addition, the mind of the actor must be highly disciplined, for he must work consistently on several levels. He must be able to concentrate completely and totally on his role during performance keeping his focus on the character's intentions as he moves from scene to scene in the play. Added to this, he must concentrate on the audience and its reaction being aware of the effect he is creating with his performance and adjusting the performance as required to move the audience to laughter or tears.

The Voice

One of the major means of communication for the actor is the use of his voice which must be flexible and capable of adjusting not only to the various attitudes of the characters he will play, but also to the characters themselves. A forced voice reflects a lack of training on the part of the actor and often makes the audience uncomfortable and aware of the actor at work. This can be fatal to the actor's ability to create believability on stage, for an audience which senses the artist at work often misses the object of his work. In such a case, the audience ceases to experience the play, experiencing the players instead. In many cases, actors are required to sing in today's theatre making the development of the voice that much more important.

Along with the development of the voice comes the refinement of diction and the ability to reflect various characters according to social status, ethnic and national background. The actor must master dialects and accents or regional speech patterns. A good actor is a student of people. As an artist, he is an imitator of others and just as his bodily movements must reflect the character he is playing, so must his speech.

The Body

The second means of communicating with the audience is through the use of the body. An actor's body must be as flexible and responsive as is the body of a highly trained athlete. Just as each one of us reflects our moods, attitudes, and intentions through bodily response, so must the actor reflect his character's mood, attitudes, and intentions through the use of the body. The requirements for flexibility can be taken to extremes in some cases. For instance, in the script for *Elephant Man,* the author, Bernard Pomerance, prints a warning to directors and actors regarding the role of John Merrick, the "elephant man." It reads, "No one with any history of back trouble should attempt the part of Merrick as contorted. Anyone playing [it] should be advised to consult a physician about the problems of sustaining any unnatural or twisted position." Using slides of the original John Merrick who was an actual person, a doctor describes Merrick while the actor playing the role, clad only in a loin cloth and quite natural and well-developed in appearance, slowly changes his bodily positions until they equate those described by the doctor and illustrated by the slides:

> The most striking feature about him was his enormous head. It's circumference was about that of a man's waist. From the brow there projected a huge bony mass like a loaf. . .The osseous growth on the forehead, at this stage about the size of a tangerine, almost occluded one eye. From the upper jaw there projected another mass of bone. It protruded from the mouth like a pink stump, turning the upper lip inside out, and making the mouth a wide slobbering aperture. . .The deformities rendered the face utterly incapable of the expression of any emotion whatsoever. The back was horrible because it hung, as far down as the middle of the thigh. . .The right arm was of enormous size and shapeless. . . .The right hand was large and clumsy–a fin or paddle rather than an arm. . .The lower limbs had the character of the deformed arm. They were unwieldy, dropsical-looking, and grossly misshapen. . .To add a further burden to his trouble, the wretched man when a boy developed hip disease which left him permanently lame, so that he could walk only with a stick.

From Laurence Hutton, *Curiosities of the American Stage* 1891

Edmund Kean (1787?-1833) as Hamlet.

In addition, the actor is often called upon to perform highly skilled physical feats on stage. In the last act of *Hamlet*, for instance, the actors playing Hamlet and Laertes fight with daggers and swords. In *The Taming of the Shrew* Petruchio and Kate are not only a match intellectually, but physically as well. In their first scene together, the two battle intellectually, verbally, and physically in their contest for domination. Actors are often called upon to trip, fall, collapse, etc., all of which require complete and total bodily control if they are to be done convincingly without causing harm or injury to the actor. In many cases, actors are required to dance. Again, they must be able to do so with ease and control if their efforts are to be convincing to an audience.

If the physical requirements made upon the actor were for film only, his task would be simplified, for scenes can be shot time and time again until the director has the specific effect he is seeking. In live theatre, however, the actor must be capable of performing his feats convincingly not only in the rehearsals, but also in each and every performance.

The Method

Along with training his body, voice and mind, the actor must learn the basic techniques of entering and exiting the stage, standing and sitting, opening to the audience and closing oneself off from the audience. He must learn how to give scenes to other actors and to bring the attention back to himself when his character must dominate the scene. He must develop the skill of memorizing sometimes long and complex scripts and making his lines so much a part of himself that he does not need to remember them, but can allow them to come naturally from the actions of the play.

The actor must be capable of giving the illusion to the audience that what it is seeing is occurring for the first time at this time. Though the audience must have the security of feeling that what it is viewing has been well and carefully prepared, it must also feel that it is totally spontaneous. It was in an effort to achieve this and to help the actor adapt to the demands of the realistic plays being written at the end of the 19th century that Constantine Stanislavski began to develop and continued to refine what has come to be known as "the Method." It was also Stanislavski's hope that by following his "method" the actor would be able to find inspiration for each performance as he repeated a role time and again.

Because Stanislavski's approach to acting took place over many years, which is reflected in the four books he wrote on the subject, it was adopted at least in part by many actors and acting teachers in varying stages of its development. Taking their information from various sources, these practitioners of the art of acting each developed their own interpretations of the Method. In the United States Lee Strasburg and Stella Adler developed conflicting approaches to acting, each claiming that his/her approach was "the Stanislavski" approach. In the meantime, others throughout Europe and England developed their own versions of the Method which Stanislavski admitted should be altered or changed by those adopting it according to their own differing artistic and cultural background.

In *History of the Theatre* Oscar Brockett summarizes Stanislavski's approach as follows:

1. The actors' voice and body should be thoroughly trained so that they may respond efficiently to all demands.
2. The actor should be schooled in stage techniques since he must be able to project characterization to the audience without any sense of contrivance.
3. The actor should be a skilled observer of reality, out of which he or she builds a role.
4. The actor should seek an inner justification for everything done on stage. In doing so, the actor depends in part upon "the magic 'If'" (that is, the actor says, "If I were this person faced with this situation, I would. . .") and "emotion memory" (a process by which the actor relates the unfamiliar dramatic situation to some analogous emotional situation in his or her own life, although Stanislavski was eventually to downgrade the importance of emotion memory).
5. If the actor is not merely to play himself or herself, he or she must make a thorough analysis of the script and work within the "given circumstances" found there. The actor must define a character's motivations in each scene, in the play as a whole, and in relation to each of the other roles. The character's primary "objective" becomes the "through line" of the role, around which everything else revolves.
6. On stage the actor must focus attention upon the action as it unfolds moment by moment. Such concentration leads to the "illusion of the first time" and will guide the actor in subordinating his or her ego to the artistic demands of the production.
7. An actor must continue to strive to perfect understanding and proficiency.

In America, a great deal of emphasis has been placed upon "emotion memory" especially by Lee Strasburg and his fellow teachers at the Actor's Studio in New York City. The approach taken here and by Strasburg's disciples often involved complicated exercises in which the students were required to delve into their inner feelings in detail in an effort to understand themselves, their background and the reasons for their actions. Stella Adler, who also advocated the teachings of Stanislavski, found such an approach to be dangerous and destabilizing for the actor. She recommended that the actor approach the role from the outside working to its inner core and that the actor rely more on his imagination to create the emotions within himself needed for a role than upon his own personal and painful experiences.

Junius Brutus Booth in the title role of Shakespeare's *Richard III*.

There are dangers in interpreting Stanislavski's "emotion memory" too literally. In this country the "method" actor has displayed a tendency to exaggerate emotional identification. This has given rise to what has sometimes been called the "sweat-shirt" school of acting in which the actor becomes so involved in his role that he loses control. Even before the advent of the Stanislavski "method" this happened on occasion. Junius Brutus Booth, father of the great Edwin Booth and the more notorius John Wilkes Booth, often became so involved in his portrayal of Richard III that he drove his dueling opponent off-stage, out the stage door, and down the street running for his life as Booth pursued sword in hand.

Another theory of acting is based on what is referred to as the James-Lange theory. This states that if the actor can recreate the physical response associated with an emotional condition, he will stimulate his psyche to respond with the proper emotion. In this case, the actor works from the outside in. He analyses how he has responded to his emotions physically in the past–his body position, muscle response, vocal reaction–and attempts to recreate that. According to this theory, if he has accurately observed these reactions and is exact in his physical reproduction of them, his emotional state will change accordingly.

Preparing a Role

The first requirement for the actor to consider is the function of the character within the entire play. Therefore, he must read and study the play carefully. In the early days of the theatre, and even today in some cases, the actor was provided with **sides**. A "side" is a script containing only the lines the character speaks and the phrase or sentence which immediately precedes that line–the **cue** line. Today, the actors are provided normally with a complete script which makes their lives much easier and the play more readily understood. Normally once the play is cast the director brings the entire cast together to read through the play with the director explaining his approach and the approach each actor should take to his role.

At this point the actor is in a position to make an in depth-analysis of the role. Using the levels of characterization discussed in Chapter 6, he can create at least a basic image of the character he is to portray. This image may change during the rehearsal period as he discovers more about his and others' characters and understands better the director's interpretation of the total work.

Once the actor has an understanding of his character and the play, something which will develop further as rehearsals progress, the director begins to **block** (arrange) the movements of the actor within the environment of the play and in relation to other characters on stage. These rehearsal can be tedious at times, but they are necessary if the correct character actions and relationships are to be established.

During the blocking period, the actor starts memorizing his lines within the context of the play itself and in relation to the movements he has been given. In some cases, the actor is expected to have the lines memorized prior to blocking rehearsals. Prior to the early 20th century, actors were often expected to memorize their lines, whether from side or script, prior to any rehearsals. In fact, in some cases, there were very few, if any, rehearsals and the actions in the play were carried out according to a tradition the actor was expected to know from his past experience.

From this time on in the rehearsal period–normally two to four weeks in the professional theatre and about five weeks in educational theatre (professional actors are committed to full-time dedication to their work whereas student actors normally have classes and assignments to fulfill)– the interpretation of the characters, the line readings, and the movements are refined and, hopefully, perfected. This is still a time of discovery for both the actor and the director and major changes may occur during this part of the rehearsal period.

As the play enters its final rehearsals, the actors and directors devote themselves to perfecting all that has gone before and particularly to establishing the rhythm of the entire play. The refining of rhythm can rarely be accomplished until the actors are line and movement perfect.

In understanding his character, the actor must consider not only the character's actions on stage, but what he has been doing prior to appearing in the scene, why he enters the scene, where he is going, and what he is going to do when he leaves the scene. He must develop an understanding of the character's wants and desires–his **motivations**, his purposes and how everything he says and all he does are done to achieve those purposes. *Hamlet,* for instance, opens with the two sentinels, Francisco and Bernardo. One has been standing guard, the other has come to relieve him. Both have previously seen the ghost of Hamlet's father. Each is apprehensive not knowing what to expect in the dark of night. Each challenges the other in the darkness to establish identities. They are guards, but their anxious attitude is not the result of a human threat but of some supernatural force. This has naturally raised questions and fears within them which they feel they must share with others and which they hope others will resolve for them. Francisco, in particular, wants to leave and hopes to be relieved from the watch. He is cold and, more importantly, does not want to witness another visitation by the ghost. Bernardo, who has come to relieve him, is reluctant to be out on such a night and certainly does not want to see the ghost again. The actors playing these roles must get these

'WHAT'S MY MOTIVATION?'

Excerpted from *The Small Theatre handbook*, by Joann Green, illustrations by Leo Abbett, c 1981, with permission of The Harvard Common Press ideas across to the audience in twelve brief speeches. Only by considering these factors prior to appearing on stage and through imagination recreating them within their minds will the actors be prepared to communicate them to the audience.

The preparation referred to above must be repeated by the actor for each performance. Off-stage, prior to his entrance, he must concentrate on his character, the character's attitude and purpose, and allow these to consume him. His techniques for communicating with the audience must be so completely a part of him that he will use them subconsciously. His conscious actions and attitudes must be those of the character he is portraying. Only then can he give a performance which creates "the illusion of the first time every time."

Finally, as Geraldine Page states, the role must consume the actor, not the reverse:

> "When you take the character over and use the character, you wreck the fabric of the play, but you can be in control of the character without taking the character over. When the character uses *you*, that's when you're really cooking. You know you're in complete control, yet you get the feeling you didn't do it. You have the beautiful feeling that you can't ruin it. You feel as if you were tagging along on an exciting journey. You don't completely understand it and you don't have to. You're just grateful and curious."

> ...the whole process of an actor's or director's work–including his performance–is one that requires enormous self-mastery and often also great physical endurance. This work cannot be replaced by means of general words and moods.
>
> The thing that lies at the base of an actor's or director's creativeness is work, and not moods or any other popular slogans such as "flights," "down beats," "triumphs."
>
> Stanislavski

> It's when you start to rehearse, with other people, that things begin to happen. What it is exactly, I don't know, and even don't want to know. I'm all for mystery there. Most of what happens as you develop your part is unconscious. Most of it is underwater.
>
> Kim Stanley

> Acting is in many ways so unique in its difficulties because the artist has to use the treacherous, changeable and mysterious material of himself as his medium. He is called upon to be completely involved while distanced–detached without detachment. He must be sincere, he must be insincere; he must practice how to be insincere with sincerity and how to lie truthfully.
>
> Peter Brook

> There is a story about Dustin Hoffman and Lawrence Olivier when the two were appearing together in the film *The Marathon Man.*
>
> Olivier was getting into make-up when Hoffman arrived obviously worn-out, breathing heavily, sweating, hoarse.
>
> Olivier looked at Hoffman and exclaimed "Whatever happened to you?"
>
> "I've been running," puffed Hoffman.
>
> "Running, whatever for?"
>
> "Since three o'clock this morning!"
>
> "For goodness sakes, why?"
>
> "Because," said Hoffman catching his breath a little, "in the scene we shoot today you've been chasing me and I've been running."
>
> "My dear boy," said Olivier, "haven't you heard of a thing called acting?"

Theatre Appreciation
Class Assignment

Name:______________________________

Choosing a character from the list provided by your instructor, answer the following questions:

1. What special skills, physical and/or vocal are required of the actor performing this role?

2. Studying the character's first entrance, answer the following:

   A. Where has he been?

   B. What has he been doing?

   C. Why does he enter?

   D. What does he want?

3. What is this character's attitude toward the other characters on stage?

Remove from text to hand in to instructor.

17
The Performance Space

In its most elemental form, the theatre needs space only for the actor and for the audience. As the theatre has developed throughout the ages, however, its physical facilities have evolved to meet a wide variety of needs, not the least of which has been the desire to provide for audiences a wider range of spectacles. Just as the Greek theatre provided a place for the worship of the gods through drama, so has the theatre of later eras been designed to satisfy society's wants and needs.

From E. Guhl and W. Koner, *The Life of the Greeks and Romans* 1876.

The ruins of the ancient Roman theatre in Aspendos, Turkey. Note the wall around the orchestra which protected the audiences from the gladiators and wild animals used in some events here.

When the Romans conquered Greece and adopted the Greek theatre, they adjusted its physical elements to serve their tastes in entertainment. Retaining walls were constructed around the orchestras so that gladiatorial combats could be staged within the confines of the already established theatres. In some cases, the orchestras were redesigned to allow them to be sealed so they could be flooded with water in order to provide for the staging of **naumachiae** (staged sea battles). The **skene** (scene) building and **logeon** (stage) were moved closer to the audience so that the action on the stage could be emphasized, the chorus no longer being of major importance since under Roman rule the presentations were only nominally in honor of the gods.

During the Middle Ages, when drama was first presented in the church, the church architecture itself dominated the arrangement of audience and actor with **mansions** or **sedes**, scenic pieces, being placed around the nave of the church with the audience turning in place to follow the action. When this proved to be unsatisfactory and the large crowds could not be accommodated, the presentations were moved outside with the mansions being transferred to a wide stage or situated on several levels with all set pieces being in view simultaneously. A similar arrangement may be viewed today at Oberamergau, Germany, and at Spearfish, South Dakota, where passion plays are still mounted on a fairly regular basis.

The Elizabethan stage, discussed in Chapter 11, was a direct descendant of the simultaneous stage of the Middle Ages now in an architectural arrangement with a variety of playing areas. Such arrangements made possible the showing or suggestion of a large number of locales which were required for the panoramic stories being told in the medieval and Elizabethan theatres. In France the use of simultaneous stage settings was continued in the indoor theatres such as the Hotel de Bourgoyne for which the scenic designer Mahelot constructed scenery.

In universities, provisions were made for theatrical presentations by erecting a platform at the end of a large hall. Scenic embellishments were added with great simplicity.

From Jacques Burdick, *The Theatre* Newsweek Books, 1974

A performance for Louis XIII at the Palaise Royale. Note the provision made for the King's seating, the large area in front of the stage for dancers used in the court performances, and the proscenium stage with its scenery.

Court entertainments mounted during the Renaissance required large performance spaces with adequate provision for the audience and special arrangements for the king and his honored guests to view the production. Since these presentations included miraculous appearances and disappearances, some dialogue, a great deal of music and dancing, the arrangement was somewhat similar to that of the Greeks in that a stage was erected at one end of the court ballroom with machinery for the special effects and a large open area, similar to the orchestra, in front for much of the action and the dancing incorporated into the performance. Special seats were provided for the King similar in placement to those provided for the priests of Dionysus hundreds of years earlier.

It was also during the Renaissance that the court architects began designing scenery in perspective and looked upon the stage as a three-dimensional picture which achieved its best effect when it was framed. Taking the term from the Greek **proskenium**, these architects devised a **proscenium** which would frame the picture and separate the stage from the rest of the theatre. The proscenium could also serve the purpose of hiding the machinery required for the special effects the court audiences had come to expect. Because of its efficiency in providing a place for the actors, the scenery, the machinery, and the audience, the proscenium theatre is still with us today and is the dominant arrangement for the theatre throughout the Western world.

Today's theatre is, as stated earlier, eclectic. Just as we have a wide variety of dramatic forms and, as we shall see later, styles, we also have a variety of theatrical arrangements. These may be placed into five groups: (1) proscenium, (2) arena, (3) thrust, (4) flexible and (5) found space. In all cases, these spaces provide for both the actor and the audience. Additionally, these theatres normally provide auxiliary spaces such as the box office, lobby, rest rooms, offices, light and sound control rooms, dressing and make-up rooms, and storage rooms for properties, costumes, lights, and scenery.

The commercial theatre today is often designed on the proscenium concept. In this country, many of the theatres are designed to house only one play at a time. Since the theatre is rented on this basis, storage facilities are minimal and little or no shop space is contained in the theatre structure which is often placed on parcels of expensive real estate making it necessary for the theatre to contain only those elements which are absolutely necessary and will produce financial income. In state-supported theatre and those which are supported not only by box office but by grants from various sources, the architects have been allowed the freedom to create more elaborate facilities often containing more than one performing space, shops for the construction and storage of scenery and costumes, and ample provisions for audience comforts. Often the facilities include restaurants, exhibition rooms, and expansive lobbies. These theatres often present plays in repertory, changing the offering every few days and rotating the offerings among the several plays chosen for the repertory season.

From Allardyce Nicoll, *The Development of the Theatre* Harcourt, Brace & Co., n.d.

A Renaissance stage for the production of a play by Terence. Composed of a simple platform with several draped doorways labeled with character names, such stages were erected in large halls for the performances.

From *Appleton's Journal* (1870)

Booth's Theatre, constructed by actor Edwin Booth, featured a proscenium arch behind which was an unusually well-equiped stage with a revolve, traps, full stage house for flying scenery and ample off-stage space for storing scenery.

Proscenium

The proscenium theatre with what is sometimes called the "picture-box" stage is generally the normal theatre to be found. Its arrangement allows the seating of large audiences and the mounting of elaborate and spectacular productions. The picture frame itself provides for the masking of backstage areas where sets and properties are stored during a performance and where machinery is placed to enable the efficient and rapid change of sets stage spectacles often require.

In the ideal proscenium stage, off-stage (the **wings**) space on either side of the proscenium opening is equal to the width of the opening itself, allowing for wagons containing full sets of scenery to be stored until required. In some cases, the stage floor is on an elevator which can lower the current set into the basement beneath the stage while a wagon from **right stage** or **left stage** is rolled into place behind the proscenium arch with the new setting on it. At the Metropolitan Opera House in Lincoln Center there are four complete stage floors: (1) the first is that which is immediately behind the proscenium arch and

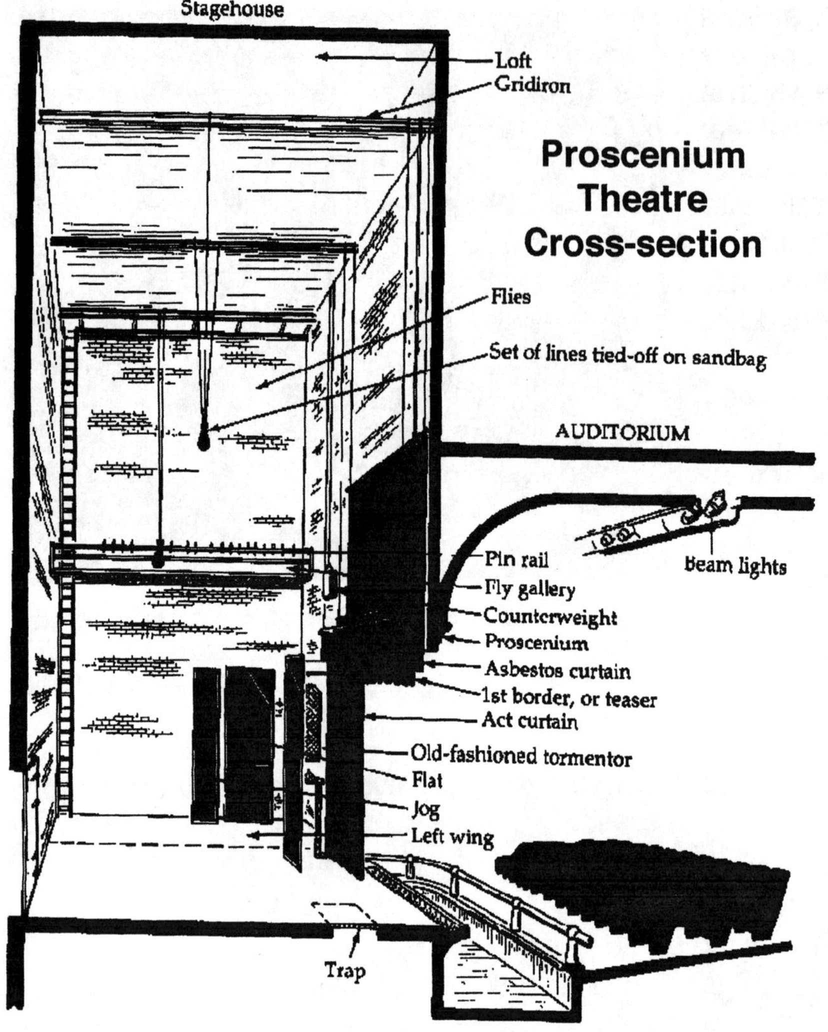

may be lowered to the basement, (2) the second is on right stage in the wings, (3) the third is left stage also in the wings, and (4) the fourth is **up-stage** ready to be rolled forward when the first is lowered out of sight. A system for changing scenery is available above the stage in the **stage house** which allows for overhead scenic pieces and **masking** units to be flown in to complete each set as it is wheeled into place. If more than four sets are required, a set can be changed when its platform is off-stage while the action is taking place on the set on stage. In addition, the floors of all the stages are **trapped** to allow for appearances and disappearances from and to the area beneath the stage. Immediately behind the proscenium arch is a curtain, the **grand drape,** which may be drawn or lowered across the opening to mask scene changes. In many proscenium theatres there is also an **orchestra pit** between the stage and the first row of audience seats. The floor of this pit is often on a elevator so that the height of the orchestra in relation to the stage may be adjusted or the pit floor itself may be raised to stage level, thus bringing the action forward to the audience.

The proscenium theatre also provides us with another convention, that of the "invisible fourth wall." This became important in the late 19th century with the presentation of the more realistic plays. In this situation, the audience is removed from the action and is within the confines of the auditorium peering through an opening, the proscenium arch, which reveals another and very different world. Actors working with this convention must adhere to it closely by not moving out of their designated scenic environment. Any movement which brings them through the "invisible fourth wall" immediately destroys the illusion that has been created.

Arena Stage

The architecture of the arena stage is relatively new in modern stage architecture, but dates back to the time of the archaic Greek period when the chorus chanting Dithyrambic odes performed, it is believed, in threshing circles with the audience arranged around the circle. Some morality plays apparently were presented in an arena arrangement during the Middle

Ages. In the modern era, the arena theatre is generally dated from the 1930's when universities, particularly the University of Washington, with few funds available to construct traditional theatres, adapted "found space" into an arena concept with the playing area in the center of the auditorium and the audience seated around the acting space. Entrances were made through aisles in the auditorium which, by convention, came to represent exits to some specified locale.

Courtesy of the School of Drama, University of Washington

The Penthouse Theatre at the University of Washington. The aisles provide entrances for both the audience and the actors. Small windows are for the support crew–lights and sound. Note intimacy of audience arangement.

The arena arrangement provided for a greater intimacy between the audience and the actor, but limited the use of scenery and properties. If scenery of any kind was to be used, it usually was reduced to a basic low-cut silhouette of the walls of a room. Furniture also needed to be low in order to allow the audience to view the actors without interference. Directors soon found that they were required to move the actors more often in this arrangement in order to allow the entire audience to better view the total action of the play. At the same time, it was discovered that the action could be more realistic, for the actor was not required to take into account his relationship to the audience.

Not all plays can be presented effectively in the arena environment. Plays requiring extensive stage settings and large casts are automatically excluded from this performance space or have to be altered drastically because of adjustments made for the audience/actor relationship. Settings must be simplified, particularly if rapid changes of scenes are necessary. All property and scenic changes take place before the audience and can potentially destroy the overall rhythm of the performance. Yet, for single-set plays or plays requiring no specific representation of locale, the arena arrangement can be very effective. The immediacy and naturalness of the performance is greatly enhanced by the audience/actor relationship.

Audiences, of course, are required to accept a new set of conventions. In spite of the fact that an audience member seated on one side of the arena can see other members of the audience opposite him, he must ignore any actions or reactions by, and the very existence of, those across from him. With carefully controlled and focused lighting and good acting, this convention is not a major difficulty, however. In some cases, the Casa Mañana in Fort Worth, for instance, the arena is used for major musicals and the seating capacity is greatly enlarged over the seating of the early arena theatres. Though this may be acceptable from a commercial standpoint, the actor/audience intimacy is greatly reduced under such circumstances and this major benefit of the arena arrangement is negated.

Thrust Stage

Courtesy of the Guthrie Theatre, Minneapolis

Chekhov's *The Three Sisters* directed by Tyrone Guthrie in the Guthrie Theatre in Minneapolis. Note the arrangement of the stage in relation to the audience in this thrust theatre.

In recent years, further experimentation with the actor/audience arrangement has been made, resulting in the development of the thrust stage. In many ways the thrust arrangement is reminiscent of the arrangements made for the court masques and intermezzi. In this arrangement, the stage is sometimes backed with scenery on one side while the acting area "thrusts" out into the audience, which is seated on three sides. Entrances are often made from the back of the thrust and from audience aisles in the theatre itself. The arrangement brings the actors closer to the audience than is often possible in the proscenium theatre and still allows for the use of some scenery. Scenic units placed on the thrust, however, have the same limitations as those used for the arena arrangement. Thrust theatres often have a greater seating capacity than arena theatres, though actor/audience intimacy is lessened as more rows of seats are added.

Marco Marcola, Italian (Veronese), c. 1740-1793, An Italian Comedy in Verona, oil on canvas, 1772, Courtesy of The Art Institute of Chicago, Gift of Emily Crane Chadbourne

A Commedia troupe performs in "found space" on a temporary stage. Painting by Marco Marcola, 1772.

Flexible Space

In many university, regional, and community theatres, the auditoriums are designed to be flexible. That is, the seating can be arranged in a variety of ways so that the theatre space can be used as an arena, thrust, or perhaps even a proscenium. This allows producing organizations a flexibility in the manner in which their season of plays is mounted with each actor/audience relationship being determined by the manner in which the play is being staged.

Found Space

Throughout the history of the theatre, actors have acted wherever an audience could be assembled. Though it was usually far more convenient for all concerned to have a permanent arrangement available, there have been and still are occasions when that could not be provided. Just as the Greeks "found" the threshing circles ideal for their very early dramatic efforts, the Commedia dell'Arte players found city squares or even cross-roads and market-places possible performance areas. During the late 1960s and into the 1970s, avant garde groups in this country and Europe, often working without any home base and with little or no financial support, began producing wherever there was a place for the actors to act and for the audience to gather. Old warehouses, factories, empty stores, basements, deserted churches, etc., were often pressed into service. In many cases flat-bed trucks were pulled into city parks or even parked on the street for performances with the audience gathered and standing around. In larger cities, it was and is not unusual for street performers to work wherever an audience can be found and the city ordinances will permit (or wherever they can get away with it).

The Performance Group's *Commune* 1970, performed in an old warehouse/factory. The audience was seated wherever space could be found. Photo by Elizabeth LeCompte.

Conclusion

In spite of their many and sometimes major differences, all these performance spaces must provide certain basic accouterments. There must be provision for the audience to secure tickets and to enter. In many cases, elaborate lobbies are an integral part of the overall design. This is particularly important in Europe and some American opera houses where the intermissions are relatively long and the lobbies become a social gathering place for audience members during intermissions. One must always consider that the performance begins when the audience member walks into the theatre, not just into the auditorium, but into the theatre itself. It is here that the audience member may be given his first introduction to the production. The lobbies may also serve as a waiting area for late comers who often are not seated until there is a scene or act break so that audience members will not be annoyed or interrupted during a performance. In some cases closed circuit television may be provided so that late comers may see what is happening on the stage during the wait. In addition to the lobbies, adequate provision is usually made for the audience's physical comfort. Restrooms are designed to provide ample facilities for the number of people who will be attending a performance.

Within the theatre itself the seating must be arranged so that all audience members have a clear and unobstructed view of the acting area. Designers and directors take into account how the audience is seated when planning a production so that audience members will be able to view the total stage picture as much as possible. Aisle lights are usually provided for safety purposes and all doors to the auditorium are required to open out in case an emergency evacuation is necessary.

Arrangements must also be made for the control of lighting and sound. Usually a booth is provided from which the operators can view and hear the performance. An intercom system is normally a part of the total design so that backstage personnel can readily communicate with the lobby or with the light and sound operators. Speakers are normally located in dressing rooms and the **green room** so that actors can hear the progress of the performance while waiting for their **cues**. Auditoriums are normally provided with thermostat-controlled air conditioning systems which must be large enough and well enough regulated to keep the temperature even and the air fresh at all times. In proscenium theatres, a fire-proof curtain is normally required. (Since most theatre fires occur on or back stage, such a curtain, which is heat and smoke activated, will automatically seal the stage house off from the audience.)

In all cases, with the possible exception of found space, audience comfort is of primary importance. If the audience is not comfortable, a favorable response to the show will be diminished. Nothing should exist or occur within the theatre which distracts from the action taking place within the acting area–the stage.

Sectional drawing of the Madison Square Theatre with the elevator stage designed by Steele Mackaye. From *The Scientific American*, April 5, 1884.

With this proscenium theatre, two settings could be completely set at one time and the stages either raised or lowered into the proper position behind the proscenium. Provision was made to allow the setting to be changed on either the upper or the basement levels.

18
Scenery & the Scenic Designer

"The essence of a stage setting lies in its incompleteness. . .It contains the promise of completion, a promise that the actors will later fulfill. It is charged with a sense of expectancy. . .By itself it is nothing. In connection with actors it can become a work of art, filled with dramatic life."

Robert Edmund Jones

Background

Scenic design has become an important part of the total theatre experience only since the time of the Middle Ages. There is little information regarding scenery in the Greek and Roman theatres. We know that there was some, for it is stated in several sources that Sophocles was the first scene painter. We also have some words referring to scenery such as **phylakes** and **periactoi**. However, we have little information telling us what the scenery was or where it was actually placed. It is highly probable that such scenery was more symbolic than representational.

The setting for the Valenciennes Passion Play. This play, presented in the late Middle Ages, featured a **simultaneous** stage setting. Each locale is represented by a **mansion**. The conventions of the time relied on the audience's acceptance of the location as indicated by the mansion from which the actors entered.

From Kenneth MacGowan and William Melnitz, *The Living Stage*, 1955

Beginning with the **mansions** in the medieval cathedrals and continuing with the presentation of mystery, miracle, and morality plays outside the church, there is evidence that some of the scenic units were highly developed and elaborate. Little or no mention is made of scenic designers, though there is evidence that at least a few made a living creating the mansions and wagon stages for the more elaborately mounted productions.

It was with the Renaissance and the court festivals that theatre architects became truly important and well known in the theatre. One of the earliest published works regarding design and stage effects was written by the Italian designer Sebastiano Serlio (1475-1554) and published 1545. Though he was not the first scenic architect or designer, Serlio's *Architettura* was the first work to devote a section exclusively to the theatre. Much of his work was derived from descriptions of the Roman stage by the architect Vitruvius in his book *De Architectura*. Following Vitruvius' very brief description, Serlio devised three settings for the three kinds of plays being presented by Renaissance actors: tragedy, comedy, and the pastoral. In Serlio's world, stage settings were generic, that is, they were designed not for specific plays, but for the three forms

From Kenneth MacGowan and William Melnitz, *The Living Stage*, 1955

Serlio's design for tragedy, c. 1545. Note the forced illusion of depth accomplished through his use of painter perspective.

of drama commonly accepted.

From Allardyce Nicoll, *Development of the Theatre* Harcourt, Brace, n.d.

An court performance in Florence, Italy, as recorded by Jacques Callot, an **intermezzi**, from about 1616. Note the perspective scenery on the stage in the background with the action taking place on the ballroom floor. This is similar to the arrangement of the present

It was with the Italian court **intermezzi** of the 16th and 17th centuries (called the **ballet de cour** in France and the **masque** in England) that the scenic designers began many of the trends which are still present in the theatre today. The intermezzi, which had originally been created to occur between scenes of tragedies and pastoral plays, became so popular that they became a form of theatre in their own right. Produced in the courts of Europe and England to celebrate special occasions such as the birth of a prince, a visiting dignitary, or in honor of the life of a ruler, the intermezzi were elaborate productions featuring music, dance, dialogue and poetry. For these the resident court architects devised a variety of scenes and elaborate machinery to create almost magical scene changes, appearances and disappearances of gods and goddesses. During this period designers learned the skill of developing settings using **forced perspective** thus creating the illusion of greater depth on stage. By the middle of the 17th century the intermezzi had been merged with the popular opera and the scenic devices and settings became standard in the presentation of those musical works.

Toward the end of the 17th century, the theatre having completed its move to indoor auditoriums in both Europe and England, the designers began developing a group of **stock** settings for plays. These included such settings as a throne-room, street scene, grotto, dungeon, garden, and drawing room which were used whenever a play required one or more of the sets to aid in establishing locale. Just as the costumes of this period were generally contemporary, so were the sets with little or no effort being made to establish period, mood, or ethnic origin.

Courtesy, National Bibliotique, Vienna

A perspective setting for an opera by the Italian Bibiena family. By the early 1700s, designers had learned how to use very complex perspective with multiple vanishing points.

In 1771, the great English actor/manager David Garrick employed the French artist Phillippe Jacques DeLoutherbourg (1740-1812) to design settings for pantomimes and other spectacles for London's Drury Lane. Between 1771 and 1785, DeLoutherbourg introduced reproductions of actual locales for these productions, one of which was *Omai, or a Trip Around the World* (1785) for which he mounted a scenic "travelogue" based on Captain

Cook's voyage. This started a vogue in England for productions featuring "local color" and influenced English stage design throughout the following century.

The theatre has always responded to events shaping or reflecting world history. By the end of the 18th century, archaeologists had been active in Greece, Turkey and Egypt discovering and uncovering many ancient ruins. This began the **antiquarian** movement in Europe and England, an almost fanatical devotion to the publication and distribution of archaeological discoveries. Antiquarianism was reflected in the theatre by an increase in the number of attempts to stage plays using authentic historic settings. In this case, the designers became researchers seeking to recreate actual locales on the stage. Plays which did not require such literal representations were often altered so that the set designs could be advertised as having been derived from authentic sources. One of the earliest of these was a production of *Macbeth* staged by the English actor Charles Macready and set in 10th century Scotland. During the 1850s, Charles Kean, actor/manager of London's Princess Theatre, mounted several of Shakespeare's plays using historically accurate stage settings and costumes.

Probably the most noted of the antiquarian directors was Duke George II, the Duke of Saxe Meiningen, referred to in Chapter 15, who carefully researched his productions traveling to museums and libraries throughout Europe to secure his information. In particular, his productions of Shakespeare's *Julius Caesar* and Schiller's play about Joan of Arc, *The Maid of Orleans*, reflected his desire to mount historically accurate productions and were a major influence on the theatre throughout the world.

The 19th century is often referred to as the century of pictorial realism in the theatre. In order for this to take place, the profession of scene painting became more and more important. Sets, composed primarily of **wings** and **drops**, were carefully painted to create elaborate three-dimensional illusions. Under the lighting then in use, gas, the illusions were often startlingly real. With the advent of the electric incandescent lamp in the theatre in 1881, however, much of this would change. The brilliance of electric light revealed the artificiality of the painted sets destroying the illusions the scene painters strove to create. In addition, the growing emphasis on environment as an influence on character created a growing desire to reproduce accurately on stage the actual three-dimensional environments in which the characters existed. No longer were the illusions of the scene painter acceptable, now audiences expected fully functional three-dimensional sets to be seen on the stage.

New York Public Library, Billy Rose Theatre Collection, Astor, Lennox and Tilden Foundation

A set for *Electra* by Edward Gordon Craig who stressed a simplicity of design using suggestion rather than reproduction.

There was no way, however, for the stage to compete with photography, and theatre artists began to fret under the limitations of the realistic and naturalistic presentations which often rejected the products of the imagination and stifled creativity. By the end of the 19th century, therefore, theatre artists began to experiment more and more with suggestive and symbolic stage settings. Two men are often credited with stimulating this new movement in the theatre, Adolph Appia and Edward Gordon Craig. Both advocated stage settings which were more suggestive than real. Both stated that two-dimensional scene painting should not be used in the theatre, but that settings should be three-dimensional as are the actors. Both saw the function of the setting as being primarily to create a mood or feeling for the play; i.e., an attempt to capture the illusive "spirit" of the play rather than to give the play a literal environment. The influence of Appia and Craig is still highly evident in today's theatre where many designers work in **symbolic** and **impressionistic** styles rather than realistically. Today, the photographic realism of the late 19th and early 20th century is usually more appropriate for the motion pictures than the living theatre.

The Scenic Designer

The scenic designer or set designer in the modern theatre works closely with the director of the play in order to achieve a visual interpretation of the script. He normally has a background in art with training in design, drawing, rendering, model-making, etc. He usually has training in art history and a thorough knowledge of the various periods and styles of the discipline. In addition, he has a thorough background in theatre history and dramatic literature, their periods and styles. He is often required to have a knowledge of the history of architecture, decoration and furniture as well.

It is the responsibility of the designer to create the proper environment for the characters and the action of the play. Though his work may be more symbolic than literal, it often needs to evoke a feel for the period in which the play is set and must complement the mood of the play. Following a thorough study of the play and in consultation with the director, the designer is expected to create a setting which will allow for the arrangement of stage pictures as conceived by the director and also allow for the necessary actions (movements) of the play to occur. If multiple sets are required by the play, it is the responsibility of the designer to create them in such a way as to allow for efficient changes to take place so that the rhythm of the play can be maintained.

The world to be created by the designer is the world of the play, not necessarily the world of real life. It is also a world which is incomplete until the actor is placed within it. As Robert Edmund Jones says in *The Dramatic Imagination*, "By itself [the stage design] is nothing. In connection with actors it can become a work of art, filled with dramatic life...Scenery is not there to be looked at. It is really there to be forgotten. The drama is the fire, the scenery the wind that lifts the fire and makes it bright."

The designer's responsibility, therefore, is to reflect the **tone** and **mood** of the play. The set must also indicate the **time** and **place** of the action if that is important to the play itself. Once that has been established, all elements of the design must be consistent. In addition, the set must provide opportunities for many kinds of actions so that a variety of meaningful stage pictures may be created upon it by the actors and so that their movements will not be hampered. As artistic as the set should be, it must also be practical. If literal and usable aspects of the setting are necessary for the action of the play; for instance, if a window must be raised or lowered or a door opened and shut, the design must provide for that. Finally, the design must be consistent in style with the play itself or with the interpretation of the play as it has been agreed upon by the artistic staff responsible for the final production.

The **stage** and **hand properties** are also a responsibility of the scenic designer. The stage properties include all the furniture and probably the set decorations which must complement the set with regard to period and style and yet provide for the necessary actions of the play. The hand properties are those smaller items, not a part of a costume, directly handled by the actor and often brought onto the stage by him.

In preparing his design, the scenic designer must answer a number of basic questions. These are factors with which he will have to deal in planning many aspects of his design and will have to be answered before the design can be finalized:

1. What is the shape and size of the stage? Will the theatre be proscenium, arena, or thrust? That is, what will be the actor/audience relationship?

2. What will be the relationship of audience to stage with regard to the theatre's **sight-lines**? How is the seating arranged? Will the audience look up to the stage, down on it, or be on eye-level with it? How much can, will and should the audience see?

3. If multiple sets are to be used, how will they be shifted within the confines of the particular theatre's architecture? Is the theatre provided with mechanized means for changing sets such as adequate **flies**, a **revolving stage**, a wagon arrangement, or will it be necessary to change sets purely by manpower or by a combination of manpower and machine?

4. Will the architecture of the theatre need to be changed to accommodate the production? In the cases of *Sweeney Todd, Starlight Express,* and *Cats* the interiors of the theatres in New York City were altered considerably.

5. Are there special effects which must be provided for the play to make its statement?

6. Of what materials will the set be constructed? Will traditional construction techniques making use of canvas stretched on wooden frames (**flats**) or more unconventional techniques using steel and plastics be more suitable? Will painted **drops** be required and, if so, how will they be hung and changed?

7. Will modern stage techniques be used or will the play be mounted in an historic style requiring the construction of machinery not normally found within the modern theatre?

8. What budgetary limitations have been placed on the production?

9. How much time is available for the building, assembling and rehearsal use of the settings?

Having met with the rest of the artistic team, having the answers to these questions, and having conducted his research, the scenic designer is ready to move on in the process of creating his design. This includes drawing up a to-scale ground plan (see Chapter 15), developing a carefully rendered perspective drawing of the set(s)or possibly making a to-scale model of the set for both his and the director's use. Once he has received approval from the director, the designer proceeds to create **builders' elevations** for the technical director and his stage carpenters and **painters' elevations** for the scene painters. If various properties must be constructed, plans must also be developed for these. As the building and painting of the set proceeds, the designer normally supervises making sure his plans have been followed and that the colors he has chosen have been matched by the painters. Throughout the process, the designer is in constant contact with other members of the artistic team coordinating his efforts with theirs. When the final rehearsals take place, the designer is normally present in order to arrange for any changes which may be needed and to instruct the stage crew regarding setting up the sets and stage properties and conducting the scene shifts, if any.

Forms of Stage Scenery

Just as we have dramatic forms related to the structure of plays, there are scenic forms directly related to the structure and design of stage settings. The designer may make use of these and others devised from his own imagination and experience. Just as more than one dramatic form may exist within a play, so may the designer use several scenic forms in combination. These scenic forms will reflect several aspects of the production of the play dealt with by the artistic staff in the early stages of planning:

The basic forms of stage scenery are indicated below:

Full-Stage Settings

Box Setting: This form of setting utilizes complete scenery using two or three walls (two walls being called a **corner set**), the side walls extending to the proscenium arch. Masking flats are used behind doors and a full ceiling is often used. See the illustration of the Belasco production of *The Auctioneer* on page 110 for an example of a box setting in use.

Exterior Setting: This requires the use of the full stage. In designing it, the designer first creates an arrangement which will completely mask off the back stage areas, then he considers the set's decorative possibilities. Overhead, he often uses **borders** which mask the fly system, etc. Often the set is completed with the use of a **drop** or **cyclorama** at the rear.

Wing and Drop: This setting makes use of a painted drop at the rear of the stage with **wings** masking the side areas of the stage. Because of its arrangement, this kind of setting is often used to represent exteriors. It is particularly popular for ballet or other theatrical pieces in which large groups of people must be moved on and off stage rapidly.

Unit Set: The unit set makes use of basic scenic pieces which are changed from one position to another throughout the play to provide a variety of compositions and to indicate various changes of locales.

Skeleton Set: This set consists of framework scenery upon which scenic units are hung or mounted and changed frequently and quickly. It not only indicates the locale in which the action

From David A. Welker, *Theatrical Set Design*, Courtesy of Allyn and Bacon, Publishers

Examples of the use of a unit set. In this case, the sets above are for Garcia de Lorca's *Blood Wedding* The arches remain the same from set to set. Changes are made by adding **plugs** in the arches and through the use of decorative pieces and furniture.

is taking place, but it reveals the basic structure of the stage setting. In some cases, it may be abstract and be seen as a kind of skeletal stage sculpture. As a style, this is often referred to as **constructivism**.

Minimum Settings

These are settings which are suggestive using only elements of the locale being represented. Masking is handled through the use of drapes (**legs**) on either side of the stage and either a full stage curtain or cyclorama at the rear.

Cut-Down: contains scenic units not normal in height although the scenery usually has a complete floor-plan from proscenium side to proscenium side.

Selective: The scenery is of normal height, but often only portions of walls are used. This is sometimes called **suggestive**.

Fragmentary: small irregularly shaped sections of a complete setting often painted rather than three-dimensional. These pieces are often not normal in height. Used on the proscenium, arena and thrust stages.

Projected: Makes use of an optical projector. Normally requires the use of a cyclorama or rear projection screen. On occasion a series of projectors are used with a variety of screens standing on or hung above the stage.

Profile Setting: This setting consists of two-dimensional, irregularly shaped frames painted in a non-realistic fashion. There is seldom an attempt at presenting a literal three-dimensional form.

Simultaneous: Specific stage areas set to represent specific locales which remain constant throughout the play. When the action of a scene begins in one area, the entire stage, by convention, represents that locale. (See Medieval theatre discussion, Chapter 11)

Courtesy the University of Texas at Austin

The Good Woman of Setzuan as mounted at the University of Texas at Austin with design by John Rothgeb and directed by Francis Hodge. This production made use of small platform units, cut-down elements of scenery, and projections. All locales indicated in the script were played on this set making it a **simultaneous setting** as well.

Theatre Arts Prints, 1935

A formal platform stage setting for *Antigone* as designed by Arch Lauterer for the Cambridge Festival Theatre. Note the use of platforms and steps with the central column–all provide for a range of stage pictures through the placement of the actors.

Formal: This form of stage setting is normally non-representational and, therefore, does not reveal a specific locale. It is composed of a variety of ramps and platforms which remain constant throughout the play. As a style this is called **formalism**.

Styles of StageScenery

The manner in which a particular play is written or presented is usually referred to as the "style of the play." Styles are used in order to help plays attain their various purposes. Though we may attempt to classify a style, it should be understood that often the playwright, designer, or director may use more than one style at the same time within a presentation. **It is rare that such a thing as a pure style is used.**

Definitions of Scenic Styles

Stylization: Stylization establishes the mode of the play. It is external to the play itself, although not irrelevant to the play. It endeavors to provide a scheme of decoration in some way characteristic of the particular author, or his theme or intention, or the spirit of the play.

I. Historical and Literary Styles:

These styles are the product of a particular historic period and reflect that period either in a direct effort to imitate and/or simulate the era through the writing, or to recreate the conditions under which the play was originally produced.

Classicism: A style in which the element of reason takes precedence over the element of emotion. Classicism is orderly and controlled. It can be a narrow defender of tradition or a major agent in the preservation of the best that the experience of the race has discovered.

The Billy Rose Theatre Collection, New York Public Library for the Performing Arts, Astor, Lenox and Tilden Foundations

The Broadway production of Lerner & Lowe's *Brigadoon* (1947) made use of highly stylized scenery representing the Scottish countryside designed by Oliver Smith. This is also a good example of an exterior setting making use of **wings** and a **drop**.

Romanticism: A style in which the element of emotion takes precedence over reason and passion over fidelity to fact. It is distinguished by a love of nature, freedom of the individual, sentimentality over the past, strong use of the imagination, emphasis on the strange and far-away. It suggests an escape from reality, disunity, and lack of restraint. It is loose in structure and tends to border on the sensational.

II. Representational Styles:

These styles attempt to give the viewer the impression of the real.

Naturalism: A style which is representational and not interpretive. It is also a more exaggerated kind of realism. Naturalism is prosaic and deliberate. A product of "scientific determinism," human personalities are usually presented as products of heredity and environment. It rejects all selectivity and is often presented on stage as "a slice of life." Because of the subject matter often discussed, many see naturalism as a pessimistic view of life, though some critics see the very discussion of naturalism's subjects as a hope for future understanding and, ultimately, change.

Realism: A style in which there is a passion for fidelity to fact, in which life is presented on the stage as it is presumably lived. There is no sharp design apparent in realism. Human personalities are sometimes presented as products of heredity and environment. Too often, realism tends to become too photographic and verges on the naturalistic. Realism is sometimes defined as "selective naturalism" and requires a degree of selectivity and interpretation.

Theatre Arts Prints, 1935

A realistic stage setting for Elmer Rice's *Street Scene* as mounted at the Stadttheater, Mainz, Germany. Note the multi-level arrangement of the New York apartment house created for this production.

III. Symbolic Styles:

These styles make use of abstract forms which stand as symbols for ideas or as interpretations of reality.

Symbolism: The use of imagery and fancy in writing and in the theatre and painting, etc. Symbolism seizes on some aspect of an object and dignifies it with imaginative, fantastic, or esoteric qualities so that it may represent some philosophic, religious, or social abstraction.

Impressionism: A highly personal manner of expression in which the author presents characters, scenes or moods as they appear to his individual temperament rather than as they are in actuality. Impressionists feel it is more important to retain the impressions an object makes on the artist than to preserve the appearance of the object by precise detail and realistic finish.

Courtesy of the Jo Mielziner Estate

Jo Mielziner's setting for the first act of Arthur Miller's *Death of a Salesman* Mielziner combines **constructivism** in the framework of the house and **projection** in the overlay of the leaves. The projection, used during the flashback scenes, adds **symbolism** to the setting since it suggests the peace and happiness of Willy's earlier years. Overall, the set is **impressionistic** in that it gives an impression of Willy's environment rather than a literal duplication of it.

Expressionism: A style presenting an intellectual abstraction of nature. The expressionist presents actuality as modified by his personality plus an intellectual concept. Distortion is used as an emphasis of the essential quality of the object obvious primarily to the artist. Expressionism often deals with the subconscious and may be a cry for help. Using the expressionistic style, the artist often presents us with a view of the world as seen through his own eyes or through the eyes of the protagonist.

IV. **Non-Representational Styles:** The following styles do not attempt to present a specific idea or to represent a specific place. They do provide a background against which the various nuances of the play may be revealed. They may also be considered "forms" of stage scenery.

The Billy Rose Theatre Collection, New York Public Library for the Performing Arts, Astor, Lenox and Tilden Foundations

Robert Edmund Jone's design for the banquet scene in *Macbeth.* Note the distortion used to help the audience view the scene through the eyes of the protagonist, Macbeth. This is an example of expressionism in scenic design.

Formalism: This manner of producing a play is principally applied to scenic art, although it may be used in other phases of the production. Formalism demands the complete suppression of the stage setting as such and the substitution of a purely formal background. The setting is not a part of the play, but signifies only the "essential theatricality of the playing space."

Plasticism: An attempt to establish a three-dimensional effect in the theatre. This often entails the use of a platform or sculptural stage or a space stage in which the background is in darkness and the characters seem formed or molded according to the author's impression. Using light, the space is molded and modeled through changes in spatial relationships.

Constructivism: Another manner of designing the setting for a play in which the setting consists of numerous levels produced by ramps, scaffolds, stairways, etc. Sometimes called a skeleton setting, this style does not attempt to hide the structural underpinnings of the set, but rather these elements are used as a part of the visual design.

Theatricalism: No attempt to hide the fact that the play is taking place in the theatre. It is highly presentational in style, the acting is often directly to the audience, the lighting is in full view, and scenic and property elements are not used to create an illusion of a realistic locale. In fact, illusion is eliminated in true theatricalism. In serious works it promotes an intellectual response since the audience is constantly reminded of the artificiality of the presentation. In entertainment pieces, it denies reality and is used to encourage the audience to sit back and relax - to escape to the "magic of the theatre."

Theatre Arts Prints, 1935

An expressionistic version of the setting for Elmer Rice's *Street Scene*. Note how the buildings are distorted with the distortion carried out in the placement of the rubble on the forestage. Here we see the environment through the eyes of the play's interpreters rather than those of the protagonist.

Theatre Arts Prints, 1935

A constructivist stage setting for the Russian comedy *The Inspector General* by Gogol as presented at the Cambridge, England, Festival Theatre.

Conclusion

The work of the scenic designer is of extreme importance in the modern theatre. Whether his setting is extremely complex or very simple, it is often this designer who first establishes the play's locale, style, mood, and period in the eyes of the audience. It is the scenic designer who provides opportunities for actor movement, for interesting stage pictures, and for the physical necessities required for the play to occur. Like other artists involved with the play, he is a part of a team. His work must complement that of the director, costumer, and lighting designer so that all efforts contribute to the final effect the audience experiences.

Bertold Brecht's *Mother Courage* as staged at the Kammerspiele, Munich, under the direction of Brecht. The play requires little in the way of a set design with the exception of Mother Courage's very complex wagon laden with the wares she hawks to the opposing armies. The play is a strong indictment of greed, selfishness, and materialism. The design is by Teo Otto.

From Hanns Braun, *The Theatre in Germany* 1952

Theatre Appreciation
Class Assignment

Name____________________________________

Using a play assigned by your instructor, answer the following questions which would be considered by the scene designer:

1. In what period is the play set?

2. What is the overall mood of the play?

3. What specific elements in the set are required by the author of the play?

4. Which of these elements are "practical;" i.e., must be used by the actors?

5. What pieces of furniture would be appropriate for the set?

6. What set or property changes might be required, if any?

7. What color(s) would be appropriate for the set? Why?

Remove from text and hand in to instructor.

19
Costuming & Costume Design

A costume is any item of or related to clothing worn by the actor on stage. It may be drawn from some historic period, contemporary fashion, or from the imagination of the costumer. Off stage, it is "dress," but on stage it becomes a costume. Its function is to aid the audience in identifying the character, set the mood of the play, and establish the locale and period in which the play is set.

Historical Background

Just as the position of scenic designer in the theatre is of relatively recent origin, so is that of the costume designer. Certainly there were those who designed and provided costumes for actors from the time of the Greeks on, but the creation of the position of costume designer as such began in the theatre in the early 19th century.

We know that specific costumes were worn in the classical Greek period. The actors were apparently provided with exaggerated versions of customary Greek costume, with **cothurnos** (high soled boots), with the **onkos** (headdress), and with **masks,** which were often a part of the onkos. From vase paintings, it is evident that the Greek choruses, particularly in comedies, were elaborately dressed. Aristophanes calls for choruses of birds, horses, frogs, and others in his scripts. Other than the readily apparent fact that someone must have devised and constructed such costumes, we are given little or no information. Since much of the information concerning the Roman theatre reveals that the Romans adopted many of the plays and production methods of the Greeks, it can be assumed that Roman costuming for comedies and tragedies was very similar. In most cases, for both the Greeks and Romans, the costumes were adapted from contemporary dress.

A vase painting from the time of the ancient Greeks shows a musician accompanying a chorus of men riding horses as might have been seen in Aristophanes' comedy *The Knights.*

During the Middle Ages surviving records indicate that the costumes worn by actors in mystery, morality, and miracle plays were also adapted from contemporary dress though there are indications that some of the costumes were adapted from the ritual dress of the clergy. The most imaginative costumes, however, were those created for the devils who led sinners to Hell or tortured them in Purgatory or Hell. The elaborate dress for such characters is well shown in the following description from an early 16th century French manuscript:

"Then the show of devils was made in the town square. These devils were all clad in skins of wolves, calves, and rams, surmounted with sheep-heads, bull-horns, and cockscombs; girdles of thick skins from which hung cows' bells or mules' bells with horrible noise. . ."

From Allardyce Nicoll, *The Development of the Theatre* Harcourt, Brace & Company, n.d

Medieval devil costumes at Zurich.

Medieval producers also indicate that actors were often dressed in specific colors to symbolize their character. "Cain is to be clad in red garments, Abel in white," states one set of instructions. The costume, or lack of it, could go to extremes. According to one account of a 14th century play in France, a woman disguised as a monk was, on death, revealed to be a man "totally nude."

Maurice Sand's painting of Giangurlogo, one of the Commedia dell'Arte Zannis, in his adopted costume. Note the mask. See p. 114 for other Commedia characters.

During the Renaissance, the actors were generally expected to provide their own costumes. Many of these were drawn from contemporary dress. In the case of the Commedia dell'Arte, the actors, playing their set roles, each had a costume specifically designed for their characters. Harlequin was, of course, seen in the costume composed of multi-colored diamond patches. Pierrot was dressed all in white. Pantalone was dressed in a black outfit similar to that worn by Venetian merchants of the period. The most elaborate costumes were to be found on the mythical figures often presented in the court spectacles.

From Allardyce Nicoll, *The Development of the Theatre* Harcourt, Brace & Company, n.d

Inigo Jones' (1573-1652) design for a costume for a knight masquer in *Oberon* a court masque presented in 1611 for James I of England.

In the public theatres of the 17th and early 18th century, actors generally wore contemporary dress no matter the time or locale indicated by the play script. There are indications that on occasion an actor might add a costume piece representative of the period and/or locale of the play, but this apparently was more the exception than the rule. Nor was there any effort to coordinate the costumes worn on stage. If one character did adopt an ethnic or period piece of dress, that did not necessarily mean that the other actors would follow suit. On the Elizabethan stage, records show that ethnic and some period items were often used and that actors usually dressed according to the social rank or status of their characters. Shakespeare refers to an "ass's head" and a "lion" in *A Midsummer*

Night's Dream. Shylock apparently dressed in the appropriate costume for a Jewish money-lender and Portia in lawyer's robes for the trial scene in *The Merchant of Venice.* According to the diary of Henslowe, manager of the Fortune Theatre, the theatre's wardrobe contained "1 lion skin. . .1 bear skin. . .1 bores head. . .1 dragon. . .1 lyon's head. . .1 black dogge. . .1 great horse."

The traditions of the Elizabethan stage were carried on during the Restoration and into the 18th century in England and in France. The actors still provided their own contemporary costumes and occasionally supplemented them with ethnic or period accessories. The appearance of women on the Restoration stage in England brought a major change in the attitude toward dress, however. There are many recorded cases of the newly arrived actresses vying with each other in the area of dress. In a number of reported incidents, actresses playing maids would totally outdress the actresses playing the ladies they were expected to serve. On more than one occasion this competition brought backstage bickering among the ladies and sometimes resulted in gowns being ripped off the offending actress by her colleague while waiting for an entrance.

From Rowe (ed.), *Shakespeare's Plays* 1809

An 18th century production of *Hamlet* Note the contemporary dress worn by the actors.

By the middle of the 18th century in France and Germany, greater attention began to be paid to stage costume. Still, such attention was normally placed on the leading characters with the others in the cast wearing contemporary dress. In Germany, toward the end of the century, the newly popular *sturm und dram* (storm and stress) dramas which were often set in specific historic periods encouraged actors to begin to accumulate costume pieces which were somewhat authentic for the character and the period in which the play was set. Slowly but surely, actors began to acquire wardrobes of authentic period costumes. By the early nineteenth century and for the decades which followed, such a wardrobe became the actor's most treasured possession. Even in the early 20th century, actors were often chosen by producers as much for their wardrobes as for their talent.

The rising interest in antiquity as seen in the **antiquarian** movement discussed in the previous chapter was to prove as great an influence on the costuming of plays as it would on the stage settings. In 1823, James Robinson Planché persuaded John Phillip Kemble, the great British tragedian, to allow him to "habit" a new production of Shakespeare's *King John* with authentic costumes for the entire cast, not just the leading characters. In 1834, Planché published what he claimed to be a complete history of costume in England. In that same year, he assisted Charles Macready in that actor's production of an "authentic" *Macbeth.* Planché's work was to influence a growing list of actor/managers in the following years who would attempt to mount historical works in the correct period dress. It was often spectacular and not always successful. It should be noted, however, that in many cases designers of the 19th century adapted their historical costumes to the ideal silhouette of their own period so that often their costumes were really adaptations of the current fashions.

The drive toward authentic costuming on stage would be furthered by the work of Duke George, the Duke of Saxe Meiningen, who not only designed authentic locales for his productions, but created authentic costumes for them as well. His actors were required to study paintings of the past to understand how the costumes were to be worn and the various poses appropriate to them. His own armory in his palace constructed authentic historic chain mail and plate armor as well as weapons. In preparation for his production of *The Maid of Orlean,* the Duke had material woven using looms and yarn similar to that used during the time of Joan of Arc. Knowing that the characters in the plays were comfortable in their native dress, the Duke required that all costumes, including armor, be constructed and available for use when rehearsals for a play began. Actors were required to rehearse in costume in order to become familiar with the movements and postures influenced by the costumes well in advance of performances.

With the 20th century, the interest in accurate and artistic stage costuming continues and grows as theatre artists experiment with a variety of styles. Rather than relying on actors to supply their own costumes, directors, producers and costumers create costumes for each character according to the needs of the play. This practice brings more unity to the productions in interpretation and style.

The Costumer

The costume designer must be a skilled researcher with a knowledge of the various periods and nationalities, or the ability to go back into history and find the information necessary. Like the scenic designer working with a period play, the costumer may attempt, a la Duke George, to literally recreate the dress of a particular time, but is more likely to design an interpretation or impression of the original in order to interpret the play better. Some plays, of course, do not require historical authenticity, but depend on the designer's imagination to create a variety of fantasy costumes. In any case, the costumer must have a knowledge of basic sewing skills, the ability to draft patterns, a knowledge of fabrics, dyeing techniques, millinery skills, and other craft skills.

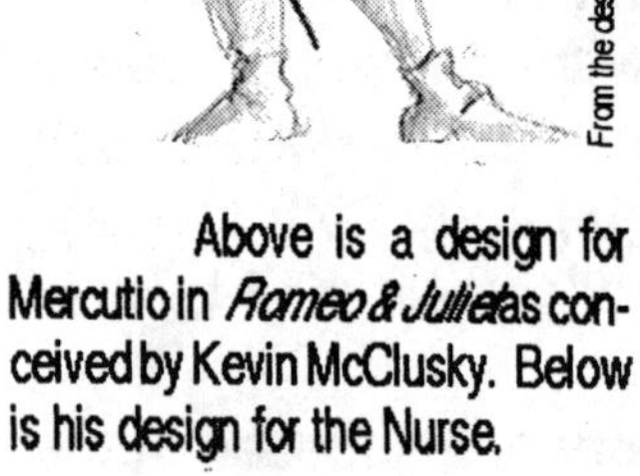

Above is a design for Mercutio in *Romeo & Juliet* as conceived by Kevin McClusky. Below is his design for the Nurse.

In dealing with a particular play, the costume designer works closely with the director and the scene and lighting designers in order to allow all efforts to be coordinated so that one basic interpretation of the play will take place. Normally, the designer sketches or renders each costume required and submits it to the director for approval with appropriate swatches of material attached. Once the costume renderings have been approved, the actors are carefully measured, patterns are drafted, materials purchased, and the actual assembling of the costumes takes place. In the professional theatre these tasks may be assigned to a number of individuals with the designer supervising all aspects of the work.

In some cases, particular costumes restrict or influence the actor's actions. It is therefore necessary for the designer to consult with the director regarding the movements he will require of each actor throughout the play so that the costumes will make the necessary allowances. For period plays, the costumer often works closely with the director assisting actors in period movements and in the actual use of the costumes on stage.

From the designer's collection

Velta Hargrove's design and its realization for a costume in the 18th century play *The Mistress of the Inn.*

In designing the costumes, the designer must consider each character's age, nationality, economic status, attitude, relation to other characters, and the overall style upon which the artistic staff has agreed. Often family groups are given one color which will help the audience to identify relationships. Individuals with differing social functions are first revealed to the audience through their costumes. The attitude of a character is usually reflected in his choice of clothing, in the individual items of which it is composed, its color, and the kind of fabric worn. With some exceptions, it is **not** the responsibility of the costumer to "make the actor look good," but rather it is his responsibility to help the actor reveal the character more readily to the audience.

(Note: In some cases, the costumer is charged with the responsibility of correcting some deficiencies in an actor's build which would detract from his overall impression on the audience. For instance, screen actor Errol Flynn was "blessed" with spindly legs which did not provide an acceptable silhouette when the actor had to don tights. The MGM costume designer devised a set of "falsies" to pad out Flynn's legs and thus correct the problem.)

Stephen F. Austin State University Collection

The realization of the design above.

Another aspect of design is to be found in the area of costume changes. Costume changes are often necessary to indicate a change of time from one scene to another or a change of social function for the character. Sometimes, therefore, an actor is required to totally change his appearance. This often entails complex and rapid costume and/or makeup changes. The design of the costume must be created in such a way as to make the changes possible in the time available. Action on stage cannot wait for a half-dressed actor to complete his change!

The costumer must also consider the total stage picture. He must be aware of color combinations and their aesthetic effect. The cut or line of the costumes also influences the total composition just as every line in a painting influences the total effect of the work. The fabric used will also have its impact because different fabrics reflect lights differently. The cut of the costume and the material chosen will have an impact on the artistry of the shifting movements of the actors on stage.

Parts of the Costume

The costume itself for each actor may be divided into five elements:

1. **Undergarments**: Each period has its own set of undergarments except for the Greek and possibly the Roman when undergarments were rarely worn. These undergarments, whether they be loose or form fitting, influence the hang of the costume on the actor. Corsets (for both men and women), hooped petticoats, paniers, braziers, briefs, or boxer shorts all have an impact on the final silhouette of the actor and on his movements. Undergarments often dictate the final silhouette of the actor.

2. **Outer garments**: This is the part of the costume which the audience sees. It is also the part of the garment that the actor must learn to handle with confidence. It includes blouses, skirts, suits, robes, shirtwaists, vests, coats, capes, etc. It is this part of the garment which often identifies the character for the audience and establishes his age, nationality, economic status, and the play's historic period.

3. **Footwear**: Footwear also helps to identify the age, nationality, and economic status of the character and the play's historic period. For the actor, it has a major influence on movement. Anyone who has suddenly had to shift from wearing flat tennis shoes to shoes with heels is aware of the change in movement dictated by footwear. Each historic period can be identified to some extent by the footwear of both men and women.

4. **Headwear & headdress**: This includes not only hats and scarves, but hair styles as well. Hair styles and headdresses change rapidly from one decade to another and must be so designed as to be in keeping with other costume elements.

5. **Accessories:** Each individual adopts a number of accessories which he adds to his costume. Some of the accessories are purely personal while others may reflect a specific period. These include purses, billfolds, jewelry on the costume itself or on the individual, ties or neck-scarves, cigarettes and cigarette cases and holders, snuff boxes, swords, daggers, guns and gun-belts, and other items related to social status, personal taste, or occupation. For the actor, these items become an important part of the character, often helping to separate one individual from another. They also provide opportunities for **business** on stage which adds to the believability of the action viewed by the audience. They are the final details which give a richness to the stage picture and action.

Up to this time, we have been discussing the "normal" in stage costuming. Often, the costumer is required to create the abnormal as well. For George Bernard Shaw's *Androcles and the Lion*, a lion is necessary. Thornton Wilder's *Skin of Our Teeth* requires a dinosaur and mammoth on stage during the first act. Karel Capek's *R.U.R.* requires several actors to appear as robots. Aristophanes' *The Birds* needs a full chorus of birds as well as several major characters who are also birds. In fact, for this play the costumer not only has to create birds, but must costume several actors to appear as Olympian gods, and others as normal human beings. Futuristic plays may require not only unusual costumes for human beings, but the creation of alien forms and creatures.

Theatre Appreciation
Class Assignment

Name______________________________

Choosing a character from one of the plays you have read or one specified by your instructor, answer the following questions related to costume design:

I. Name of Play: ________________________ 2. Character:________________________

3. Period in which the play is set:____

4. Country:___________________ 5. Character's nationality:____________________

6. Character's social position:____

7. Character's occupation:____

8. Character's attitude:____

9. Character's function in the play:____

10. How many costumes would the character need due to:

a. Changes in activity? ____________________

b. To indicate passage of time?______________

11. What color(s) would be appropriate for the character?

12. Of what elements would the costume consist? Be as specific as possible.

Remove from text and turn in to instructor.

20
Lighting and the Light Designer

One of the major changes to take place in the theatre occurred when the theatre moved to indoor playing spaces. Suddenly, it was necessary to provide adequate lighting so that the actors and the scenery could be seen. As can easily be imagined, early lighting was extremely primitive and consisted primarily of braziers, torches and candles. Non-directional, the lighting usually illuminated the audience as well as the actor. Toward the end of the Renaissance, however, lighting became more sophisticated as the scenic architects (designers) attempted to create special effects. By this time oil lamps had been introduced to theatrical use and the designers attempted to illuminate specific areas of the stage through the use of these lamps backed by polished basins which could act as reflectors. For color, designers introduced the use of bottles of colored water which would be placed in front of the light and, to some extent, allow a tint to be given to the whitish-yellowish flame.

Iron cresset

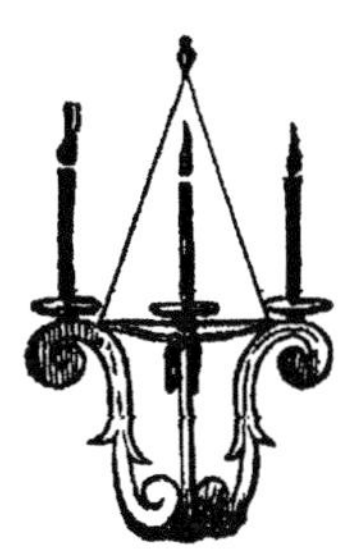

Candelabra

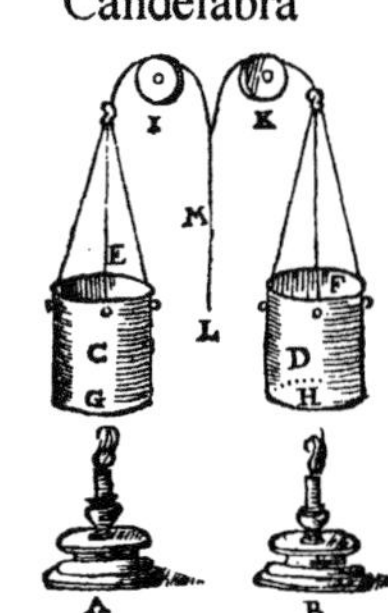

Candles with dimming capability

A "float"- a wick forced through a cork floating in oil

Argand oil burner

Placement of the lighting instruments was critical. Records show that by the late 1600's the stages were lit through the use of oil lamps backed by small reflectors placed along the front edge of the stage. Additional lamps were mounted on poles behind the wings on either side of the stage. Overhead lighting was generally provided by candle chandeliers. Auditoriums were illuminated by wall sconces and chandeliers which remained burning throughout the performances. Though the greatest concentration of light was on the stage, the audience was still in full light throughout the performance.

From the author's collection.

Moliere's *The Imaginary Invalid* as presented before the court of Louis XIV in 1674 in the gardens of Versailles. For this production, a temporary stage was erected at Versailles. Note the candelabra hanging over the stage, the orchestra pit, and the special seating for the King and his court. The original engraving plate for this is still in existence and has been preserved in the lithographic office of the Louvre in Paris.

David Garrick, the actor/manager of the Theatre Royal in Drury Lane, London, is generally credited with introducing stage lighting hidden from the audience. Working with the designer DeLoutherbourg, Garrick apparently introduced the use of a new lighting instrument called the Argand Oil Burner which had been invented in France in c.1785. This ancestor to the more recent kerosene lamp had a glass chimney which greatly improved air flow causing a brighter, whiter and steadier light. It soon replaced the oil lamps and candles as the preferred source of illumination.

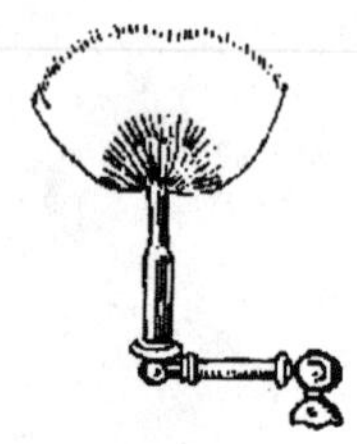
Gas jet designed for a flat flame

By the beginning of the 19th century, it had been discovered that coal, when heated, produced an inflammable gas which could be fed through leather tubes and controlled by valves. Brighter than oil and kerosene lamps, the gas lamp was introduced to the theatre first in Philadelphia in 1816 at the Chestnut Street Theatre. Covent Garden and Drury Lane in London adopted the gas lamps for their stages in 1817. Since there was no central supply source for gas, those desiring to use it had to install their own manufacturing plants. It was not until the 1840s that gas became widely available.

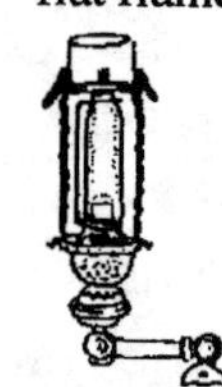
Gas jet with silk mantle providing brighter and whiter light.

Gas was a major improvement. Not only did it give a brighter light than oil lamps and candles, but it could be controlled so that lighting could be dimmed or brightened through the use of a gas board which consisted of a series of valves controlling the amount of gas distributed. Also, since it did not use a wick, it did not have to be constantly tended. (One of the conventions of the earlier theatre to which audiences had become accustomed was the black-clad figure of the "wick boy" who moved about the stage trimming smoking wicks whenever necessary throughout the performances.) Improvements in gas burners in the years following its introduction brought stronger light to the stage and in the 1880's an incandescent mantle made the light even brighter and whiter. An added benefit came with the use of gas: now the lights in the auditorium could be dimmed during the performance.

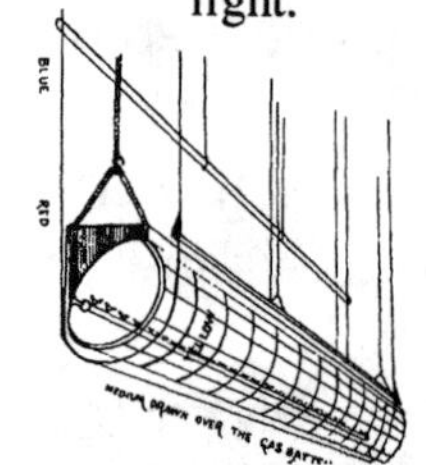
Gas batten lights with silk color media

Gas wing lights with wire cannisters to protect from flame

By 1840, another source of illumination for the stage had been introduced, the **lime-light**. Invented by Thomas Drummond in 1816, the lime-light made use of a cylinder of lime against which the flame from combined hydrogen and oxygen gasses was directed. Heated, the lime gave off a brilliant, yellowish beam of light which could be directed with the use of a reflector and lens. First used in the theatre in 1837, it was adopted by the 1850's primarily for special effects such as sunlight or moonlight. It was not long, however, before stars began requiring the use of the lime-light as a follow-spot. Because of the color of its light, it was complimentary to the human complexion. Well after the introduction of electricity to the theatre in 1881 the lime-light was still in use. The great English actor Sir Henry Irving brought his own set of lime-lights with him to the United States when he toured here in the 1890s. This required one railway box-car loaded with tanks of gas. Unfortunately, the lime-light was extremely expensive to use since it required constant attendance for each instrument to keep the flame in correct alignment with the lime. The expense and

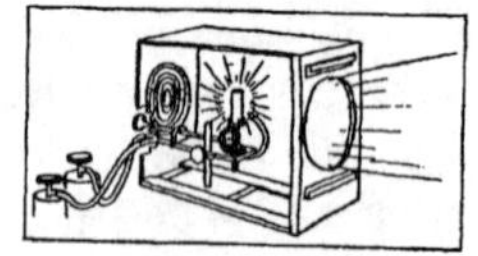
Limelight

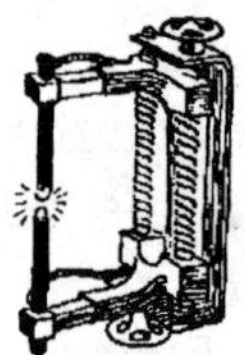
Carbon Arc

inconvenience of operating the lime-light brought about that instrument's demise about the time of World War I.

Edison's Incandescent Lamp

In addition to gas and the lime-light, another source of illumination was introduced to the theatre in the 1840s. This was the carbon arc spot light. The carbon arc, which gives light as a result of a spark of electricity leaping a small gap between two rods of carbon, was first demonstrated in 1808 by Sir Humphrey Davies. Due to a lack of a satisfactory source of power for this instrument, however, it was not introduced to the theatre until the 1840s when it "played the role" of the sun in an opera by Meyerbere at the Paris Opera House. It remained in use in the theatre, primarily as a follow-spot, until the 1980s when it was replaced by the more powerful xenon lamp. For many years, however, actors opted for the lime-light, the light from the carbon arc being harsh and unflattering.

Combination gas and electric control board at Proctor and Turner's Theatre in New York City in about 1895.

By the mid 1800s, therefore, the theatre had at its disposal lights which could be controlled in intensity, focus, and to some degree color. However, all of these light sources carried one constant danger with them–fire. The average life-span for a theatre during this time was no more than ten years. In addition to fire, there was the constant danger that the gas jets might not relight once the gas had been turned off, but would release a toxic flow of gas into the theatre. If audiences were not asphyxiated, as some were, by the gas, explosions could easily occur, and some did, when attempts were made to relight the instruments.

In 1879, Thomas Edison in the United States and J. W. Swan in England developed the first incandescent lamps or light bulbs. These lamps, making use of carbon filaments, gave off a brighter light than that of the gas jets. They were also considerably safer. On December 26, 1881, audiences attended performances of the Gilbert and Sullivan operetta *Patience* at the first theatre to be fully illuminated by the incandescent lamp–the Savoy Opera House in London. In a dramatic presentation, D'Oyly Carte, the manager and owner of the Savoy, went before the audience to explain the safety of the new lighting device. *The London Times* reported as follows:

> The comparative safety of the new system was pointed out to the audience by Mr. D'Oyly Carte. . . who enveloped one of the lamps in a piece of highly inflammable muslin. On the glass being broken and the vacuum destroyed, the flame was immediately extinguished without even singeing the muslin.

The London Daily News exulted with the following commentary:

> A herd of wild elephants suddenly turned loose among the intricate details of the fine

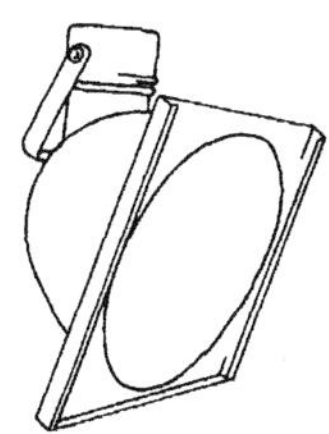

Flood Light

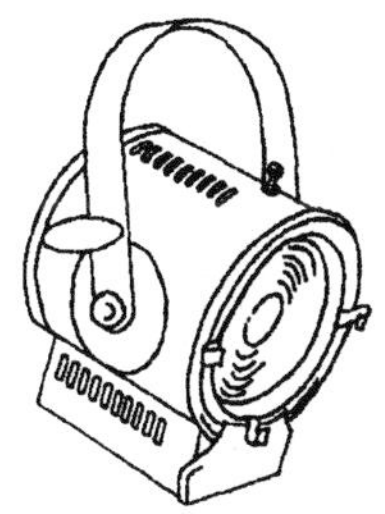

Fresnel Spot Light

woodland scene of the second act of *Patience* might trample down "ground rows" and literally destroy whole "battens" and hanging "wing-lights" scattering literally hundreds of lamps among the wreck of inflammable canvas and frail woodwork, but be assured, they could not set fire to the Savoy stage while lighted, as it will be tonight, only by this means.

Since the use of electricity was so new and the source of power supply not always dependable, as a precaution the Savoy was also "tubed" for gas. This was common practice for the next twenty years.

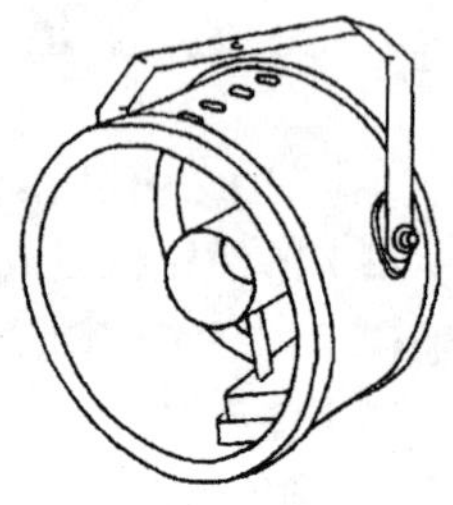

Beam Light

With the introduction of the incandescent lamp in London and the following year at Boston's Bijou theatre, theatres throughout the world began making use of the new lighting techniques. By 1900, every major theatre in every major city was illuminated in this manner though theatres in outlying and rural areas continued to use gas into the 1920s.

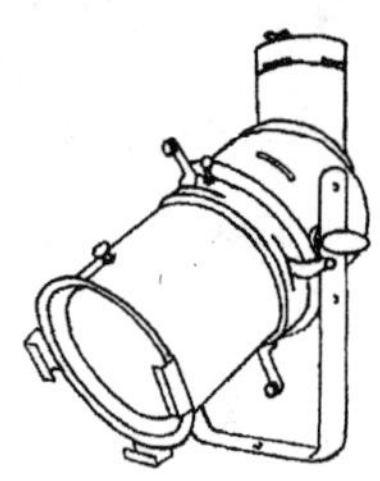

Elipsoidal Spot Light

During the first decade of the 20th century, major improvements were made in the instrumentation for lighting the stage. Incandescent lamps could be housed within box-like instruments and, with the addition of a lens and reflector, could be aimed wherever light was needed. The intensity of the light could be controlled by adjusting the amount of electricity going to the instrument. The color of the light could be controlled either by dipping the lamp in a clear color lacquer substance, or by placing a sheet of colored gelatin, called **gel**, in front of the instrument.

The incandescent lamp and the instruments developed for it now provided the theatre with potential control over the three main elements of stage lighting: intensity, direction, and color.

Scientific American 1896

Light board at the Paris Opera House, early 20th century. Note the control board at bottom left, the prompter in his box on the right, and the performers on stage.

Lighting the Stage

Even before the advent of electricity and the incandescent lamp, lighting designers divided their lighting into two elements: **general** stage lighting and **specific** stage lighting. General lighting was achieved through the use of instruments that more or less flooded the stage with light such as foot lights, strips of lights, and flood lights. These instruments were more or less non-directional providing only general illumination for the entire stage. They did achieve one of the primary objectives of stage lighting–allowing the actor and the action of the play to be seen by the audience. Specific lighting was achieved through the use of a variety of spot lights which could selectively emphasize various areas of the stage. Since World War II, much of our stage lighting has been in the category of the specific. Rarely now do lighting designers use strip, flood or foot lights, preferring to have the greater control the use of spot lights provides.

In an early text on stage lighting by Samuel Selden and Hunton D. Sellman, the authors discuss in detail the specific functions of light for the stage. The authors narrow their list to five major functions which are as follows:

Functions of Stage Lighting

Selective visibility: Just as the director arranges the stage picture in such a way as to force the eye of the audience to focus on the most important actions and reactions, so does the lighting designer. He achieves this by selectively lighting the stage, contrasting light against dark, shadow against light. Though all of the stage will normally be in view, the intensity of light on various areas of the stage will vary according to the needs of the scenes and the specific center of action. If done subtly, the effect will appear to be natural to the audience even though its attention is being guided by the lighting design. More obvious is the use of the follow-spot which singles out a specific actor.

An example of "selective visibility" in the Stephen F. Austin State University production of *The Dresser.* Here, lighting designer Kevin Seime has concentrated the light on the action of the play thereby focusing the audience's attention on the principal actors, others and the sets being left in relative darkness.

Revelation of form: Modern lighting is used to accent the three-dimensional attributes of the stage, the various items, and the individuals on it. Through the judicious placement of lighting instruments, a careful choice of colors, the angles of the light beams, and a variety of intensities, the stage and the actors can be modeled. This becomes an important element in the total design of the stage picture and is usually accomplished through the careful coordination of efforts between the lighting and the set designer. With modern equipment, such modeling can be altered throughout the course of the performance, accenting the action as it moves from one area of the stage to another and contributing to the overall mood created by the total stage picture. The revelation of form becomes a prime objective for the lighting

From the author's collection.

The murder of Caesar from *Julius Caesar.* Note the use of light to complement the set design while yet focusing attention on the action. In this case, the actors silhouetted in the foreground become a part of the overall scenic design. The production was staged at Stanford University under the direction of A. N. Vardac with sets by Wendell Cole and Lighting by O. G. Brockett and W. K. Waters.

designer working with the dance. In this case, the three-dimensional dancer's body must be revealed if the performance is to be fully effective.

Psychological mood: The intensity, color, and directional quality of light can aid in establishing the mood of the play and can have a psychological impact on the viewing audience. Comedy, for instance, often requires bright, warm lighting. The colors used often are predominantly the warm tones such as ambers and pinks. Tragedy, on the other hand, often depends on "moody" lighting. For this dramatic form, strong contrasts of light and dark areas are often appropriate. Often cool colors predominate, i.e., blues and greens. Whereas lighting designers often try to keep the angle of the light at about 45 degrees, greater angles may produce more dramatic effects.

A stagehand operates a keyboard switch device to create the illusion of fireflies flitting through tall grass for a 19th century presentation. One of many attempts to create the illusion of nature through stage lighting.

Illusion of nature: Often the lighting designer is required to suggest actual natural lighting effects to the audience. Moonlight filtering through a window, a sunrise or sunset, the light from a fireplace or lamp, stars in the sky, the glow from a television set, illuminated windows in a building at night, etc., are but a few of the effects he may be expected to create. If the play has a realistic interior setting, he will be required to study the arrangement of the set and design the lights to complement the placement of lamps and windows. If the play has a realistic exterior, the designer will be required to imitate the natural lighting provided by the sun, moon, streetlamps, etc. In such cases, the designer must adapt himself to the style of the production so that his lighting is consistent with it. If he does not, he will defy the conventions and destroy the believability of the production.

Symbolism: In certain productions, the lighting may be used symbolically. This is often done through the choice of colors made, the angles chosen for the light beams, and symbolic projections. The angle of the light beam can produce a symbolic illusion of the psychological condition of the characters. Colors can readily be chosen for their symbolic meanings such as red for blood or death, purple for royalty, green for envy, etc. Projections of symbolic patterns on the set may also communicate abstract concepts to an audience and contribute to the communication of the production's ideas. The effects are particularly important if the scene is non-realistic. An attempt to combine symbolic lighting with lighting designed to reproduce that of nature, however, can often be confusing to the audience.

The Lighting Designer

The lighting designer needs a broad artistic background with a thorough understanding of composition, shading, and color as well as an understanding of the play, its meaning, and the action within it. He needs to have a firm understanding of the psychological effect of light and color on the audience and how those elements may be employed to further enhance the interpretation of the play. From a technical standpoint, the lighting designer must have an understanding of electricity and its properties, of lighting instrumentation, of colors and color media, and of control systems including computers.

As a designer for a particular production, the lighting designer's responsibility is to understand the play itself and the interpretation of the play as decided upon by the director and the total artistic staff. In order to achieve this, he will not only study the play and its obvious requirements, but will also study the set design and the theatre in which the performance will take place so that he can use the facilities as effectively and efficiently as possible to complement the stage arrangements envisioned by the scenic designer and the director. In conjunction with this, he will often attend rehearsals to note entrances and exits, areas of the stage as they are being used by the actors, scenes requiring specific lighting shifts, mood changes the director and actors are attempting to achieve, and verbal cues related to the lighting of the stage. For each scene, he will attempt to create a design which will emphasize the time of day, the locale, necessary shifts of focus, and the mood for the audience. Of major importance will be the rhythm of the play which the director and actors are trying to establish, for the planning and timing of the lighting cues will either complement or destroy these when the play is in performance.

In working with all these elements, the lighting designer attempts to coordinate his design with other members of the artistic staff. He will check colors with both the scenic designer and the costumer to make sure that the gels he uses to tone the lights complement both the set and the costumes as well as the actors' complexions. The colors also will help to establish the locale of the action and will have a direct psychological, if not symbolic, effect on the audience.

Having accomplished the above, the designer is ready to lay out his light **plot**. Here he enters the actual design phase. At this time he carefully chooses each instrument he will need, plans its placement for optimum effect, and chooses the color of gel which he will use. He will plan how the instruments are to be controlled, whether singly or in groups. Usually, he will divide the stage in overlapping areas so that he can emphasize different parts of the stage at different times during the performance. Added to these areas, he will include any specific **specials**, that is, special effects or limited areas used for a particular scene or action, that will be needed. This done, he will supervise the **hanging** of the lights making sure that each instrument is focused to cover the area for which it is designated.

After the lights have been hung, plugged into their dimmer circuits, and focused precisely, the designer begins writing cues for the light board operator. The cues indicate which of the instruments are to be used at what times and at what intensity. They also indicate the speed at which light changes are required to occur. The writing of the cues completed, the cues are then refined during rehearsals with the actors and sets on stage. At this point fine adjustments in light balance can be made and the timing can be set with greater accuracy.

Though the primary function of the lighting designer is to make sure that the actors can be seen, just as important is the artistry with which he carries out his responsibilities. His contribution can bring the set to life, focus the attention of the audience on particular actors, create the mood and feeling of the play, establish the locale and time of the action, and support the rhythm of the play through the cueing of the light shifts.

Theatre Arts Prints, 1935

Noel Coward's *Cavalcade*(1931). The production made use of space staging with the lighting not only iluminating the actors, but providing an important element in the design.

Theatre Arts Prints, 1935

(Above and below) Two scenes from the Seattle Repertory Playhouse production of Henrik Ibsen's panoramic epic *Peer Gynt*. The production made use of a platform unit setting with major changes of emphasis and design provided by the lighting.

Theatre Arts Prints, 1935

Class Assignment
Theatre Appreciation

Name______________________

From a play assigned by your instructor, discuss briefly the use of lighting to accomplish each of the five **functions of stage lighting.**

1. **Selective Visibility**: In a scene you select, indicate where the emphasis should be placed through lighting the scene.

2. **Revelation of Form**: Are there any elements within a specific scene which would benefit through emphasizing their three-dimensional shapes? If so, what are they?

3. **Psychological mood**: Choosing a specific scene, what is the mood the playwright is attempting to achieve? How can lighting (through direction of color) assist in achieving this.

4. **Symbolism**: What colors or selected directions of lights may be used to symbolize the ideas of the play in a specific scene?

5. **Illusion of nature**: Are there any motivated light cues to be found in the play which come from natural or man-made lighting sources? If so, what are they?

Remove from text to hand in to instructor.

21
Makeup

Theatrical makeup can . . ., as an integral art of the characterization, illuminate the character for the actor as well as for the audience and provide the actor with an extraordinarily effective means of projecting a subtle and striking character portrait.

Makeup does not create a character; it only helps to reveal it. No makeup is complete without an actor underneath. And a makeup which is conceived as a work of art in itself, unrelated to a specific performance, no matter how brilliant the execution may be, is worse than useless–it can destroy the actor's characterization.

Richard Corson

Background

Certainly for the Greek and Roman actor makeup was of little interest, for during those classical periods the actors wore masks which would be replaced only much later by the made-up actor's face. The masks worn by the devil and demon characters in medieval plays served a similar purpose. The same may be said to be true for the Commedia dell'Arte actors who also wore at least half-masks. The young lovers in the Commedia troupe, however, probably did use makeup, but only for the purpose of accenting their natural appearance. In this case, they were adapting the normal makeup for men and women of their own era. Little reference is made to the use of makeup in the theatre until the latter part of the 18th century when the French actress, Mlle. Clairon, abandoned the use of liquid white on the face which was then customarily applied by "ladies of quality" and went before her public "barefaced." She did say, however, "I am not against giving every assistance to Nature. . .I had remarked in others, that nothing was so injurious to the expression of the features as having pale lips or pale ears. A little art gave them the appearance of florid health: I darkened the color of my eyebrows, as the character I was to perform required; I did the same thing to my hair, with different colored powders; but far from concealing, in the least degree, those features which give animation and expression to the countenance."

Greek & Roman Masks

As the theatre auditoriums grew larger and larger during the 18th and 19th centuries, makeup became an important skill which had to be acquired by the actors. The further the actor was from the audience, the fewer details of the actor's face the audience could see. Without the help of makeup, subtle and even natural facial expressions would be lost. The curl of the lip or the raised eyebrow could no longer be used to communicate a response beyond the footlights. With makeup, however, facial features could be accentuated and communication made possible.

Another factor which brought about the need for makeup was the lighting. The dimness of the candles, oil lamps or gas lights and their lack of directional control was of little help to the actor and of no help at all when the theatres of the 19th century grew to house audiences of between two and three thousand. Though the introduction of the incandescent lamp was of help, it became a hindrance as well. Too much light could actually "bleach-out" the actors' features. The carbon arc follow spot particularly all but flattened the actors' faces, rendering them expressionless in the eyes of the audience. Makeup could help in such situations and was relied upon greatly by most actors.

Makeup, of course, has always been a necessity for actors portraying roles well out of their own age range, sex, race, or basic human characteristics. In some cases, the makeup for particular characters became almost as traditional as did the costumes for those characters. A young man assuming the role of an older character uses makeup to assist in the portrayal, and a beardless youth can acquire age by applying a beard and/or mustache to his face. A male actor playing the role of a woman uses makeup to accent the feminine qualities in his face. An actor assuming the role of a creature other than human, Caliban in *The Tempest,* for instance, relies on makeup to help him project his character.

With the advent of the motion pictures and now television, makeup has become a fertile field for theatre artists. The demands of the camera are such that makeup must be applied with the skill of a portrait artist and, in some cases, that of a sculptor. Though such fine makeup is not required for the stage and, indeed, the actor often does not have time to apply it, the basic techniques used are to be found in all three media. The true makeup artist knows that his job is to apply the right makeup for the eye of the audience, whether that eye be the camera, the man in the first row, the eleventh row, or the back row of the theatre.

Purposes of Makeup

Stage makeup is usually divided into two categories: **straight makeup** and **character makeup.** Straight makeup is makeup which is applied to accentuate the features of the actor so that they may be better seen by the audience. Character makeup is makeup which attempts to alter the natural features of the actor in order to help him appear older, of different racial origin, or to give him facial attributes which he does not possess but which are required by the character, the bulbous nose of Cyrano, for instance.

The first and primary purpose of theatrical makeup is to **help make the features of the actor visible** to the audience. Both lighting and distance, as indicated above, can "wash" out an actor's features to such an extent that his expressions may not be apparent. By emphasizing the facial features, that is the face's bone structure, the eyes, and the lips, the makeup artist can assist the actor as he attempts to convey the ideas, responses, and feelings of his character. It is **not** the purpose of makeup to make the actor beautiful unless the character is supposed to be physically attractive. It **is** the purpose of makeup to assist the actor in communicating with the audience.

As master makeup artist Richard Corson states in the quotation at the beginning of this chapter, the overriding purpose of makeup is to aid in **visually establishing the character** the actor is portraying. Makeup alone cannot accomplish this, but it can contribute to the actor's efforts to appear as the character before the audience.

Makeup is also important in helping to establish the **style and mood** of the play. Though it may contribute little to the realistic play, it assumes major importance in stylized presentations in which the actor must represent a non-realistic interpretation of life. Characters in expressionistic plays, for instance, often become representatives of human types and lose their human individuality. In some cases, actors are asked to play roles outside of the normal human condition such as animals, robots, aliens, etc. For any of these, makeup becomes extremely important.

Makeup is sometimes used by the actor to assist him in **visualizing himself as the character**. Lawrence Olivier, one of the greatest of the twentieth century British actors, has claimed that he does not truly know his character until he has developed the character's "looks;" that is, the curl of a lip, the furrowed brow, the twist of an eyebrow, the conformation of the nose.

Though makeup can assist the actor in his visual portrayal of a character, it is no substitute for the actor's ability to imbue himself psychologically and intellectually with the character's attributes. In fact, many actors are so accomplished that they can portray a character convincingly without elaborate makeup. Jose Ferrer, playing the role of Cyrano de Bergerac, absentmindedly forgot to apply his "Cyrano nose" for one of his performances. So convincing was his portrayal of the character that neither the audience nor his fellow actors noticed the mistake. In the 1920's, John Barrymore was able to portray both Dr. Jekyll and Mr. Hyde believably with no change in makeup at all.

The Makeup Artist

For centuries, actors have been responsible for their own makeup in the live theatre. The ability to design and apply makeup is normally considered one of the skills which must be acquired by every aspiring actor. In some cases, however, the style of the production or the complexity of the makeup require that a specialist, **the makeup artist,** be employed to design the makeup and instruct the actors in its application. It becomes the responsibility of this artist to design the makeup for the entire cast in a play so that a consistency will exist in the style of makeup used. Usually, the makeup artist also serves as a teacher, training the individual actors in the application of the makeup. In the motion pictures and television, actors usually are made-up by professional makeup artists since the camera is very unforgiving and requires a delicacy of precision in the application of makeup that the actor can rarely achieve on his own.

The makeup artist works like a portrait painter might work in altering the features of his subject. The actor's face becomes the canvas and the makeup the paint. Often, the artist must transform the actor's face by changing its basic shape or conformation. He therefore brings into play the skills of a sculptor as he creates **prostheses** which may be added to the actor's features. One of the major challenges lies not only in creating an appearance which is appropriate to the character, but one which will be flexible enough to allow the actor to change expression at will.

As are the other designers, the makeup artist is but one member of the design team. He must therefore coordinate his efforts with the total concept and style of the production. His makeup and the colors chosen for it must be designed in such a way that it works under the lighting which will be used. Any exaggerations or designs which move away from reality must be viewed in context with the total production concept so that all elements will work in harmony.

The Actor/Makeup Artist at Work

William Dills was a stock company character comedian during the first decade of this century. As such he appeared in a wide variety of roles, many of them stereotypes for which he developed basic makeup designs. Here are examples of his makeup artistry.

As the Yorkshire Man

William Dills as himself

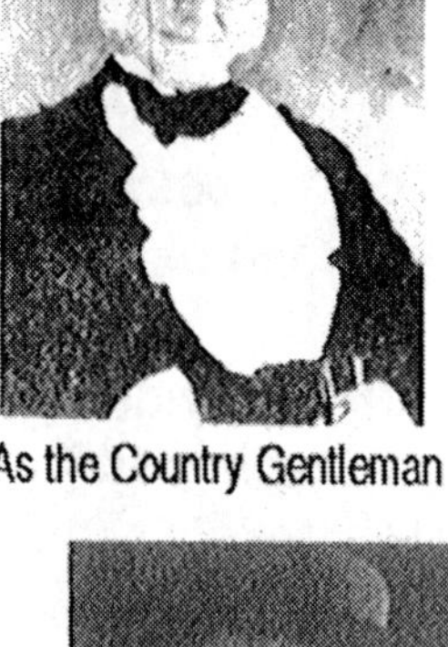

As the Country Gentleman

As the "Piccadilly Dude"

As the Chinaman

As a Country Bumpkin

As the stereotypical African-American

As Another Country Bumpkin

Reprinted from the author's collection

22
Sound

Background

Sound in the theatre may be divided into two categories, sound effects and music. The latter is perhaps the oldest and most consistently used sound in addition to the actors' voices still in use. We know from historic documents that in the Greek theatre the playwright engaged a musician to compose and perform a score for his plays. We also know that there was extensive use of music in the Roman theatre, particularly for the mimes. The medieval theatre is said to find its roots in the antiphonal chants sung during the rituals performed in European cathedrals. Provision was made in the architecture of the Elizabethan theatre for a "musician's chamber" on the third level above the apron of the stage. Etchings of productions of Moliere's plays as performed before Louis XIV show an orchestra, and we know that several of Moliere's plays had incidental music composed by the court composer Jean Baptiste Lully. The very word melodrama comes from the French and means a "play with music" such as those performed in Paris in the 19th century with scores written by many of the leading composers of the day. Such performances also took place throughout England, Europe and the United States as well.

The history of sound effects, however, is more clouded than is the history of the use of music in the theatre. Very little is said concerning them during the Greek and Roman periods. During the Renaissance, however, some theatre architect/designers do indicate that a variety of devices were used to create the sound needs for an illusion of reality during performances. On the top level of the Elizabethan theatre there was a special room set aside for creating the sound of rain and thunder. Cannons were sometimes shot from the roof of the theatre in order to provide the illusion of battle. Indeed, it is said that Shakespeare's theatre, the Globe, burned down as a result of such an effort when a spark from the gun-powder used fell onto the theatre's thatched roof, smoldered there, and finally set the theatre on fire. In Sweden's Drottningholm Court Theatre, built in 1745, there is still an operating thunder and rain machine lodged in the theatre's attic.

With the advent of recorded sound in the early part of the 20th century, an attempt was made to record actual sounds. Unfortunately, there was no way at that time to adequately amplify the recordings nor were the recordings accurate. Improvements during the 1930s and 40s, as well as experiments in the development of sound effects for radio, brought a major change to the theatre. By the 1950s, fairly accurate recorded sounds could be used with controllable amplification. Since these sounds were available on records and could be easily secured and stored, they became an important resource for the theatre. Cueing them, however, required a precision that sound operators could not always master. The result was that many technicians resorted to tried and true manual ways of creating the desired effects. (See page 172) With the development of tape recorders in the late 1950s, cueing could be much more precise. Tape is still the preferred method of handling sound effects with certain exceptions, though computer digitized sound effects are becoming somewhat more common. Such sounds as doorbells, telephone bells, knocking, gun shots, and others are normally created live in the theatre today.

Music and the Theatre

In addition to creating realistic or symbolic sound effects for a particular production, it is often the responsibility of the sound designer to choose, record, and arrange music. In some cases, particularly for professional productions, original scores are commissioned and composed. This, of course, is ideal providing the composer is aware of and understands the requirements of the play as it is being interpreted in the particular production for which he is writing. The expense of the original composition and the musicians to perform it often makes this unfeasible in non-profit operations. As a result, such productions usually rely heavily on pre-recorded music drawn from recordings readily available.

Music in the theatre often serves one or more of the following functions:

1. **Music establishes a specific era, time, or locale**: Just as sound effects rely upon the audience's familiarity with particular sounds to achieve their purpose, music may also rely on the audience's familiarity with musical styles and compositions. The sound of a "honky-tonk" piano suggests a western barroom in the late 1800s; the sounds of the lute and recorder suggest the Elizabethan period; sounds of nature included in a musical composition may establish a country or outdoor setting; martial music may suggest to the audience marching armies; particular melodies traditionally related to specific ethnic groups may establish both a period and a locale, and Christmas carols or other appropriate selections may be used to indicate time. Here the sound designer relies not only on his knowledge of the history of music but also on the instruments used in various periods and countries.

2. **Music establishes a specific mood for a play**: Music appeals primarily to an audience's emotions. Its rhythm, pace and harmony produce marked psychological responses within an audience. It is necessary, therefore, for the sound designer to have a thorough understanding of the play and its requirements so that the music chosen complements the mood the director and actors are attempting to establish.

3. **Music establishes a tempo and pace:** As discussed in Chapter VIII, each play has its own rhythm which dominates the characters and affects the responses of the audience. The music chosen to introduce scenes or underscore them is also chosen to establish and reinforce the overall rhythm of the play.

4. **Music may be required to fulfill the demands of the playwright:** In some plays, the playwrights refer to specific selections of music, often songs or pieces which trigger specific plot actions. For instance, in *Blithe Spirit* Noel Coward asks that the Irving Berlin song "Always" be played on the phonograph on stage at certain times by the characters. The song is used to provoke the appearance of the ghost of the protagonist's dead wife and lead the story forward.

5. **Music may be used to <u>point</u> certain actions of characters or to prepare the audience for upcoming events**: Though not used in live theatre to any great extent, occasionally music is chosen to identify characters and may be used in relation to their action or their entrances. This may be seen particularly in the motion pictures, the "Jaws Theme" for instance, which signals the imminent appearance of the shark.

6. **Music may be used to underscore dramatic action**: On occasion it is chosen to reinforce

the mood and drama of a specific segment of a play. In realistic productions, however, the introduction of music for this purpose often defeats the illusion of reality that the director and actors and have been attempting to create. If it does and if it calls attention to itself and away from the action of the play itself, it is counterproductive. Music which is unmotivated can detract from a play in the same way as unmotivated movements, light cues, and other elements. Unlike the motion pictures, which are a mechanical means of reproducing life, the introduction of music to underscore a live-action performance can often seem unrealistic unless the style of the production has been carefully developed to allow for the use of an outside source of sound, in this case music, to be introduced.

7. Music may be used to provide a brief, relaxing respite for the audience between scenes or acts: For many years, professional theatres boasted the presence of "house orchestras" which provided musical accompaniment for the melodramas and a variety of musical selections during the intermissions between acts of plays. This practice has been largely abandoned, for many feel that such use of music may well distract the audience from the mood of the play itself. Stanislavski, in fact, banned the orchestras from the Moscow Art Theatre for this very reason. If music is used between acts of plays, it is chosen carefully to complement the play in some way.

Sound Effects

Sound effects are normally required by the script to aid in the telling of the story. If so, they are carefully chosen from recordings or created live and cued precisely to the action of the play and the actors' lines. Used judiciously, they provide an added depth to the total impact of the play on the audience and may, in fact, allow the play to be told on several levels. Actions taking place off stage may be represented by the proper sound effects, thus allowing the audience to be aware of such actions as well as those of the actors on stage. Actions on stage may be triggered by specific sound effects such as the chiming of a clock, a doorbell or telephone. In such a case as this, the timing of the cue is crucial, for the very progress of the play may be thrown into disarray if the effect is either early or late. In the case of sound effects, the source of the amplified sound becomes highly important to the believability of the performance, therefore sound designers normally provide a variety of speakers placed in different locations on and back stage so that directional sound may be used.

Amplification of Actors

In certain circumstances, particularly musicals, the sound designer will also be responsible for amplifying the voices of the performers. With current technology, it is now possible to secrete a microphone on each actor/singer. The sound designer can then not only support the voices through amplification but can adjust the volume for each performer in relation to the others on stage, thus compensating for the vocal quality and power of the performer to some extent. This practice is of great importance to the performer who may have to act and sing a role as many as eight times a week. Since all these voices are often fed into the same speakers, however, there are problems for the audience in that, unless the production has been carefully mounted, the identity of the speaker at a particular moment may not be readily evident. Only in rare cases are actors' voices artificially amplified in plays.

The importance of the sound designer is readily evident when one considers the impact sound has on a performance. The judicious choice of both music and effects, careful use of amplification, and precise cueing can enhance the mood, style, atmosphere, and final impact of a production.

Mechanical (Hand Operated) Sound Effects

(a) Wind machine - canvas stretched over wooden drum. (b) Rain - shot in wooden drum. (c) Rain - shot in tray with wire screen (d) Thunder sheet - sheet metal. (e) Rumble cart. (f) Falling rubble after an explosion. (g) Wood crash. (h) Gun shots. (i) Slap stick. (j) Horses hoofs - cocoanut shells.

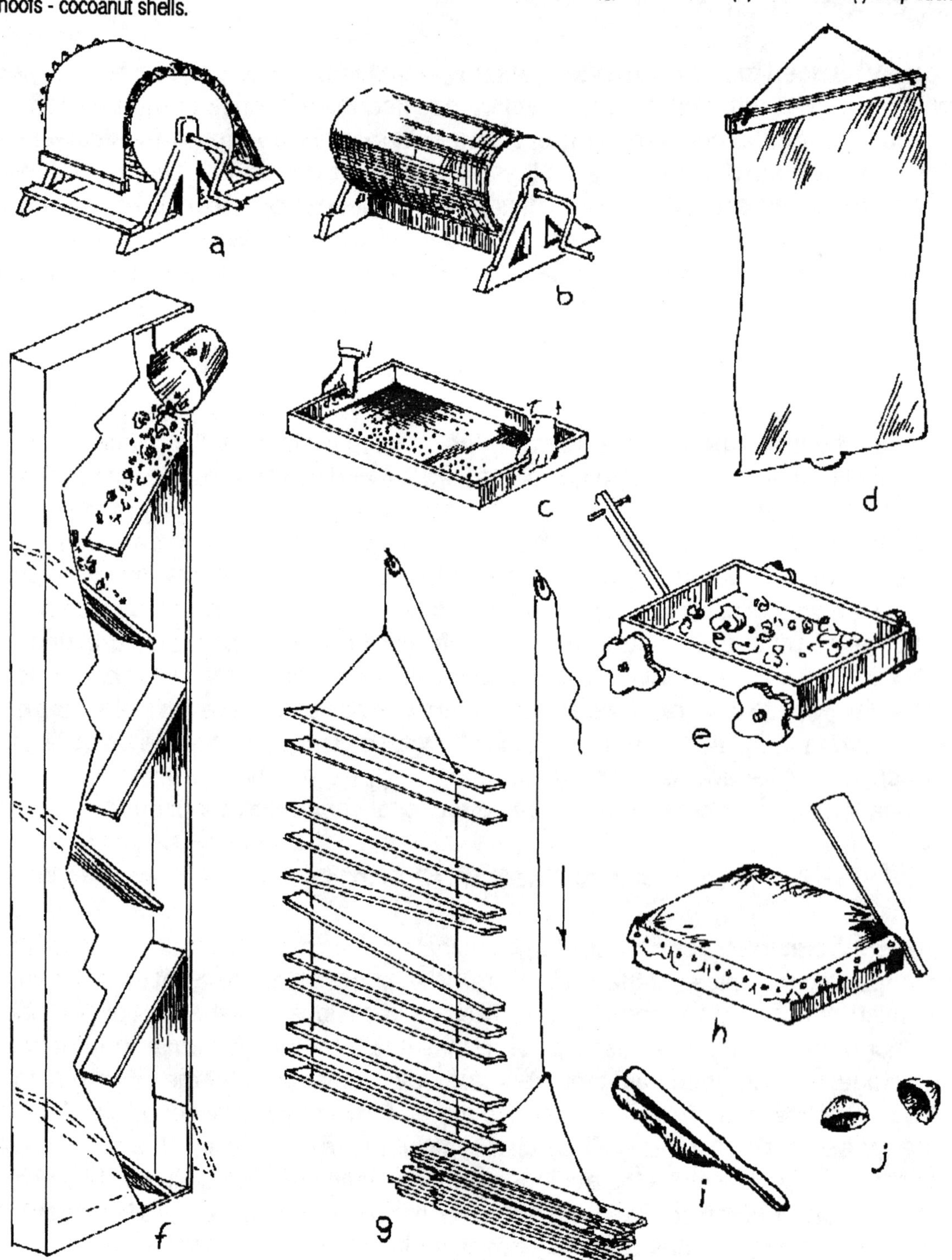

From W. Oren Parker and Harvey K. Smith, *Scene Design and Stage Lighting* Holt, Rinehart and Winston, 1963.

23
Putting It All Together

At this point, we have discussed the play as it may appear in its various forms and the various artists involved with its creation as a living piece of theatre. Though implied throughout, we haven't discussed the **process** by which the play comes into being as a living, vibrant creation.

Discussing a process is always a difficult undertaking, for by dryly outlining a series of occurrences as they take place from the beginning to the presentation of the finished piece, the performance, one can often remove the magic from the actual artistic endeavor. And there is a magic if all involved do their jobs with skill, discipline, and enthusiasm. A well-produced play with well-trained and talented actors, interesting and motivated choreography and stage pictures, appropriate sets and costumes, and a receptive audience will create a world of its own into which all concerned will immerse themselves for, perhaps, several hours. It does not matter whether the style is realistic, classical, impressionistic, etc. What does matter is that this particular world within which the characters find themselves becomes equally a world in which the audience is a part.

The preparation of a play begins with the playwright. As indicated in earlier chapters, he may have a particular theme he wishes to investigate, he may have a story to tell, and he may have characters he wishes to reveal. Probably all of these elements form the motivation behind the writing of the script. His source may come from myths and the history of the past, from observations of the actions of those around him, or from his own personal experiences. In any case, the manner and way in which he structures his play, reveals his characters, and resolves the situations in which they find themselves will be influenced by his attitude toward life and the world about him. His play, therefore, becomes a metaphor for life and the human condition as he sees it. From these elements, he develops a script which will form the basis for the efforts of all the others involved in placing the play on the stage.

Once the play has been chosen, it is placed in the hands of the artistic production team: the director and the set, lighting, costume, makeup and sound designers. By studying the script, each details the challenges found within it. The director then calls the first of several production meetings to discuss the play and share with the other members of the artistic team his **concept** regarding it. The concept usually includes a statement of what the playwright is attempting to say; that is, the theme, and how best this may be revealed to the audience. Each member of the production team shares his concept with the others. Finally, the various approaches to the play are melded to form one primary concept to which all will dedicate their efforts. If there are disagreements, the director acts as mediator; and, in the final analysis, the director makes the choices and chooses the direction the entire team will take in preparing to mount the play.

This first meeting of the production team is the most important, for during it the approach and style of the production will be determined. The result of the meeting forms, therefore, the basis for future decisions relating to all aspects of the production. It is here that the theme of the play is focused upon. At this time, the style of the production is established and guidelines for all on the artistic team are delineated. This does not mean that changes cannot be made, but such changes are carefully considered so that all elements of the production remain consistent to the central concept.

Additional meetings prior to the beginning of the rehearsal period deal with the realization of the agreed upon concept in more detail. The designer brings his designs to the meeting for comments, suggestions and approval. Often he will have developed them based on a **ground plan** provided by the director. In some cases, he will offer a variety of suggested ground plans from which the director can choose. Only when the ground plan and the basic arrangement of the scenery has been agreed upon can the actual rehearsals of the play begin, because only then will the director know the space in which he will place and move the actors. The costume designer will also present **renderings** or pictures of the costumes for the director's considerations. Some of the costumes may influence the actors' movements or the design of the set. (For a play set in the 18th century or mid-19th century, for instance, the use of large skirts with hoops or other supports may require doorways larger than normal. Helmets, hats, wigs, and footwear which increase the height of the actor will require scenery that makes adequate allowance for such accessories.)

From H. D. Albright and Lee Mitchell, *Principles of Theatre Art*, 1968

Above is a sample ground plan. Drawn to scale, this shows the arrangement of the setting on the stage. Platforms are indicated by their height. It is through using this that the director can begin his preliminary blocking of the play. When rehearsals begin, this plan is taped out on the rehearsal floor at actual size. Below is a perspective sketch of the set evolving from the above ground plan.

Casting the Play

Choosing the actors to appear in the production is normally the responsibility of the director. As indicated in Chapter 14, this is often influenced by the producer in the professional theatre. In educational and community theatre, this may also be affected if a guest artist has been employed to appear. For the director, casting decisions are probably the most important he will make. As one director stated, "I find my main job as a director is to compensate for the mistakes I have made in the casting." Though the talent of the actor is normally of primary importance, there are other elements which the director must consider:

Appearance

This includes sex, height, weight, race, carriage, etc. The character's first impression on an audience results from his appearance. The director will also want to have actors of contrasting physical qualities to assist the audience in readily remembering and identifying each character.

Voice

This includes vocal range and quality. As with physical appearance, the director seeks to have a range of voices within his cast. This also assists the audience in recognizing a character and may help to reveal the character's personality.

Personality

As much as one would like to assume that an actor can totally sublimate his personality to that which is required by the role, this is rarely the case. Generally, the actor selects an aspect of his personality which complements the role and emphasizes that in his performance.

Skills

If the character the actor is to play is required to demonstrate specific skills, this must be taken into account by the director when the cast is being chosen. For instance, does the character need to speak in a dialect or language other than his own; does the character need a knowledge of dance–tap, ballet, modern dance, etc.; does the character need to sing or play a musical instrument; does the character need to fence, box, be an expert in martial arts?

Finally, the director attempts to place on stage a cast of contrasting actors who not only complement the roles to which they are assigned, but complement each other.

In some cases, particularly in the professional theatre and certainly in the motion pictures and television, the director is assisted by a Casting Director, whose primary responsibility is to search out the actors most appropriate for each role and bring them to the director's attention.

The Rehearsal Period

The organization of rehearsals, their length, and the number of rehearsals varies considerably from play to play and from production unit to production unit. In the professional theatre, a rehearsal period of three weeks for a play followed by several "tryout" or "preview" performances is often the norm. Musicals normally require more time. In some cases, the rehearsal and preview period may extend over several months. When Sammy Davis, Jr., appeared in a musical version of Clifford Odets' play *Golden Boy*, over seven months were devoted to rehearsals and preview performances as the script was both rewritten and redirected several times. This is rare, however, for the expense of such an extended period of preparation would make the initial production cost prohibitive in all but the most unusual cases. New scripts will require more time in rehearsal than will established scripts, for it is during the rehearsal period that the playwright, director and actors spend many hours reworking the original script. (An untried manuscript is rarely totally stageworthy and often requires extensive rewriting.)

In the educational theatre, the rehearsal period is often determined as much by the school calendar as it is by the needs of the play or musical. Normally, four to four and a half weeks are devoted to the preparation of a production. The scheduling of daily rehearsal time is also heavily influenced by the academic calendar since the actors are also students and must maintain their class attendance and prepare homework assignments as well as rehearse the play and build the sets and costumes. Whereas professional actors may devote as many as eight hours a day in actual rehearsal, a student-actor often cannot afford more than three or four hours a day. The hours indicated for both professional and amateur actors do not include preparation time for rehearsals during which the actors must learn their lines, attend costume fittings, make promotional appearances, etc.

Community theatres face many of the same time-limit problems as those found in educational theatre. Actors in community theatres are also part-time actors who work full-time to earn a living. They have family responsibilities and other community activities which place demands on their time and energy.

Generally the total rehearsal period may be divided into three blocks:

1. The introductory and blocking rehearsals
2. Review and refinement rehearsals
3. Final polishing rehearsals in which all elements are joined

At the first rehearsal, the director discusses the agreed-upon concept for the production and how it relates to the actors and their interpretations of their roles. Usually this also includes a read-through of the entire play during which the director will comment on the play, its background and meaning. This is followed by a series of blocking rehearsals during which the actors learn their movements and positions on stage for each scene. It should be noted that no two directors work in exactly the same way. What are being outlined here are the usual steps taken during the overall rehearsal period.

Once the play has been blocked, a series of reviews are conducted in an effort to refine the actions and motivations for each actor singly and in conjunction with others. Line readings are carefully worked so that the proper interpretations may be given throughout the play. During this period, the actors work to "get off book;" that is, memorize their lines so thoroughly that the lines become a part of them and their character. Actors often work in substitute costumes and use substitute properties during these rehearsals. Toward the end of this period, great care is taken to develop the rhythm and timing within each scene and the play as a whole.

The third part of the rehearsal period is devoted to combining all the elements. By now the sets and properties, though probably not complete, are at least partially usable. Any costume pieces or adequate substitutes for them should be available if they will affect the actors' movements and the rhythm of the play. The actual properties the actors will use in performance are normally made available to them.

During the final days of the third block, full technical rehearsals are scheduled in order to set all scene and property shifts, all light cues, costume changes, and sound cues for the production. It is at this time that the designers and technicians, who have been preparing the technical elements of the play, have an opportunity to rehearse them and learn their responsibilities for the performances just as the actors have been doing for the past several weeks. On occasion this group of final rehearsals will be divided allowing the sets and properties to rehearse first, with lights and sound being added next, and finally the costumes. When the costumes join the rest of the technical elements, the preparation of the play is in its final stage. In amateur theatre, at least three full-dress rehearsals, often with makeup as well, are normally scheduled. At this time all elements have been put together and it is now the responsibility of the director and his artistic staff to make sure that each element complements the others and that all carry out the agreed-upon concept.

The final rehearsals are normally closed to individuals having no responsibility with regard to the production. (Earlier rehearsals are usually open by invitation only or through prior arrangement with the director.) One of the dress rehearsals, however, may be used as a "preview" performance for an invited audience. This is occasionally done in order to provide the actors an opportunity to get a "feel" for audience reactions prior to opening night. In the professional theatre, preview performances may be mounted for several weeks if the play is new, for this gives the playwright and director an opportunity to gauge audience response and make such changes as are deemed necessary. This is particularly important if the play is a comedy, for much of the timing of the play is dependent on audience response and the actors' ability to handle it.

Working closely with the director may be a dance and/or fight choreographer depending on the demands of the script. In each case, their work is designed and prepared in such a way as to complement the style of the rest of the production. The choreographers study the script, discover the function of the dances or fights within the plot and design them in such a way as to contribute to the overall story of the play. They also train the actors in the required movements. Both the choreographers and the director are actually teachers as well as creative artists.

The Stage Manager

In the previous paragraphs a great deal of attention has been paid to the activities of the director in relation to the actors. While the director and actors have been occupied in rehearsals, other members of the production team have been hard at work preparing the elements for which they are responsible. Though regular meetings of all the members of the artistic team are held, there are many occasions when additional communication is desirable. It is the job of the stage manager to act as a liaison between the director and his fellow artists. In addition, the stage manager attends all rehearsals making notes of the director's instructions to the actors.

When the rehearsals enter their final block, the stage manager takes on more and more responsibility until, finally, he takes full charge of the rehearsals backstage. With his assistant, he is responsible for seeing that the sets are in place and ready prior to the **opening of the house**, that the lights and sound have been checked to make sure all are working properly, and that any special effects required are ready. He also checks on the actors, warning them about elapsed time before the performance is to begin and generally acts as a trouble-shooter as necessity demands. During the actual rehearsal, he and/or his assistants make sure the actors are in place for entrances and that the technical crew is prepared for upcoming cues. His primary responsibility during the rehearsal, however, is to give cues for all technical effects; that is, scene shifts, lighting changes, and sound effects.

The stage manager fulfills all the above responsibilities during performances. Under performance conditions he is in full charge. The director may attend performances and may give notes to the cast members after performances, but usually he is expected to work through the stage manager who is there to carry out the director's requests (demands?). If a new actor must join the cast, it is the stage manager's job to teach him his blocking and line readings. If a new technician is employed, it is the stage manager's responsibility to train him. Always, though, the stage manager is expected to remain faithful to the original interpretation of the play and the original direction as it has been set. In the professional theatre, the stage-manager has an additional responsibility, for he is the on-site representative of Actors' Equity and must make sure that all of that union's rules and regulations are observed.

The Designers & the Rehearsal Period

Throughout the rehearsal period, the designers have a similar relationship to the technicians as that of the director to the actors.

The Scenic Designer

The scenic designer presents his building plans for the sets and costumes to the technicians who will build them. If he has a technical director, that individual is responsible for supervising the construction of the various elements in strict accordance with the original designs. In some cases the technical director may also serve as draftsman and prepare the building drawings for the stage carpenters and property men. Once the sets have been built, they are turned over to the scene painters who, following the directions of the designer, paint the scenery. Often the designer is present to supervise the mixing of paint so that the colors will accurately meet his specifications. He will usually be present as well to supervise the final texturing of the set.

Once the set has been completed and the theatre is available, the set is moved onto the stage where the performances will take place. At this time, the designer supervises any finishing touches which may be needed. Working with the stage manager, he organizes and rehearses scene and property shifts so that all will go smoothly when the technical rehearsals take place.

The Lighting Designer

The lighting designer, working from ground plans and elevations provided by the scene designer, lays out a **light plot** for the show making provision not only for lighting the actors, but also lighting the set and providing for any needed shifts in lighting. Often, he attends rehearsals of the play to watch actors' movements and find which areas of the stage need to be emphasized at specific times. Working with the stage manager, he develops cues for the entire show which the stage manager enters in his master script; for the stage manager will be responsible for instructing the light board operator concerning the exact time at which each cue should be activated. In the meantime, the lighting designer works closely with the set and costume designers to make sure that the colors he selects for his lights will complement both the set and costumes.

The lighting designer supervises his electricians who hang, focus, and gel the instruments required by the light plot. Once this has been accomplished (usually only after the set has been placed on stage), he works out the individual specifications for each light cue and begins the job of training his chief electrician in the handling of the board. This is done in conjunction with the stage manager and the director and can only be completed when the actors are on stage rehearsing the play.

The Costume Designer

The costume designer, having presented his sketches and material swatches to the director and to the rest of the production team during the early production meetings, proceeds to take the measurements of the actors and to instruct individuals on the costume construction crew in the areas of pattern drafting and construction. If the production is professional, the designer usually has a pattern drafter and cutter as well as experienced seamstresses on staff to assist with this work. The designer also arranges for the purchase of the materials needed for the production and supervises any dyeing required. If the costumes require that the actors adopt period movement, the costume designer often works with the actors and the director in developing the movement skills that will be needed. He may also instruct the actors in the proper handling of period costume props such as fans, snuff boxes, canes, etc.

Often the costume designer will mount a costume parade prior to the first dress rehearsal. This will give him and the director the opportunity to see the costumes under the lights and to make arrangements for any adjustments which they find to be necessary. During the dress rehearsal period, the designer makes notes regarding alterations any costumes may require and any movement problems which arise so that these may be solved prior to the public performances. He also checks on all costume changes required throughout the play and makes arrangements for a wardrobe crew to be on hand to assist with the changes if necessary.

The Makeup Designer

In many cases the costume designer also serves as makeup designer. Whether or not this is the case, the individual charged with the responsibility of creating the makeup provides detailed designs for each actor prior to the dress rehearsal period and instructs the actors in the application of the makeup if necessary. If the makeup is complex, such as that used by the actor playing the Phantom in *Phantom of the Opera,* the designer or a trained assistant is present prior to each performance to assist in its application. As with all other elements of the design, the makeup is created to blend in with the overall style of the production.

The Sound Designer

The sound designer, having studied the script and consulted with the director, uses the rehearsal period to find or create appropriate music and sound effects, keeping in mind the agreed-upon style of the presentation. Once having collected and/or arranged the sound score for the production, the designer proceeds to record it and cue it in such a manner that it may be used most efficiently during the final rehearsals. If certain sound effects are needed earlier in the rehearsal period–music for a dance, for instance–it is his responsibility to provide them. Prior to the beginning of technical rehearsal, the sound designer works with his technicians to prepare the equipment, placing the speakers as required and arranging his amplification equipment for the various cues he will have during the performances. In the final rehearsals, he will work with the director and his technicians to set each sound cue and all sound levels for the production. Just as the rest of the technical support crew rehearses with the actors, so do the sound technicians at this time if not before.

Conclusion

The theatrical performance begins for the audience when a decision is made to attend a specific performance. At that time each audience member unknowingly becomes a participant. Tickets are purchased, plans are made, clothing chosen, all in anticipation of the culmination of a kind of ritual. As the audience members enter the theatre, they are greeted by box office and ticket personnel, given programs, and shown to their seats. Often there is music carefully chosen to prepare them for what is to come. The lights are dimmed, specially selected music played, the theatre goes dark, the curtain rises, and the audience is transported into a new and different world. Whether the play is designed to show man as he can be, is, or should be, the audience becomes involved in the scenes placed before it on the stage and the ideas demonstrated before it. This is the culmination of the effort it has put forth to attend and of the efforts expended by many individuals to place before it situations, ideas, emotions and lives with which it can become involved. If the elements are brought together as they ideally can be, both on stage and in the audience, the final aim of the theatre will be realized–**entertainment**.

"It's good enough for Broadway but not for an 'off-Broadway' production"

Glossary

Above Upstage or away from the audience. A performer crossing above a table keeps it between himself and the front of the stage.

Acting Area One of several areas into which the stage space is divided in order to facilitate blocking and the planning of stage movement.

Ad Lib To improvise lines of a speech, especially in response to an emergency, such as a performer's forgetting his lines or being late for an entrance.

Aesthetic Distance Physical or psychological separation or detachment of the audience from the dramatic action, regarded as necessary in most kinds of theatre in order to preserve illusion.

Antiquarian A student of antiquity.

Antagonist The chief opponent(s) of the protagonist in a drama

Apron The stage space in front of the curtain line or proscenium; also called the forestage.

Arena A type of stage which is surrounded by the audience on all four sides; also known as *theatre-in- the-round.*

Aria A melodic composition sung by a soloist in an opera or operetta.

Asbestos Curtain A fire-proof curtain originbally made of asbestos. It hangs immediately behind the proscenium arch. In case of fire, it automatically drops separating the auditorium from the stage where most theatre fires occur. A safety device required in proscenium theatres.

Backdrop A large drapery or painted canvas which provides the rear or upstage masking of the set.

Backstage The stage area behind the front curtain; also, the areas beyond the setting including the wings and dressing rooms.

Ballad Opera See p. 67.

Ballet de Couer An elaborate French court entertainment including song, dance and music. Popular in the late 16th and the 17th centuries.

Batten A pipe or long pole suspended horizontally above the stage upon which scenery, drapery or lights may be hung.

Beam Lights Stage lighting coming from instruments hung in the ceiling of the auditorium.

Below Opposite of **above**, toward the front of the stage.

Blackout To plunge the stage into total darkness by switching off the lights; also the condition produced by this operation.

Blocking The arrangement of the actors' movements on stage with respect to each other and the stage space.

Book (1) The spoken (as opposed to sung) portion of the text of a musical play. (2) To schedule engagements for artists or productions.

Border A strip of drapery or painted canvas hung from a batten top mask the area above the stage; also, a row of lights hung above the stage.

Box Set An interior setting using flats to form the back and side walls and often the ceiling of a room.

Courtesy The Library of Congress

Edwin Forrest (1806-1872) in the title role of Shakespeare's *King Lear.*

Bunraku Japanese puppet theatre

Burlesque See p. 88.

Business Obvious and detailed physical movement of an actor to reveal character, aid action, or establish mood (e.g., pouring drinks at a bar, opening a gun case, etc.).

Catharsis A Greek word, usually translated as "purgation," which Aristotle used in his definition of tragedy. It refers to the vicarious cleansing of certain emotions in the members of the audience through the representation of such emotions on stage.

Center Stage A stage position in the middle acting area of the stage or the middle section extended upstage and down stage.

Chorus In ancient Greek drama, a group of performers who sang and danced, sometimes participating in the action but usually simply commenting on it. Also, performers in a musical play who sing and dance as a group rather than individually.

Climactic Plot Also called a "linear" plot. Each action leads directly to the next. See p. 35.

Complication The introduction into a play of a new force which changes or threatens to change the direction of the action or the fate of the protagonist. It often produces conflict or is produced by conflict.

Conflict Tension between two or more characters that normally leads to a crisis or a climax. May be a conflict of personalities, ideas, things. It is necessary in all good drama.

Convention An understanding established through custom or usage that certain devices will be accepted or assigned specific meaning or significance on an arbitrary basis; that is, without requiring that they be natural or realistic. "An agreed upon falsehood." Ex.: Though an actor in the Greek theatre might play several characters in one production, the audience identified him as a specific character by the mask he wore.

Counterweight A device for balancing the weight of scenery in a system which allows scenery to be raised above the stage by system of ropes and pulleys.

Cross A movement by a performer across the stage in a given direction.

Cue Any prearranged signal, such as the last words in a speech, a piece of business, or any action or lighting change that indicates to an actor or stage manager that it is time to proceed to the next line or action.

Cue Sheet A prompt-book marked with cues, or a list of cues for the use of technicians, especially the stage manager.

Curtain (1) The rise or fall of a physical curtain which separates a play into structural units such as scenes or acts. (2) The last bit of action preceding the call of the curtain.

Cycle Play A collection of short medieval plays based on stories from the Bible. Often performed on wagon stages in England, the Lowlands, and Spain. See p. 80.

Cyclorama A large curved drop used to mask the rear and sides of the stage. Often painted a neutral color or blue to represent the sky or open space. It may also be a permanent stage fixture made of plaster or similar durable material.

Denouement Sometimes translated as "the tying up of loose threads," it literally means "The knot is untied." The moment in the play when the final suspense is satisfied.

Deus ex Machina Literally means "the god from the machine," a resolution device used in Greek drama. Denotes in modern drama a conclusion based upon an arbitrary action or introduction of a new character to resolve the problems.

Didactic Theatre Theatre which has as its chief aim teaching. Often associated with propaganda theatre. See p. 89.

Dimmer A device which permits lighting intensities to be changed gradually.

Director In American usage, the interpreter of the play. Responsible for the overall continuity and coordination of all the artistic elements in the play. The American director is the equivalent of the British *producer* and the French *metteur-en-scene.*

Down Stage The front of the stage toward the audience.

Drop A large piece of fabric, generally painted canvas, hung from a batten to the stage floor, usually serving as a backing.

Ensemble Playing Acting which stresses the total artistic unity of the performance rather than the individual performances of specific actors and actresses.

Entrance The manner and effectiveness with which an actor comes into a scene. The actual coming on stage. The physical opening for an entrance.

Epic Theatre A form of drama chiefly developed by Brecht. So-named because of the scope of the action included and the manner of presentation. See p. 90

Epilogue A speech addressed to the audience after the conclusion of the play.

Episodic Plot Also referred to as a "panoramic" plot. See p. 35.

Exit A performer's leaving the stage, as well as the preparation for his leaving.

Exposition The imparting of information necessary for an understanding of the story but not covered by the action on stage. Events or knowledge from the past.

Flat A single piece of scenery, usually of a standard size, made of canvas stretched over a wooden frame.

Fly Loft or Flies The space above the stage where scenery may be lifted out of sight by means of ropes and pulleys when it is not needed.

Follow Spot A large, powerful spotlight with a sharp focus and narrow beam which is used to follow principal performers as they move about the stage.

Footlights A row of lights in the floor along the front edge of the stage or the apron; once a principal source of stage light, now rarely used.

Forestage See apron

Forced Perspective A design technique employed by scenic artists to create the illusion of greater depth than is actually being occupied by the sets.

Front of the House the portion of the theatre reserved for the audience. Sometimes referred to as the *house.*

Gauze See *Scrim*

Gel A thin, flexible medium used in lighting instruments to give color to the light. Originally made of thin gelatin, now mostly made of plastic.

Grand Drape A full stage curtain situated immediately behind the proscenium arch. Often used to mask full-stage scene changes.

Grid A metal framework above the stage from which scenery may be hung and on which are mounted pulleys, etc.

Hand Props Small props carried on or off-stage by actors during a performance. See *props.*

Inner Stage An area at the rear of the stage which can be cut off from the rest of the stage by means of a curtain. Thought to have been used at Shakespeare's Globe.

Intermezzi A popular Italian court entertainment during the late 16th and early 17th centuries. See "ballet de couer."

Kabuki Japanese popular spectacle theatre.

Kyogen Japanese comic Noh play

Left Stage The left side of the stage from the point of view of a performer facing the audience.

Light Plot a diagram indicating the arrangements of the lighting instruments in the theatre, the areas on which they are focused, and the speficific instruments and color media to be used.

Courtesy The Library of Congress

Edwin Forrest in the title role of *Richard III.*

Lime Light A spot-light invented in the 19th century and used by many actors. Its source of light came from a cylinder of lime heated to a white-hot temperature by a mixture of compressed gases. See p. 156.

Linear Plot See "climactic plot," p. 35.

Mansion A scenic unit representing a specific locale used in medieval staging. Several mansions were used in multiple and simultaneous staging. See p. 81.

Masque A popular English court entertainment during the late 16th and early 17th centuries. See "ballet de coure."

Mask (1) To cut off from the view of the audience, e.g., scenery masks the backstage area (2) A face covering in the image of the character portrayed. May cover the entire head.

Masking Anything used to mask above the set and backstage from the audience.

Method See Stanislavski method.

Minstrel Show A comedy/musical revue originally featuring Afro-American performers and later white performers in black-face. Now in disrepute, it was popular from about 1870 to the late 1930's. See p. 68.

Miracle Play A medieval play based on the life of a saint. See p. 80

Mise-en-Scene A French term referring to the arrangement of all the elements in the stage picture (sets, props, costumes, actors, etc.) either at a given moment or throughout the entire production.

Morality Play A medieval play in which good and evil traits are personified. See p. 80.

Multi-Media A theatrical production using a variety of media; i.e., live actors, motion pictures, slides, music, television, etc.

Multiple Setting A form of stage setting common in the Middle Ages in which several locations are represented on stage at one time; more accurately called *simultaneous setting.*

Mystery Play A medieval play based on stories from the Bible, both Old and New Testaments. Passion plays and cycle plays are also mystery plays. See p. 80

Noh Japanese court drama.

Offstage The areas of the stage, usually the wings or backstage, not in view of the audience.

Onnagata Japanese female impersonator in the Kabuki plays.

On-stage The area of the stage in view of the audience.

Open A term in stage movement of the actor. Means to turn toward or face the audience.

Opera Literally means "work" in Italian. In this case, a musical work in which a drama has been set fully to music. See p. 66.

Operetta A "little opera" or "light opera" in which spoken dialogue is incorporated into the action along with musical numbers. See p. 67.

Option A term used to describe a short-term contract giving a producer the right to mount a specific play.

Orchestra (1) In Greek theatre, the circular area in front of the stage, *logeon,* in which the chorus was thought to perform. (2)Auditorium ground-floor seating.

Pace The rate at which a performance is played. May also be called *tempo.* Also, to play a scene or an entire play in order to determine its running time.

Panoramic Plot Also referred to as "episodic." See p. 35. Ex.: *Hamlet*

Passion Play A medvieval mystery play based on the the last seven days in the life of Christ. See p. 80.

Platform A raised surface on the stage floor serving as an elevation for parts of stage action. Sometimes called a level.

Platform Stage An elevated stage which does not make use of a proscenium.

Plot As distinct from story, the patterned arrangement of events and characters for a drama. Incidents arranged for maximum dramatic effectiveness.

Point of Attack The moment in the story when the play actually begins.

Producer In the American theatre, the person responsible for the business side of the production.

Prologue An introductory speech delivered to the audience by one of the performers.

Prompt To furnish a performer with missed or forgotten lines or cues during a performance.

Prompt book The script of a play indicating the performer's movements, light cues, sound cues, etc.

Props Properties. (1) **Set Props:** furniture and set decorations. (2) **Hand Props**: anything handled by the actor. These are placed on stage and used as necessary. (3) **Costume Props**: usually accessories which complement the costumes but must be handled by the actor; i.e., canes, swords, purses, etc.

Proscenium The arch or frame surrounding the stage opening in a box or picture stage.

Protagonist (1) For the Greeks, this referred to the "first actor;" (2) The principal character in a play, the one whom the drama is about.

Rake An upward slope of the stage floor from down stage to up stage

Recitative Sung-speech. Most often found in operas in which the dialogue is sung to a musical accompaniement. The musical line is composed to reflect the speech pattern of the character rather than a specific melody.

Reversal "The hunter becomes the hunted." A sudden switch in the fate of a character which leads to results contrary to those expected.

Revolving Stage A large turntable on which scenery is placed in such a way that, as it moves, one set is brought into view while another one turns out of sight.

Revue A musical/comedy variety show. See p. 68.

Right Stage The right side of the stage from the point of view of the performer facing the audience.

Scenario The outline of the play containing the occurrences in each scene. Does not include dialogue.

Scene (1) Stage setting. (2) The structural units into which the plays or acts of the plays are divided. (3) The location of the play's action.

Scientific Determinism A philosophic movement derived from Darwin's observations and based on the premise that man's behavior is derived from heredity and environment. See p. 87.

Scrim A thin, open-weave fabric which is nearly transparent when lit from behind and opaque when lit from in front.

Script The written or printed text of a play or other theatrical production.

Set The scenery, taken as a whole, for a scene or an entire production.

Slapstick A type of comedy or comic business which relies on ridiculous physical activity—often violent in nature—for its humor.

Sound Plot Sometimes called a "sound score." The notes arranged by the sound designer to indicate the various effects and music required for the production. Includes also the methods by which the sounds will be achieved and the specific cue for each effect.

Spill Unwanted light from stage lighting instruments which falls outside of the area for which it was intended.

SRO "Standing Room Only" meaning all seats for a production are sold.

Stage House The stage floor and all the space above it up to the grid.

Stan'slavski Method A set of techniques and theories about the problems of acting which promotes a naturalistic style stressing "inner truth" as opposed to conventional theatricality.

Stock Characters Normally stereotypical characters which appear in a series of plays. Ex.: dumb blond or jock, smart-mouth servant, absent-minded professor.

Stock Sets Basic sets which may be stored and used repeatedly in a variety of plays. Ex.: interior, garden, woodland, grotto, throne room, street scene.

Subtext A term referring to the meaning and movement of the play below the surface; that which is implied and never stated. The meaning and thoughts, unuttered. Often more important than the surface activity.

Supernumerary An actor who helps to complete the stage picture by being a part of a crowd. Does not have lines other than joining in with the crowd reactions.

Teaser A short horizontal curtain just behind the proscenium used to mask the fly loft and possibly lower the height of the proscenium.

Tragic Flaw A character's chief weakness which brings about his ultimate downfall.

Trap An opening in the stage floor, normally covered, which can be used for special effects.

Unities A term applied to theories of drama espoused during the Renaissance. They include the unities of time, place, and action.

Unity A requirement of art. In drama, this refers to the unity of action in the play's structure or plot. It may also refer to a unity of style adopted for a production.

Upstage At or toward the back of the stage. Dates from the time when the stage floor was raked up and away from the audience.

Wagon Stage (1) A low platform mounted on wheels for moving scenery. (2) A stage used during the Middle Ages for the mounting of episodes of the *cycle plays* in England and the *auto sacrementales* in Spain. Literally a large wagon fitted with scenery, etc.

Walk-on A character which has no lines, but only appears on stage.

Wings (1) Left and right offstage areas; (2) narrow pieces of scenery normally standing parallel to the proscenium. Used to form the sides of a set.

SELECTED READINGS

Aristotle: *Aristotle's Poetics,* S. H. Butcher (trans.), New York, 1961
Atkinson, Brooks: *Broadway,* New York, 1974
Bay, Howard: *Stage Design,* New York, 1974
Benedetti, Jean: *Stanislavski: An Introduction*, New York, 1982
Benedetti, Robert: *The Actor at Work*, Englewood Cliffs, 1971
Bentley, Eric: *The Life of the Drama,* New York, 1964
_____, *The Theory of the Modern Stage*, Baltimore, 1968
Boardman, Gerald: *Oxford Companion to the American Theatre*, New York, 1991
Brecht, Bertolt: *Brecht on Theatre*, John Willett (trans.), New York, 1965
Brockett, Oscar G.: *History of the Theatre*, Boston, 1994
_____, *The Theatre: An Introduction,* New York, 1969
_____ and Robert J. Findlay, *Century of Innovation: A History of European and American Theatre and Drama Since 1870*, Englewood Cliffs, 1973
Brook, Peter: *The Empty Space,* New York, 1968
Burdick, James: *Theatre,* New York, 1974
Carlson, Marvin: *Theories of the Theatre*, Ithica, 1984
Catron, Louis E.: *The Director's Vision*, Mountain View, CA, 1989
Clark, Barrett H. (ed.): *European Theories of the Drama*, New York, 1965
Clurman, Harold: *On Directing*, New York, 1972
Cohen, Robert: *Acting Power*, Palo Alto, 1978
Cole, Toby: *Playwrights on Playwriting*, New York, 1961
_____and Helen Kritch Chinoy: *Actors on Acting*, New York, 1970
Corrigan, Robert (ed.): *Comedy: Meaning and Form*, San Francisco, 1965
_____ (ed.): *Tragedy: Vision and Form*, San Francisco, 1965
Corson, Richard: *Stage Makeup*, Englewood Cliffs, 1981
Dukore, Bernard (ed.): *Dramatic Theory and Criticism: Greeks to Grotowski*, New York, 1974
Dean, Alexander: *Fundamentals of Directing*,New York, 1941
Esslin, Martin: *The Theatre of the Absurd*, Garden City, 1969
Fergusson, Francis: *The Idea of a Theatre*, Princeton, 1949
Gassner, John: *Masters of the Drama*, New York, 1954
_____ and Philip Barber: *Producing the Play & The New Scene Technician's Handbook*, New York, 1941
_____and Edward Quinn: *The Reader's Encyclopedia of World Drama*, New York, 1969
_____and Ralph Allen (eds.): *Theatre and Drama in the Making*, 2 vols., Boston, 1964
Hodge, Francis: *Play Directing, Analysis, Communication and Style:* Englewood Cliffs, 1971
Jones, Robert Edmund: *The Dramatic Imagination*, New York, 1941
Kuritz, Paul: *The Making of Theatre History*, Englewood Cliffs, 1988
Lahr, John and Jonathan Price: *Life-Show*, New York, 1973
Law, Jonathan, et. al.: *Brewer's Theatre: A Phrase and Fable Dictionary*, London, 1994
MacGowan, Kenneth and William Melnitz: *The Living Stage: A History of World Theatre*, Englewood Cliffs, 1955
Miller, Arthur: *The Theatre Essays of Arthur Miller*, New York, 1978
Nagler, Alois M.: *Sourcebook of Theatrical History*, New York, 1952
Oenslager, Donald: *Scenery Then and Now*, New York, 1936
Rice, Elmer: *Minority Report*, New York, 1963
Roberts, Vera M.: *On Stage: A History of the Theatre*, New York, 1974
Schechner, Richard: *Environmental Theatre*, New York, 1973
Southern, Richard: *The Seven Ages of the Theatre*, New York, 1961
Stanislavski, Constantin: *An Actor Prepares*, Elizabeth Reynolds Hapgood (trans.), New York, 1936
Watson, Jack and Grant McKernie: *A Cultural History of the Theatre*, New York, 1993
Wickham, Glynne: *The Medieval Theatre*, Cambridge, England, 1974
Wilson, Edwin and Alvin Goldfarb: *Living Theatre*, New York, 1991
Wilson, Garff B.: *Three Hundred Years of American Drama and Theatre*, Englewood Cliffs, 1973